CATHOLIC HISTORY FOR TODAY'S CHURCH

CATHOLIC HISTORY FOR TODAY'S CHURCH

How Our Past Illuminates Our Present

John W. O'Malley, SJ

A SHEED & WARD BOOK

ROWMAN & LITTLEFIELD
Lanham • Boulder • New York • London

Published by Rowman & Littlefield
A wholly owned subsidary of The Rowman & Littlefield Publishing Group, Inc.
4501 Forbes Boulevard, Suite 200, Lanham, Maryland 20706
www.rowman.com

Unit A, Whitacre Mews, 26-34 Stannary Street, London SE11 4AB

Distributed by NATIONAL BOOK NETWORK

British Library Cataloguing in Publication Information Available

Library of Congress Cataloging-in-Publication Data
O'Malley, John W.
Catholic history for today's church : how our past illuminates our present / John W. O'Malley, SJ
pages cm
Includes index.
ISBN 978-1-4422-5002-4 (cloth : alk. paper) — ISBN 978-1-4422-5003-1 (electronic)
1. Catholic Church—History. 2. Catholic Church—Doctrines. I. Title.
BX945.3.O43 2015
282.09—dc23
2015006433

Printed in the United States of America

"The past is not dead. It's not even past."

—William Faulkner, *Requiem for a Nun*

CONTENTS

PART III: THE CHURCH AT LARGE

INTRODUCTION

This book is a collection of essays about aspects of the history of the Catholic Church. My title suggests the conviction that allows me to publish the articles under one cover. I wrote them not simply to satisfy readers' curiosity about the past but also to help them see a contemporary problem or issue in historical perspective. In every case I explicitly or implicitly ask the question, "So what for today?" The conviction that underlies these articles, therefore, and that underlies virtually everything I have ever written, is that history, correctly presented, tells us how we became the people we now are and thus helps us deal with the present. History is more than an interesting pastime; it is serious business. It is especially serious business when its subject is the church.

That is how I understand my vocation as a church historian, and that is the motivation that has been at the center of my professional life from its very first moment. I study the past in order to help us live more wisely in the present. Whether we realize it or not, whether we like it or not, the past, for better or worse, holds us in its grasp. Decisions made yesterday, last year, or centuries ago have determined the contours of the world we live in. They have determined the contours of the church we live in. If we understand how, in great ways and small, we got to be the way we are, we have a new freedom in the choices that face us. But if we are ignorant of how we got to be the way we are, we are trapped within the given and are less free in our choices. We do not see alternatives.

The church is by definition a conservative institution. Its sole reason for existence is to pass on unadulterated a message received long ago. In that regard the church cannot change. We Catholics believe, in that regard, that it has not changed. It still proclaims the good news and to that extent has escaped the ravages of time. But the church is a historical reality. It lives in time and space. It lives in the lives of its members, each of whom is the product of a certain time and culture.

Et Verbum caro factum est—"and the Word was made flesh." Even if at one level the church transcends history, on another it is, like its Lord, incarnated in history. If so, it can be studied the same way any historical phenomenon can be studied. The church has had to make decisions, and its decisions have given it certain shapes or forms.

It has also had decisions made for it by others, and those decisions have likewise given it shapes and forms. For example, few decisions were more momentous for the church than Emperor Constantine's decree granting it toleration, which led to his assuming a leadership role within the church. Not a pope but Constantine convoked the first ecumenical council, the Council of Nicaea, 325, and thus initiated a certain pattern of church-state relationships that persisted until definitively broken only by the decree "On Religious Liberty" of Vatican Council II.

It has been my privilege to dedicate my life to the study of the church, a truly remarkable institution. I have never tired of it. I am ever excited by it. No other institution in our world today has had a longer continuous history. No institution has had a richer or more complex history. It stretches across every culture from the ancient Hellenistic world centered in the Mediterranean basin to today's global, postmodern world. Its literature is in every language, ancient and modern. Its art and architecture embody a multitude of styles, both Western and other. Its members have been great saints and great sinners. Its claims sometimes reach beyond human comprehension, but at other times they could not be more lowly and human.

How can mere historians even begin to grapple with such a reality? They must, first of all, be humble and know that whatever they find in their research, they are discovering only a miniscule piece of the reality. Each historian needs to settle into a specialty and perfect the research tools appropriate to his or her specific subject. This is not a case of learning more and more about less and less, but rather a way to achieve a measure of precision in speaking about a particular aspect of the history of the church. With a firm grasp of one aspect of the history, historians are able to venture some generalizations and move beyond their specific focus to larger issues.

In my teaching I, like most American academics, have had to perform as both a specialist and a generalist. I have conducted seminars on closely defined subjects for advanced students but at the same time have been required to teach courses of much broader scope for other students. The articles in this collection reflect that reality. I originally specialized in the Italian Renaissance, fifteenth and sixteenth century, but eventually began to move into what is conventionally called the Counter-Reformation—the Council of Trent and all that! I prefer to call this complex era from the Renaissance to the Enlightenment "Early Modern Catholicism." But whatever it is called, that is where I found and still find my first academic home. The articles in this collection reflect that focus.

However, while I was writing my dissertation in Rome on Giles of Viterbo, a sixteenth-century reformer of the Augustinian order, Vatican Council II was going on less than a mile from where I was living. Like everybody in Rome at the time, I was fascinated by that event, and I began to see parallels between what was happening in the twentieth century before my very eyes and what had happened in the sixteenth century that I was learning about from books. Although at the time I never expected to write professionally on Vatican II, I published my first article on it in 1971. I have continued to write about the council up to the present, as this collection shows.

Other articles are the result of my having to perform as a generalist and to become skilled in periods and issues that stretched me beyond my specialties. Among them are a large number concerning the papacy, a subject of long fascination for me, as it is for numerous other Catholics. The papacy, important in its own right, provides a window into broader issues of church history at any given moment and thus deserves the prominence it has in this book. Nonetheless, we need to remind ourselves that the history of the papacy is not the history of the church. The latter is incomparably broader, richer, and more fundamental. It is represented here in part III.

In 1993 I published *The First Jesuits*. Since then I have written extensively on the history of the Society of Jesus and edited a number of volumes concerning the organization. I have not included any of my articles about the Society in this collection because a selection of them appeared as recently as 2013 in a volume exclusively devoted to the

Jesuits edited by Robert A. Maryks, *Saints or Devils Incarnate: Studies in Jesuit History.*

Throwing modesty to the winds, I conclude the book with an autobiographical memoir. But more than vanity motivated me to include it. The memoir will alert the reader to the limitations of the author whose works they have been reading. More important, it will remind them that in every instance history perforce passes through narrow straits of the mind and heart of the historian, and only after undergoing the filtering process of that passage does it reach the printed page.

Over the course of the years, editors of journals or other publications have asked me to write something for them for a general Catholic readership on the occasion of a notable event or anniversary. The essays in this collection represent a sample of such articles that I believe continue to be relevant, even though the specific occasions for which they were written have long since passed. In a few I have made minor editorial changes, but they otherwise appear as they originally left my pen—that is, my computer. Some are longer than others, but they are all relatively short. You will note in them an occasional repetition of ideas or information, almost inevitable in a collection like this. I ask your indulgence and suggest you simply marshal your speed-reading skills and put them into action for those sections. The book will have been a success if it whets your appetite to read more about the fascinating past and the exciting, yet difficult, present of the Catholic Church.

Part I

The Papacy and the Popes

I

THE MILLENNIUM AND THE PAPALIZATION OF CATHOLICISM

On the occasion of the millennium in 2000, the editor of America *magazine asked me to look back over the past thousand years of church history and indicate what I saw as the most salient development. I found the assignment easy because the growth of papal authority and prestige since the eleventh century is certainly the most obvious development in the Western Church. I coined the term "papalization" to capture that reality. I try to avoid neologisms, but in this case I felt it was more than justified.*

This year everyone has been trying to see the big picture. We've been bombarded with a certain type of question. Who is the man or woman of the century—better, of the millennium? What are the happenings in the past thousand years that most changed the course of history and that explain how, for better or worse, we've ended up where we are? And perhaps the most tantalizing of all—how are we different from those who went before us? Even Catholics know that, though they profess the same faith and receive the same sacraments as Christians did a thousand years ago, they are to some extent different. Then comes the final and perhaps most unsettling question—how different?

As a church historian I am on some days struck by the amazing continuity in faith and practice that has marked Catholicism through the ages. On other days I am so struck by the discontinuity, by the radical changes that have taken place, that I find it difficult to identify with the Catholic past or, in other cases, difficult to identify with the Catholic present. Probably, like yourselves, I could come up with dozens of changes in how Christians live, believe, and pray today that make us different from those of earlier times. There are certain obvious things: we worship in the vernacular, not Latin; we worship in a parish church, not in a manor chapel or in the oratory of our confraternity; we accept the Immaculate Conception and Assumption of Mary as defined dogmas of our faith; the Lenten fast, so central to Christian practice in bygone ages, has for all practical purposes disappeared; women are no longer expected to come to church with their heads covered.

We could probably go on and on, aware all the time that some differences are far more significant than others. What if you were asked, however, to single out from this long list the most important change of all, "the change of the millennium"? I don't know about you, but for me there is no contest. I would without hesitation name what I have come to call the *papalization* of Catholicism.

I coined that neologism because its very crudity shocks me to attention and because it expresses so directly the reality in question. At the beginning of the last millennium—indeed, as late as Luther's posting of the Ninety-Five Theses—relatively few Christians knew that the papacy existed, and surely only a minuscule percentage believed it had anything to do with the way they lived their lives. If the papacy figured at all in the way they conceived of themselves, it was peripherally. Even for bishops and princes it was at best a remote institution, a possible court of appeal if things got rough at home. At worst, it was a political rival and an expropriator of financial resources.

For the vast majority of Christians, however, the papacy, if they ever heard it mentioned, meant about as much to them as names like Scotus and Ockham mean to Catholics today. How and from whom would they ever have heard of it? Not from sermons. True, sermons on the feast of Saints Peter and Paul might in passing say a word about "the vicar of Peter," but even that would be exceptional. At the beginning of the millennium, in any case, there were no sermons to be heard, and even five hundred years later the record, though much improved, was spotty. This was especially true in the countryside, which is where most people lived.

During the Middle Ages catechetical instruction consisted in learning the Creed, basic prayers, and the Ten Commandments or seven capital sins, along perhaps with the Beatitudes and works of mercy. The best indication of how that content was conveyed comes from early printed catechisms, which presumably codified early teaching. The papacy is not mentioned. The obvious occasion for doing so would be in connection with the article of the Creed: "I believe in the holy, catholic church." Yet in answer to the question "What is the church?" the catechisms stated simply, "The congregation of Christian faithful, governed and illumined by God our Lord." Nothing more. Perhaps we should not be surprised the papacy is barely mentioned by St. Thomas in all his *Summa Theologiae.*

To be a Catholic today, however, as most Catholics and surely everybody else would say, is "to believe in the pope." Rare are the practicing Catholics anywhere in the world who do not know that John Paul II is the name of the current pontiff. More important, Catholics know that John Paul II "runs the church." That means, among other things, that he appoints their bishop, who is, most seem to believe, "his representative." The bishops in turn appoint their pastors. Catholics (as well as interested outsiders) know that a clear line of authority runs downward from the unquestioned CEO of the church all the way to their local parish. Every rectory, we can safely presume, somewhere prominently displays a portrait of the reigning pontiff. In the sanctuary of many churches hangs the papal flag.

Catholics also know they are supposed to "obey the pope's teaching," not just on ethereal subjects of yesteryear like repudiating Marxism but also on things as absolutely immediate to them as their sexual relations with their spouses. For many Catholics, to say that "the church forbids this or that" is the equivalent of saying that the pope forbids it. In their publications, theologians know that, quite unlike the situation in St. Thomas's day, it is as important to quote writings of the current pontiff as it is to quote Scripture.

How did such a profound revolution in consciousness and practice come about? How did an institution move from the outskirts of awareness, at best, to the defining center? How did Matthew 16:18's "Thou art Peter" become the canon within the canon for Roman Catholics and become emblematic of their very identity?

Or, really, was it not always thus? Was not the papacy always as important to Catholics as it is today? I fear that the way most of us learned the history of the church and even "Western Civ" would lead us to believe that the papacy had from the beginning, or at least from the Investiture Controversy a thousand years ago, been the determining factor in Catholic life. This is the impression left, unwittingly in many cases, by much of what we read and hear about the history of Christianity. The impression is caused in part by the almost ineradicable habit of teaching church history and Western Civ from the top downward. It is easier to teach it that way, rather than fussing with the often diffuse histories of "ordinary Christians." It is also important in history courses to give the top its due. We could hardly understand our present religious situation, for instance, if we did not study Luther and the popes who opposed him. Yet the top-down reading misleads us into thinking that just about everybody was as concerned about the popes as Luther was.

The situation is also caused in part by taking our own issues or situations as our starting point in ways that almost inevitably makes us distort the past. For the past fifty years, and especially the past twenty years, to speak of Catholicism has been to speak of the pope, or at least it has not been possible to speak of Catholicism at any length without at some point speaking about the pope. Thus interest in the papacy is at an all-time high. The number of biographies of Pope John Paul II is beyond all counting. Since 1997 four major histories of the papacy have appeared in English, beginning with Eamon Duffy's highly successful *Saints and Sinners*. In these books some popes are obviously presented as more important than others, but the general impression left on the reader is that through the ages all eyes were fixed on these leaders of Christendom.

This impression tricks us into committing the fallacy of misplaced emphasis, the easiest and most pernicious fallacy for the historian to commit: what the historian says is true, but by failing to indicate its place in a larger context, he or she implicitly distorts its significance. Even during the height of the Investiture Controversy, for instance, when the emperor's and the pope's men under arms were hacking away at each other, 95 percent of Europe's Christians did not know anything was amiss. But our history books leave us with the impression it was front-page news, though we at another level are quite aware that in the eleventh century no front pages existed.

Three factors coalesce, I believe, to account for the present situation. The first is the one I just described—that is, the way our history has been written and the way we are predisposed to interpret it. The second is the one I suggested by mentioning front pages—that is, the increasing speed of communication beginning with the invention of printing in the fifteenth century and continuing to the development of electronic communication of all kinds, including the humble telephone. Today it is possible to keep track of almost every breath drawn by every world leader, including the pope. It is possible, conversely, for those leaders to keep track of almost every breath we draw. This is new in the history of the world. This is new in the history of the church.

The third factor is the way the papacy itself changed over the millennia. There is no need to insist with this readership that from the earliest centuries the bishop of Rome held a position of special respect and claimed, sometimes effectively, unique prerogatives. Yet in the first millennium popes did not "run the church," nor did they claim to. They defined no doctrines; they wrote no encyclicals; they called no bishops *ad limina*. They did not convoke ecumenical councils, and they did not preside at them. In fact, their roles in the first eight councils were generally insignificant. In the early Middle Ages (and well beyond) the popes' principal duty, many believed, was to guard the tombs of the apostles and officiate at the solemn liturgies at the great basilicas. In that period, although some of the popes of course had a broad vision of their responsibilities and dealt about weighty matters with the leaders of society, for the most part they behaved as essentially local figures, intent on local issues.

Without doubt, the decisive turn that has led to our present situation was taken with the Investiture Controversy at the beginning of the millennium just ended—that is, the Gregorian Reform of the eleventh century. The Gregorian reformers, relying on both genuine and forged canonical sources, advanced claims for papal authority that were a curious mix of old prerogatives and startlingly new demands for submission by both secular and ecclesiastical leaders to papal decisions. The pope's right to depose emperors was among the new claims. The ancient canonical axiom that the pope was to be judged by no one unless he should be found to deviate from the faith was shortened to simply "The pope is judged by no one."

The Gregorians set a powerful ideological machine in motion. While even for them the pope was still only "the vicar of Peter," a little over a century later Pope Innocent III designated himself "the vicar of Christ." The title stuck and is today much better known than the more venerable "servant of the servants of God." As the monarchies of England and France emerged from an amorphous feudalism, the papacy developed a similarly monarchical structure and self-definition. During their residency in Avignon in the fourteenth century, the popes even led the way in the creation of effective bureaucracy.

The next great change came with the Reformation. The Protestants' utter rejection of the papacy thrust it into a new prominence in Catholic consciousness. Catholics, identified by their enemies as papists, began to glory in the insult. By the middle of the sixteenth century, Catholic catechisms had added to the traditional definition of the church the significant qualification "under the governance of Peter and his successors, the vicar of Christ." A momentous shift in self-understanding was taking place.

There were ironies. Although every Protestant church and sect utterly repudiated the papacy and wanted to obliterate the office, the Council of Trent was unable in its eighteen-year history directly to address the issue. The precise nature and extent of papal authority was too contentious an issue even among Catholics for the council to venture a statement. The council fathers went home, but the popes remained at their post. More ironies—not only had the Reformation actually strengthened the papacy in those parts of Europe that remained Catholic, but by saying nothing the Council of Trent had done the same.

Nonetheless, in important areas of Catholic life the papacy neither had nor claimed any interest. The great missionary ventures remained under the direction of the religious orders and of the kings of Spain, Portugal, and France. The establishment by the popes in 1622 of the Congregation for the Propagation of the Faith did not for a long time substantially change that situation. The universities the Jesuits established around the globe were responsible only to themselves and to their superior general.

The Enlightenment, the French Revolution, and early nineteenth-century liberals dealt heavy blows to the papacy, but again an enemy, the Risorgimento, infused new life into it. When in 1870 Garibaldi's troops entered Rome, Pius IX dramatized the event by enclosing himself within the Vatican sector of the city. Catholics throughout the world, aware through telegraph (transatlantic cable, 1866) and thence through newspapers that the pope was now "the prisoner of the Vatican," poured out their sympathy for him. They knew the pope's name, and they might even have seen a photograph of him. The cult of a papal personality began to take shape for the first time. Pius IX drew more attention to himself and boldly advanced the claims of his office through the first papal definition of dogma, the Immaculate Conception, and by being the pope under whom the dogma of papal infallibility was defined.

Popes had meanwhile begun to issue encyclicals. That is to say, they no longer were merely the judges in cases of contested doctrine; they had themselves become teachers. By the middle of the nineteenth century, publishing encyclicals had become part of the papal job description. So had the appointment of bishops. In the eleventh century the popes of the Gregorian Reform campaigned vigorously for "canonical election" of bishops—that is, campaigned for bishops to be elected by their clergy and not simply appointed by the local magnate or king. By the end of the twentieth century, the few remaining vestiges of the tradition of election had been wiped out. The pope chooses bishops—no votes, please.

Meanwhile, in 1929 the doors of the Vatican prison had swung open by virtue of the agreements between the papacy and the Italian government. Movie cameras were admitted into St. Peter's and into the Apostolic Palace, and millions on millions of people throughout the world could see Pius XI, Pius XII, and John XXIII bestow their blessings. The popes, no longer prisoners, began to travel. Jets made it easy. Popemobiles did the same.

And the rest, as they say, is history. What most fascinates me, however, is not how much the papacy changed in the course of the past millennium, but rather how much its changes have changed us. The papacy isn't what it used to be. But, largely for that reason, neither are we.

2

PAPAL JOB DESCRIPTIONS

Yesterday and Today

This piece follows naturally on papalization. As the papal job descriptions changed through the centuries, they for the most part enlarged the scope of the popes' concerns and claims of authority. Of course, no one presented the popes with a job description, as if they were applying for a job. But the popes in fact assumed that such and such was their responsibility, and they acted accordingly. The original form of this article was a lecture delivered at Saint Louis University, 9 October 2009.

Catholics know what the pope does. The Gospels laid out his job description twenty centuries ago. In the last chapter of St. John, Jesus commissioned Peter to feed his lambs and to feed his sheep. In Luke he told Peter to strengthen his brethren, and, most important, in Matthew Jesus entrusted the keys of the kingdom of heaven to Peter, the rock on which he would build his church, so that whatever Peter bound on earth would be bound in heaven and whatever he loosed on earth would be loosed in heaven. Christ intended, Catholics believe, that these responsibilities with which Jesus invested Peter be perpetuated in Peter's successor, the pope.

It is self-evident that the pope writes encyclicals and appoints the world's bishops. After all, when Pope Benedict XVI was elected, everybody wanted to know when he would issue his first encyclical, because that is what popes do—write encyclicals. It is a top item on today's papal job description, taken for granted just as it is taken for granted that the pope appoints bishops.

But should we take these activities for granted? Writing encyclicals and appointing the world's bishops may be valid implementations of Christ's commission to Peter, but they did not appear as such on the papal agenda until nineteen centuries after the commission was given. They are of startlingly recent vintage—as are other activities in which the pope engages that can seem to us integral to his office. Fascinating in the history of the oldest still-functioning institution in the Western world is how the job description has changed through the centuries. The description shifted as the popes took on new responsibilities and sloughed off old ones, only to repeat the process a little later and then again later still.

In this shifting scene, the institution nonetheless retained a strong identity, recognizable in every century. That identity is owed to the simple and unshakeable conviction of every bishop of Rome that he was the successor of Peter and that he therefore enjoyed an altogether preeminent authority in the church. From no later than the third century, the same principle has prevailed: the other churches and their bishops owe special deference to the see of Blessed Peter and must heed the word that comes from it.

In the sphere of practical politics, popes sometimes had to bow to pressure and make concessions regarding their Petrine prerogatives. In principle, however, they clung to their special leadership role with unyielding tenacity, admitting change in it only by way of increment. In that regard, they glided easily from being vicars of Peter, as they were until the twelfth century, to being vicars of Christ, as they began designating themselves in the thirteenth.

Within that framework, however, great variety has prevailed in the forms papal authority has assumed and in the claims the popes made about it. I will review some of these forms and claims, bringing us up to the present. I hope you find what I have to say interesting, but my purpose is not to entertain. I hope to do what good history always does: expand our horizons, enable us to see that it was not always thus, and thereby suggest that it need not always be as it is in the present—indeed, to show that it certainly will *not* be as it is in the present. Good history allows us "to think outside the box," if I may employ a current cliché.

Why is further change inevitable? It is inevitable because the popes, active agents in the cultures of their times, cannot step out of these cultures and times to live in a sphere above and beyond them. Like all of us, they are embedded in time and space. I have spent much of my academic career dealing with the problem of church reform—in the eleventh century with the Gregorian reformers, in the sixteenth with Luther and the Council of Trent, and in the twentieth with Vatican Council II. That is to say, I've been dealing with changes in church life and practice that church leaders have initiated and made operative. Some of these reforms have been extremely important, as you know, but they can seem almost insignificant in comparison with the impact that changes in culture at large have had on the church. These are changes in which church leaders had no say but that affected the church more profoundly than the changes those leaders self-consciously initiated.

Bishops and popes had nothing to do with Emperor Constantine's decision in the early fourth century to tolerate Christianity or with his almost simultaneous elevation of Christianity to a privileged place in the Roman Empire. The impact on Christianity was of tsunamic proportions. When Constantine, for instance, convoked the first ecumenical council (Nicaea, 325), he in effect made the bishops into the ecclesiastical equivalent of the Roman Senate, and he took on himself the responsibility to see that their doctrinal and disciplinary decrees were observed throughout the empire.

The translation into Latin of the Aristotelian corpus in the twelfth and thirteenth centuries radically reshaped the Christian theological enterprise. The resurgence of historical studies in the nineteenth century and the consequent application of historical methods to sacred subjects did the same. The invention of the telephone, to say nothing of radio, television, and the Internet, put new control and power of surveillance into the hands of church leaders, especially the pope. Modern medicine, nutrition, and sanitation have led to longer papacies, enabling the popes to influence the church's course with a new consistency and to leave a stronger and deeper imprint on it than was possible in the past. I will not belabor this point, but I needed to make it to establish the premise on which my lecture rests. We can now turn to a few examples of how and when popes assumed responsibilities that were new—responsibilities their predecessors did not have.

CIVIC RESPONSIBILITY

The first and most obvious of these, with which you are certainly familiar, was assuming responsibility for the physical well-being of the city of Rome, which included upkeep of the city walls and even paying the military to defend the city. Taking on this task was a development resulting principally from the erosion of the institutions of the Roman Empire. The popes moved into the gap left by leadership failure.

Constantine himself invested the clergy with certain quasi-civic functions, which established a basis for the later development. This is well known. But the precondition even for Constantine's actions and then for the popes' assuming such mundane activities generally goes unnoticed and is another instance of the impact on the church of realities outside it. The clergy and people elected bishops who were educated, like their pagan peers, in the literary classics of Greece and Rome that not only provided them with leadership skills but also instilled in them a sense of duty toward their city. Their education—secular, if you will—was an education in civic virtue, geared to the public weal.

Bishops in the late Roman Empire never thought to question the civic aspects of their position. They almost inevitably and unawares accepted as a mode of their job description the public servant model they had learned in school while reading Cicero's *De officiis* and similar texts. In 368, St. Basil, already bishop of Caesarea, founded a large leper colony on the outskirts of the city. In a letter to an official, he rather dismissed the accomplishment by saying that he had done no more than any well-intentioned governor was expected to do. It is a telling remark.

Basil was not a pope, but Gregory the Great was. Moreover, Gregory came from a family of Roman senators, and he, too, had received an excellent education that, along with training in eloquence, included the inculcation of the traditional Roman virtues of prudence, constancy, moderation, magnanimity, and dedication to the good of the *polis*. To these he added the characteristic Christian virtues of humility and charity, but the traditional Roman virtues he shared with all noble Romans—Christians and pagans alike. It is significant, in that regard, that before he was pope he was prefect of the city of Rome (the rough equivalent of a mayor). As pope he paid soldiers to defend the city. He drew on papal resources to bribe the Lombards, a Germanic nation that had established an aggressive kingdom in northern Italy, to keep their distance from Rome, and in 595 he signed a treaty with them in the name of the emperor residing in distant Constantinople (present-day Istanbul). "Under the pretext of being made a bishop," he noted in a letter, "I have been brought back into the world, and I devote myself to secular things to a much greater extent than I recall ever having done when I was a layman."

Gregory did not like carrying out many of the duties his position thrust on him, though he performed them extremely well. From our twenty-first-century perspective, those duties seem alien to our sense of episcopal propriety and to our principle of separation of church and state. We need to recognize, however, the positive side to this situation. These bishops, including the bishop of Rome, felt responsible not only for their flock within their cities but also for the pagans within them. Theirs was not a narrowly ecclesiastical understanding of the scope of their office and local responsibilities.

In 596 Gregory sent to England an unprecedented mission of forty monks headed by St. Augustine of Canterbury, an enterprise that bore a fruit that in its abundance surely surpassed Gregory's fondest hopes. This was the first time a pope undertook launching an evangelizing mission, and it was, with qualification, the last almost until the present. Strange to say, such missions never figured large on the papal agenda, partly because in the great centuries of missionary activity in the early modern period, religious orders and the kings of Spain, Portugal, and France took the initiative. The popes had their hands full in Europe.

The Lombards continued to threaten Rome and environs for another century and a half after Gregory. When Arian Christians first entered Italy, they gradually converted to orthodox Catholicism, but their conversion did not render them any less aggressive or less power-hungry. Their demands for tribute and their menacing armies threatened the peace of the peninsula and the effective functioning of the bishops. In 752 Aistulf, the Lombard king, appeared at the gates of Rome and demanded an annual tribute. The desperation of this situation led Pope Stephen II to do the unheard of: to cross the Alps (the first pope to do so) and to seek aid from Pepin, king of the Franks, the father of Charlemagne. Stephen appeared before the king in penitential garb, threw himself on the ground, and besought Pepin to deliver Rome from the Lombard threat. He was successful. Pepin acquiesced.

The repercussions of this event on the subsequent history of the papacy for the next thousand years and on the popes' job description are so colossal as to take one's breath away. Pepin descended into Italy with his armies, defeated the Lombards, and made a huge land grant to Stephen and his successors, which, in principle, if not immediately in fact, created for the popes their own kingdom. This Donation of Pepin, as it was called, was the foundation for the Papal States, over which the popes reigned for over a thousand years until 1870 (only a century and a half ago). The papal domain was no petty city-state. It comprised at its fullest extent about 50 percent of the landmass of Italy between Naples and Milan, stretching in the east along the Adriatic almost to Venice.

RULING THE PAPAL STATES

Only with time did the popes explicitly acknowledge the fact that, besides being bishops of Rome, they were now kings, but in fact that is what they were. The history of their trying to bring the sprawling territory they claimed as their own under control is a seesaw back and forth between a chaotic and orderly—though often resented—rule. Dealing with the Papal States consumed such immense amounts of the popes' time, energy, and resources that those dealings were often, in practice, the top item on their job description.

Why the determination to maintain a hold on this territory? The States at times served as a buffer to hold back or deflect enemy armies intent on marching into Rome. When all went well, the States were a source of considerable income. They added prestige to the person of the pope, and, in certain eras, they provided dukedoms that could be bestowed on relatives for the advancement of the family fortune and prestige. The most fundamental reason for the popes' determination to hold and control the States, however, was the conviction that they were a sacred trust, given to St. Peter and hence worth every sacrifice. The States were, like all gifts to St. Peter, a gift in perpetuity, destined to last for all time. In 1870 Pope Pius IX and his closest collaborators could not believe that God would permit the occupation of Rome and the seizure of the States by the Italian army, and Pius's successor, Leo XIII, as thoroughly convinced of it as was Pius, expended considerable diplomatic capital working for their restoration.

Altogether alien to our contemporary thinking about the church is the idea that St. Peter might be pleased with owning a lot of land. Yet Pope

Gregory VII's letter to King Solomon of Hungary (28 October 1074) leaves little doubt that that was the pontiff's persuasion. He said to Solomon:

> Your letter would have been more graciously received at our hands had not your ill-considered remarks been so grievously offensive to St. Peter. For, as you may learn from the chief men of your country, the kingdom of Hungary was long since offered and devotedly surrendered to St. Peter by King Stephen as the full property of the Holy Roman Church under its complete jurisdiction and control. . . . Neither fear nor favor nor any respect of persons shall, so far as in us lies, prevent us from claiming with God's help every possible honor due to Peter, whose servant we are.

About a century later, Pope Innocent III, in a dispute with King John of England over an episcopal appointment, put England under interdict and, when the king finally surrendered, received the kingdom of England as a fief for St. Peter.

From about the ninth to at least the sixteenth century, the so-called Donation of Constantine influenced papal thinking along these same lines. This notorious forgery, whose precise origins no later than the middle of the ninth century are still disputed, purported to be a document of the early fourth century from Emperor Constantine to Pope Silvester. In the document, the emperor granted to the pope in perpetuity, among other things, extensive lands and buildings as papal property, the right to wear the imperial insignia, and, most important, "all power" over Rome, Italy, and the western portion of the Roman Empire.

It was the Donation of Constantine that led Pope Gregory VII in 1075 to claim "that the pope alone may use the imperial insignia" and "that the pope is the only one whose feet are to be kissed by all princes." The donation was at least partially responsible for Gregory's assertion "that the pope may depose emperors." Gregory was the first pope ever to make such a claim. He acted on it a year later by deposing Emperor Henry IV, the first such deposition. Subsequent popes continued from time to time to exercise their right to depose and excommunicate rulers, but that power altogether disappeared from their list of responsibilities after Pope Pius V in 1570 excommunicated Elizabeth I of England and released her subjects from their oath of loyalty to her. The times were changing.

VALIDATING EMPERORS

On Christmas Day in 800, long before Gregory deposed Emperor Henry or before Pius deposed Elizabeth, an extraordinary scene took place during Mass in St. Peter's Basilica in Rome. At a certain point, Pope Leo III placed the imperial crown on the head of Charlemagne, Pepin's son and king of the Franks. Everything in the scene was unprecedented. A pope created an emperor, having seemingly himself decided who that emperor was to be. Moreover, a presumably legitimate emperor—more precisely, empress (Irene)—sat on the throne in Constantinople. She, stupefied, learned of the event only after the fact. Actions like this worsened already frayed relations with the Greek-speaking world and contributed to the Great Eastern Schism of 1054, which was not healed on an official level until 1965 at the time of the Second Vatican Council.

After Leo III's dramatic imposition of the crown on Charlemagne's head, popes had little control over the election of the emperor. In fact, for a long period the situation was reversed—to the point that the pope was approved, or even chosen, by the emperor. But being crowned by the pope was for centuries considered essential to validating the imperial election. Emperor validation lasted seven centuries and slipped from the papal job description only in the sixteenth century.

SOLDIERING

As you have often heard, society in the Middle Ages was supposedly divided into three categories: monks, peasants, and nobles, to each of which was attached a characteristic function—*orare* (prayer) for the monks, *laborare* (work) for the peasants, and *militare* (soldiering) for the nobles. Especially as the centuries moved on, these categories proved ever more inadequate to cover the variety of occupations in which people engaged. Nonetheless, soldiering remained the specialty of members of the upper classes who, among other things, were wealthy enough to own their own horses.

Popes were almost invariably drawn from this upper class. We should not be surprised, therefore, that some of them were soldiers, but we are perhaps surprised to learn that some of them exercised their soldiering skills as pope. Of Pope Benedict VIII (early eleventh century) it is written that "helmet on his head, a coat of mail on his body, he policed the Papal States himself." St. Leo IX, designated pope in 1049 by Emperor Henry III, was one of the most important popes of the entire Middle Ages because he launched the powerful movement that would become known as the Gregorian Reform of the church. A cousin of the emperor, he had, as a young man, led troops supplied by his bishop in an imperial campaign in northern Italy. As pope he personally led a small, ill-equipped force against the Normans south of Rome, an endeavor that ended in his surrender and capture.

Pope Julius II, the genius patron of Bramante, Raphael, and Michelangelo, is, of course, the best known of the warrior popes. He was determined to establish effective control over the Papal States, and, in 1506, in a brilliant military campaign led by himself—in full armor and accompanied by his cardinals—he wrested the important cities of Perugia and Bologna from the petty tyrants who ruled them. With that campaign won, he turned his forces a few years later against the French, who were powerfully established in northern Italy, and led his troops to drive them out with the battle cry *Fuori i barbari*, "Out with the barbarians!"

But, yes, the times were changing. With the outbreak of the Reformation a few years after Julius's death, popes came to realize they had to behave in ways that Christians of the new times thought more befitting the papal office. Nonetheless, war was on the papal agenda. The popes from the eleventh to well into the seventeenth century called repeatedly for crusades—holy war—against the Muslim infidel. In 1095 at the Synod of Clermont in central France, Pope Urban II issued a passionate call—"God wills it!"—especially to French knights to take up arms to aid Emperor Alexis of Constantinople in defending Eastern Christendom against the Seljuk Turks and, just as important, for the crusaders to continue further to free the Holy Land from "the infidel." Though it ended in a terrible bloodbath during the capture of Jerusalem, this is the only crusade in the Middle Ages that can be called successful, in that it captured Palestine and held it for a century.

But with the fall of Edessa fifty years later, Pope Eugene III called for the Second Crusade. In the wake of more serious setbacks, Pope Gregory VIII called for the Third, and in 1204, Innocent III the Fourth, which culminated in the sacking and burning of Constantinople not by the infidel Turks but by the Christian crusaders sent to defend it. The latter was an atrocity that the Orthodox have never forgotten. Innocent was, moreover, the first pope to call for a war against heretics, the Albigensian crusade in southern France.

Historians generally list five more crusades in the Middle Ages, but numbering them gets complicated. What is important to note is that funding and organizing military expeditions to the East was an absolutely major and almost constant preoccupation of the popes from the late eleventh century forward, even though they most often were unable to rally support. They devised taxes on ecclesiastics throughout Europe to help pay for actual or hoped-for military operations.

In 1453 Constantinople finally fell to the Turks, which added new urgency to the situation. Pope Nicholas V immediately announced a crusade. Nothing happened. His successors in the early Renaissance, such as Calixtus III and Pius II, were obsessed with recovering the city for Christians. Pius, discouraged by his failure to rally kings and princes to the cause, set out to lead it himself—"old and sick though I am"—only to die at Ancona on the eastern coast of Italy while awaiting ships that never came.

Were these medieval crusades offensive or defensive wars? I think it is possible to argue both sides. The crusades in the early modern period were more clearly defensive. After Constantinople fell, the Turks became more aggressive against the West, and by 1529 they had penetrated as far as Vienna. Meanwhile, their ships roamed freely over the Mediterranean, which they virtually controlled. For the popes of this period, holy war against the infidel was arguably more urgent than dealing with the Reformation. In his bull convoking the Council of Trent in 1542, Paul III refers to the Turkish threat under the rubrics of "our godless and ruthless enemy" and "our cruel and everlasting enemy."

Thirty years later, Pius V rallied Venice and Spain to a defeat of the Turkish fleet at Lepanto, a battle in which the papal galleys under admiral Marcantonio Colonna fought alongside the Spanish and Venetians. A century later, Blessed Pope Innocent XI mobilized a Holy League against the Turks that recovered Hungary and Belgrade, the last major such papal initiative.

As I just intimated, the popes from about the eighth century onward commanded their own navy, whose galleys were manned for the most part by condemned criminals and Muslim slaves. The papal armies (of which today's Swiss Guards are vestiges) were relatively small compared with those of the great monarchies. Nonetheless, they accounted for 40 percent of papal expenditures in the late fifteenth century. Papal forces fought their last battle on 20 September 1870, when they put up a token defense of Rome against the Italian troops, who then seized the city and brought an end to papal temporal power.

GOVERNING

But I am ahead of myself. For internal order within Rome and the cities of the Papal States, the popes created various police forces, the best known of which were the Pontifical Gendarmes, sometimes known in the nineteenth century as "Papal Carabinieri." During the late sixteenth century, Pope Sixtus V, determined to bring order to the States and ensure effective control of them, instituted a severe code of justice, which led during his pontificate to the public execution of hundreds of brigands. He ordered capital punishment as well for abortion, incest, sodomy, and calumny.

Sixtus went to an extreme, but the popes continued public executions until the seizure of Rome in 1870 by the Italian army. If, on your next trip to Rome, you visit the state-run Criminology Museum (*Museo di Criminologia*), just off the Via Giulia, you will find the papal guillotine, twelve feet tall. It was last used on 9 July 1870, while the first Vatican Council was in session, just two months before the seizure of the city.

In 1588 the same Pope Sixtus V reorganized the Roman Curia into fifteen departments, or bureaus, that he called "congregations," thus creating the structure of the curia with which we are familiar today. The reorganization transformed the papacy from its earlier consistorial form, according to which papal initiatives were debated in full meeting of the cardinals resident in Rome—acting as a kind of senate—to a more absolute monarchy in which heads of departments reported one at a time to the pope. While extraordinarily important, therefore, as an increase in the pope's executive powers, the reorganization also reveals how governing the States preoccupied the popes. Of the fifteen congregations created or reorganized by Sixtus, seven were for the States. They included a Congregation of the University of Rome, a Congregation of Roads, Bridges, and Aqueducts, and a Congregation of the Navy.

You are probably wondering at this point if the popes ever did anything that we today recognize as their important responsibilities. Yes, of course they did. I have belabored the other responsibilities they bore to emphasize how much the culture in which they lived determined the responsibilities they assumed and also to emphasize the extraordinary degree to which governing the States filled space on their job description for more than a millennium.

The third-century dispute between Pope Stephen and St. Cyprian, bishop of Carthage, over the validity of baptism administered by heretics or schismatics illustrates the confidence of the bishop of Rome in the special authority of his see in matters of discipline and doctrine, a confidence that would only grow stronger over the course of time. The conviction became widespread that in doctrine the Roman Church did not err. Pope Pius IX's declaration in 1854 that the Immaculate Conception of the Virgin Mary was a dogma revealed by God to be believed by all the faithful was, however, so unprecedented as to make papal definitions of dogma a new item on the job list—even though after that only one other pope, Pius XII, ever issued another such definition.

During the Middle Ages, the popes added the right to convoke an ecumenical council to the list of their responsibilities. Recognition of this right/responsibility grew gradually and was hotly contested. As you know, the Roman emperors (or empress, in one case) convoked the first eight ecumenical councils, in which the popes did not always play important roles. But the popes, like many other bishops throughout the church, often convoked local synods or councils to deal with local or immediate issues. In the wake of the Gregorian Reform in the mid-eleventh century, these Roman synods, of which there were many, began to assume more importance, because they often dealt with the tense relationship between the papacy and the German emperor and other rulers over church-state matters that affected large areas of the Western Church.

In retrospect, some of these synods began to be considered ecumenical (Lateran I, II, III, and IV, for instance). After the Council of Constance in the early fifteenth century, especially in the wake of the later rambunctious Council of Basel, popes began expressly to claim the exclusive right to convoke such councils. By the time of the Council of Trent a century later, the right was generally, though certainly not universally, acknowledged. The claim would probably have had a more difficult time growing if it had not occurred independently of the Greek-speaking church. In any case, the first Code of Canon Law (1917) enshrined the right in absolute terms: "There is no such thing as an Ecumenical Council unless it is convoked by the Roman Pontiff . . . and it is the Pontiff's right to transfer the council, suspend it, dissolve it, and confirm its decrees."

During his pontificate, Pope John Paul II canonized 482 saints and declared a whopping 1,338 individuals blessed. If the pope, and the pope alone, has an uncontested job, canonizing saints would seem to be it. Yet, as with the exclusive right to convoke councils, this right developed only gradually. Not until the middle of the thirteenth century did popes officially and definitively claim it as their own. In the early centuries, all martyrs for the faith, of which there were many, were automatically considered saints, but, because of some possibly fraudulent claims, local synods or councils undertook the examination of the evidence and pronounced on the validity of canonization. As the cult of saints who were not martyrs developed, spontaneous acclamations of sanctity became more problematic. New criteria had to be applied. In the ninth century, the legislation of the Frankish kings Charlemagne and Louis the Pious specified that in the future only the local bishop could authorize veneration and move a person's relics to a place of public cult.

In the wake of the Gregorian Reform, which entailed the popes' determination to be independent of secular rulers, papal claims developed. By the early twelfth century, authorization of cult occurred at synods or councils over which the pope presided. When Pope Eugene III in 1146 decided on his own authority to canonize Emperor Henry II, he took the decisive step. In 1215 the Fourth Lateran Council, under Innocent III, forbade any new veneration of relics anywhere without papal authorization. Two decades later, Pope Innocent IV insisted on the absolute reservation of the right to the pope because canonization entailed the solemn and church-wide cult of the saint.

Perhaps no item on the papal job description today is more important and has more immediate and profound influence on the life of the church than the appointment of bishops. Even if I devoted my lecture exclusively to sketching, in the broadest terms, the complicated and volatile history of this issue, I could not do it justice. The highlights of it, however, are these. From the earliest times, priests and people elected the bishop of their city, a principle that the popes of the fifth century, including Leo the Great, insisted on. In the early Middle Ages, under the evolving feudal system, local leaders began designating men faithful to them for the office, even though sometimes the formality of elections persisted.

The popes of the Gregorian Reform reacted fiercely against this practice, demanding free election of bishops and abbots. Their confrontation, especially with the German emperor, exploded into the Investiture Controversy, a bitter fight that, among other things, included one of the worst sacks of Rome in its history. In the end, the popes had to make some concessions, but the Fourth Lateran Council (1215) decreed that bishops would be elected by the cathedral chapter.

In a curious turn from their earlier position, the popes had, by the fourteenth century, devised means by which they themselves were able, in many places, to install their own candidates. Just a century later, however, as strong monarchies developed in France, Spain, and Portugal, the popes, in a series of separate decisions, handed over to those kings the right of appointment, something earlier popes had bitterly opposed. They of course reserved to themselves final approval, which in most cases was virtually automatic.

This arrangement, extended to other monarchs, lasted until the French Revolution, which swept monarchs even outside France off their thrones. Monarchies later returned in most places, but never to enjoy the same stability and power. (You recall that at precisely this time John Carroll, the first bishop in the new United States of America, insisted with Rome that he be elected by his clergy—the first and last time that happened in this country.) In the nineteenth century, the popes made concordats with Protestant states, in which cathedral chapters elected the bishop, having ascertained beforehand that the government had no objection to the candidate.

But in the new political situations of the nineteenth century, which included new missionary ventures, the popes bit by bit expanded their right of appointment. Pius IX viewed with horror the unification of Italy in midcentury, since it necessarily meant the end of the Papal States. However, as that unification also brought to an end other political units in Italy, it delivered into the pope's hands the appointment of bishops that had previously rested in the hands of the rulers of those states. In concordats the popes made different arrangements with governments, but the trend was ever toward greater papal control. Canon 329 of the 1917 code laid down, for the first time in history, the absolute norm: "The Roman Pontiff freely nominates the bishops."

Another canon stated that the pope could concede certain aspects of that right, but the assumption was that all authority rested with the pope.

The corresponding canon of the 1983 code (377), now in effect, is, surprisingly, not so absolute: "The Supreme Pontiff freely appoints bishops or confirms those legitimately elected."

TEACHING

Expanded Role and New Genres

In the nineteenth century the popes added teaching to their job description. They became teachers. Or, better put, they became teachers in a newly professed and more expanded way. Their principal vehicle for doing so was the encyclical. They used that medium to propose, expound, and elaborate moral, theological, and doctrinal positions in a virtually unprecedented manner. By definition, an encyclical is a circular letter and, as such, was used by popes and others from ancient times. But in the nineteenth century its significance changed to such an extent that it emerged as a new genre.

How does the modern encyclical differ from previous genres favored by the popes for their pronouncements? The premise generally underlying earlier genres like bulls and briefs was that the pope was either a judge or a dispenser of favors. He decided cases among contending parties. As St. Thomas put it, it is the pope's job *finaliter determinare*—that is, to act as court of final appeal. He conferred benefits, issued executive orders regarding liturgical practices and similar matters, and, on relatively rare occasions, on his own, condemned heretical or offensive opinions. Insofar as the pope "taught," he did so for the most part in a negative way, by condemning a wrong opinion. Although there were many exceptions, popes generally did not provide a correct opinion or develop alternatives. Pope Leo X's condemnation of Luther in the bull *Exsurge, Domine* is a famous instance. It is nothing more than a list of Luther's errors. The papal encyclicals that developed in the nineteenth century certainly did not hesitate to condemn errors, but they also elaborated on topics, as would a teacher in a classroom.

Even so, in the Middle Ages and early modern period, popes rarely on their own issued condemnations like *Exsurge, Domine*. That task fell to local or general councils and, after the thirteenth century, to the theological faculties of the universities. Remember, the faculties of Paris, Louvain, and Cologne condemned Luther independently of Leo X.

The popes' increased use of the encyclical is indicative of its growing importance. From the two issued at the end of the eighteenth century by Pius VI over the course of twenty-four years and the one issued by his successor over a twenty-three-year pontificate, we move to thirty-eight by Pius IX in midcentury and then to seventy-five by his successor, Leo XIII. Many of these encyclicals, it is true, dealt with local problems or situations, and some promoted certain pious practices. But the simple increase in number indicates a new mode of papal teaching authority that committed the popes to an increasingly large number of positions on a wide range of issues.

Meanwhile, the popes began to make use of other forms of communication to express their teaching and their views, such as addresses to groups of pilgrims, radio addresses, and homilies. Since the beginning of the jet age, the weekly audiences to thousands on thousands of pilgrims in St. Peter's Square and the journeys of the popes to every corner of the globe have provided occasions for papal speeches unknown before. Pope John Paul II issued only fourteen encyclicals over the course of twenty-six years, a relatively modest number, but the flow of other documents from him, such as Apostolic Exhortations, Apostolic Letters, and Apostolic Constitutions, was considerable, to say nothing of his homilies and other speeches.

Pius XII, in the middle of the twentieth century, was the first pope in which this phenomenon of increased communications burst notably on the scene. His speeches and other documents fill twenty volumes of five hundred to six hundred pages each. At the same time, the popes at least tacitly encouraged the congregations of the Roman Curia to issue judgments, instructions, and opinions on doctrinal and moral matters. The Holy See thus took over a function previously reserved to theologians and put itself in a competitive—potentially adversarial—relationship to them, especially when it at times seemed to be acting in a partisan way. This development helps account for the conflicts in our time between theologians and the "papal magisterium."

The Public Persona

Air, train, and auto travel have provided more occasions for papal statements, but they have, as well, made the popes into leaders of great rallies. Since Paul VI's pilgrimage to the Holy Land in 1964, which was the definitive end of the role of "prisoner of the Vatican" (a role that the popes had played after the seizure of Rome and the States in 1870), the pope, amid shouts and cheers, has presided over huge gatherings, where one of the principal aims is to stir enthusiasm and support for the office he bears. Thanks to photography and television, few indeed are the Catholics throughout the world today who do not recognize the visage of the reigning pontiff, and virtually every one of them knows the pope's name. Fostering "loyalty to the pope" has become one of the popes' principal responsibilities, just as taking that loyalty to heart now sometimes seems to be almost the core of Catholic self-definition.

This ever more public persona of the popes, coupled with the political freedom they gained by the loss of the Papal States, opened up a new role for popes as spokesmen for causes affecting humanity as a whole. Leo XIII's encyclical *Rerum Novarum* called for just wages and humane working conditions for all laborers, regardless of their religion. Benedict XV's denunciation of World War I as a "senseless slaughter" and a "hideous butchery" brought down on his head the wrath of the Allies and the Central Powers alike, but his marshaling of the Vatican's resources almost to the point of bankruptcy in evenhanded aid to the war's victims won him respect even from those outside the Christian fold. Perhaps the most striking tribute in this regard is the monument to him erected in the Muslim city of Istanbul, where the inscription reads, in part, "the great pope of the world tragedy . . . the benefactor of all people, irrespective of nationality or religion."

This new situation provided Paul VI in 1965 the opportunity to address the United Nations, where he presented himself as "a man like yourselves, your brother," and to issue his passionate appeal for peace: "No more war! War never again! It is peace, peace that must guide the destiny of the peoples of the world and all humanity." The recent (and difficult to attain) ratification in Vatican II of the declaration on religious liberty, *Dignitatis Humanae*, gave him, moreover, warrant to speak to the UN boldly about human rights: "What you proclaim here are the rights and duties of human beings—their dignity, their liberty, and, above all, their religious liberty." Actions like these of Leo, Benedict, and Paul indicate a subtle yet significant modification of values and priorities for the successors of Peter.

I hope this rapid sketch of the more important jobs the popes have undertaken in their Petrine ministry has been enlightening and has helped provide a better grasp of the papal office today. My larger aim has been, through the examination of one institution, the papacy, to drive home the point that changes in culture at large—secular culture, if you will—impact the church far more radically than we usually reckon. Even the popes have only imperfect control over the direction of the church—imperfect control even over the modes and agenda of the office they hold.

But what about the future? History takes sudden, unexpected, and radical changes that nobody could ever have predicted. In 1517, for instance, who would have thought that an obscure Augustinian friar teaching in a third-rate university in a cultural backwater known as Wittenberg would, within a few years, set Europe on its ears? All that can be said with security in 2009 is that by 2109 things will be different.

Let me conclude, however, by mentioning a startling new development made possible by Vatican II's declaration on non-Christian religions, *Nostra Aetate*. In the past, as we have seen, the popes were catalysts for holy war against the Muslim infidels. The actions of John Paul II signified not only an implicit, yet dramatic, renunciation of anything resembling that role but also the assumption of another—bridge builder, fellow pilgrim, and agent for promoting mutual respect and understanding. He met with Muslims more than sixty times during his pontificate. In 1985 he held a rally with Muslim youths in Casablanca, at which he said, "We believe in the same God, the living God who created the world and brings his creatures to perfection." He was the first pope ever to enter a mosque (in Damascus, May 2000), and he launched from the Vatican five standing dialogs with Muslim groups.

In that regard, Pope Benedict is best known for his unfortunate remarks at Regensburg, but he, too, has been trying to quell the antagonism between the two faiths that the catastrophe of 9/11 inflamed. As is well known, he in fact sees the Muslim religion as an ally with him against secularism. On 30 November 2006, he stood alongside the Grand Mufti in the Blue Mosque in Istanbul in a moment of silent prayer. Is there a more badly needed role for the popes to assume in the future than bridge builders and agents for reconciliation in a world in which hatred and distrust, often fanned by religious fanaticism, so often holds sway? John Paul II, in any case, assumed that task, and Benedict XVI gives evidence of recognizing its urgency.

"Thou art Peter." As embodied in his successors through the centuries, Peter has turned out to be a quite remarkable, versatile, and even unpredictable person.

3

CARDINALS IN CONCLAVE

A Troubled History

I published this article in 2005, just as cardinals were assembling for the conclave that elected Pope Benedict XVI. The points I made in it remain valid, I believe, even though another conclave has since elected Pope Francis.

After more than a quarter century, cardinals from around the world are once again gathering in the Vatican, soon to be sequestered "in conclave" for as long as it takes to elect a new pope. We eagerly await the results but will have no information about what happens during the conclave, because the cardinals are sworn to absolute secrecy. The whole affair, at least as viewed from the outside, will be dignified and orderly, just what we should expect from such a serious undertaking. Our present procedures evolved, however, precisely because the election of the pope was not always dignified and orderly. Often it was anything but that.

According to ancient tradition, the bishop of Rome, like all bishops, was elected by the clergy and people of the city over which he was to preside, or by the clergy with the acquiescence of the people. We have a striking example of this tradition in the well-known account of the choice of St. Ambrose as bishop of Milan in 373 or 374. As the clergy and people assembled for the election of the next bishop, Ambrose, then the chief civil administrator of the region, was present to make sure the election proceeded peacefully. After he addressed the assembly, he was greeted with the cry that he be the bishop, though he was at that point not even baptized. "Ambrose bishop!" shouted the crowd. He acquiesced to the acclamation to become one of the outstanding churchmen of a remarkable generation that included St. Jerome and St. Augustine.

Not all papal elections came off so easily. The election of St. Damasus, a contemporary of Ambrose, was rough and bloody. On the death of Damasus's predecessor, rioting broke out in Rome. Damasus and a man named Ursinus were chosen by two different factions among the clergy. The civil authorities, who favored Damasus, had to intervene to settle the dispute, but not before some thugs who supported Damasus had attacked partisans of his rival gathered in what would become the Basilica of St. Mary Major. They left over one hundred dead before finishing their rampage. Damasus, who had an extraordinarily long pontificate of eighteen years, went on to become one of the most important popes in this period of church history, especially remembered because of his friendship with St. Jerome, whom he encouraged in his translation of the Bible into Latin.

The election of the bishop of Rome, because of the political and emblematic importance of that see, continued to be especially troubled well into the modern period. While many elections took place without incident, many others were marred by rivalries among contending parties and led to confusion about who was rightly to be considered the bishop of Rome. Although it was agreed that the election lay in the hands of the "clergy and people" of the city of Rome, lack of clear procedures made manipulation of the election easy for those who wanted to seize for themselves or their families this prestigious and lucrative prize.

In this regard, the first half of the tenth century was particularly troublesome and sordid as control of the election fell into the hands of the local nobility in and around the city of Rome. Early in the century a woman named Marozia emerged as the virtual ruler of the city. She saw to the deposition of Pope John X, who in 928 was thrown into the prison of the Castel Sant'Angelo, where he was almost certainly murdered a short while later. Marozia then secured the election of her candidates— Pope Leo VI and, on his death, Pope Stephen VII. When Stephen died around 931, she gained the bishopric for her son, John XI, a young man probably only in his late teens. Only a year later Marozia fell from power at the hands of Alberic II, prince of Rome, who then controlled the election of the next five popes, the last of whom, John XII, was his illegitimate son. John XII was eighteen or nineteen when elected and would soon be known for what one historian calls "his uninhibitedly debauched life."

Meanwhile, a strong secular ruler, Otto I, emerged in the territories of northeastern Europe that would eventually be known as the Holy Roman Empire. John XII, in danger from political and military rivals after the death of his powerful father, was forced to ask Otto to help him. Otto agreed, swore to protect the pope, came to Italy with his army, and on 2 February 962 was crowned emperor by John XII in St. Peter's Basilica. First off, Otto made sure that a synod admonished the pope to reform his lifestyle. Then he insisted that henceforth the freely elected pope must, before his ordination as bishop of Rome, pronounce an oath of loyalty to the emperor in recognition of the emperor's role as overlord of the Papal States. Thus began a long era of strong imperial—that is, "German"—concern for the bishopric of Rome, the holder of which was—by reason of the oath—a vassal of the emperor.

One of the greatest turning points in the history of papal elections occurred in the middle of the next century. There were three men claiming to be the legitimate pope. In 1046 the devout Emperor Henry III entered central Italy determined to settle the dispute and to take measures to reform the church, especially the bishopric of Rome. He oversaw the deposition of each of the three rivals and then nominated Siger of Bamberg as pope. Siger died shortly thereafter, as did the man Henry designated as his successor. Then, in 1049, Henry nominated his cousin, Bruno of Toul, who took the name Leo IX. He was the first of the reforming popes who promoted the great movement known as the Gregorian Reform.

The Gregorian Reform was a complex phenomenon, but at its heart was the determination to reinstate the old canonical legislation regarding the free and proper election of bishops by the local clergy. Nowhere was this reform more badly needed than in Rome itself, and only a drastic measure like Henry's interventions could have lifted that situation out of the morass into which it had sunk. Henry nominated Leo's successor, but when Henry died in 1056 the elections in Rome threatened once again to fall into chaos. That is precisely what happened in 1059, when two claimants emerged: Nicholas II, a reformer, and Benedict X, supported by the Roman nobility.

With the help of military force supplied by friendly parties, Nicholas prevailed. His great achievement was to issue in 1059 the decree regulating papal elections that is the nucleus out of which the present system developed. It put the nomination of the pope in the hands of cardinal bishops, assisted by cardinal priests, whose choice would be ratified by the rest of the clergy and people of the city. There had, of course, previously been efforts, largely unsuccessful, to provide for the orderly and canonical election of the pope, but this decree of Nicholas II was the first to establish an administrative machinery to accomplish it.

What are cardinals, and why were they chosen to be the key players in the election process? The original meaning of the term is disputed, and much of the history is murky. But it is clear that by the seventh century the priests assigned to some twenty-five of the principal parishes in Rome were called cardinals. Especially because it was deemed fitting for the liturgies of the great basilicas like St. John Lateran, St. Mary Major, and St. Peter's to be presided over by bishops, it early became customary for the bishops from the small cities near Rome such as Ostia and Palestrina to perform that function regularly. With the beginning of the Gregorian Reform, these bishops started to take a more active role in assisting the pope in other ways as well. Although they retained their own sees, they could, by reason of the roles they were increasingly playing in Rome, be considered members of the clergy of the Church of Rome. (They were called cardinal bishops possibly because they were quasi-incardinated into the diocese of Rome.)

Thus, even for the cardinal bishops, those "outsiders," the tradition of election by the city's clergy was retained by a kind of legal fiction. That same fiction prevails to this day, for the cardinals are members of "the Holy Roman Church" (Sanctae Romanae Ecclesiae, abbreviated S.R.E.)—that is, the church of the city of Rome. For that reason each of them has a "titular" church in the city assigned to him, as if he were regularly officiating there. The reason the decree of 1059 singled out the "cardinal bishops" for the principal role in the election seems to have been twofold. First, since Rome had no metropolitan see superior to it to approve the election, the cardinal bishops discharged that office in a somewhat different way, by actually electing the pope. Second, at the time of the decree the seven "suburban" bishoprics were more or less in the hands of the reformers. The decree, besides providing the basic blueprint still in effect today, also raised the rather obscure office of cardinal to one of strategic importance for the future of the church. Thus, cardinals as we know them are a creation of the eleventh century.

For the next several centuries, the decree of 1059 was unsuccessful in putting an end to disputed elections, and popes and antipopes continued to contend for the see of Peter. The most notorious of these disputes was the Great Western Schism (1376–1415), when for a half century two sets of papal claimants, and then three, simultaneously and stubbornly insisted on their own legitimacy. The Council of Constance finally put an end to the scandal by deposing two of the claimants, securing the resignation of the third, and proceeding to the election of a new pope, Martin V, who won universal acceptance.

Even aside from such spectacular eventualities, the cardinals some-times took an inordinate amount of time—months, even years—for their deliberations. One reason for these delays was the provision made by Pope Alexander III in 1179 that a two-thirds majority of votes was re-quired for a valid election, a measure significantly modified only in 1996 by Pope John Paul II. In any case, the long deliberations led to the "conclave." The word means, as we are so often told, "under lock and key," from the two Latin words *con* (with) and *clavis* (key). When in 1268 Pope Clement IV died in Viterbo, the cardinals assembled there to elect his successor. The election dragged on for three years. As public indignation mounted in Viterbo, the civil authorities first locked the car-dinals in the papal palace; when that did not work, they put them on an almost starvation diet. (Legend has it that they also finally removed the roof.) Although not altogether without precedent, this was the first in-stance of a conclave in the strict sense—a papal election sequestered from the outside world.

Gregory X, the pope elected at this first conclave, published a bull in 1274 that made the strict seclusion of the cardinals mandatory in order to promote a more rapid election. He also obliged the electors to absolute secrecy about their deliberations. The conclave thus became official. The measure was, however, intermittently suspended by popes, with bad re-sults. It took the cardinals twenty-seven months, for instance, to elect in 1294 a successor to Pope Nicholas IV and over two years to elect in 1316 the successor to Clement V. Nonetheless, the practice of "conclave" grad-ually became normative, and, as it did, such protracted deliberations dis-appeared.

In the Middle Ages elections were held in the city where the pope died. Popes were often absent from Rome, usually in one of the nearby towns in the Papal States such as Viterbo or Orvieto. The last pope to be elected outside Rome (until Pius VII, in Venice in 1800) was Martin V during the Council at Constance. Since then all conclaves have taken place in Rome—in the church of Santa Maria sopra Minerva, then in different chapels in the Vatican, and, finally, in the Sistine Chapel, erected by Pope Sixtus IV (1471–1484).

The regulations imposing secrecy were often reiterated, but breaches were common. From Pope Pius II himself (1458–1464) we have a candid and amusing account of his election in his autobiography, published in English under the title *Memoirs of a Renaissance Pope*. Beginning in the fifteenth century, the reports sent home by ambassadors of foreign powers in Rome contained detailed information about the number of ballots taken, the votes different candidates received, and similar matters. Pius IV in 1562 had some success in curtailing these violations of confidentiality, but only in more recent elections have the conclaves been almost hermetically sealed. The concern in the most recent elections has been that electronic listening devices might be hidden in strategic places during the conclave, so those areas have to be "swept" to guard against this. Despite such measures, information somehow continues to find its way into the public domain.

In the later part of the fifteenth century, word was leaked, in fact, that several popes were elected simply because they or their promoters were able to buy votes in the College of Cardinals, an abuse that climaxed notoriously with the election in 1494 of Alexander VI, Rodrigo Borgia. A few years after Alexander died, Pope Julius II, though himself a beneficiary of the system, published a strong bull forbidding the practice. This bull seems to have been by and large effective.

Civil rulers, as we have seen, played an important role—sometimes detrimental, sometimes beneficial—in the election of the Roman pontiff. Beginning in the sixteenth century, that role took a new form. Emperor Charles V seems to have been the first to draw up a list of acceptable and unacceptable candidates, which he provided to cardinals friendly to him. In 1590 his son, King Philip II of Spain, made public a list of seven acceptable candidates, implying he would contest the election of anyone not on the list. Gregory XIV was elected from among those favored by Philip.

Thus developed the so-called veto power, or power of exclusion, that by the late seventeenth century the thrones of France, Austria, and Spain were claiming as an "immemorial right." This right allowed each of them, through a designated cardinal in the papal conclave, to veto one candidate when he seemed within striking distance of winning the election. Throughout the eighteenth and nineteenth centuries, the veto was occasionally wielded, but more often by indirection and threat than by outright action. The attempt in 1903 by Emperor Franz Joseph of Austria to block the election of Cardinal Rampolla, however, was the last straw. The new pope, Pius X, put an absolute end to the practice, forbidding any and every "civil veto . . . even if expressed in the form of a simple wish."

The most recent regulations concerning papal election were promulgated in 1996 by Pope John Paul II. These regulations built on similar ones issued in 1975 by Paul VI, which in turn built on regulations stipulated by Pius XII in 1945. Pius XI had made his own adjustments in 1922. (I have already mentioned Pius X's regulations, but not those of Leo XIII in 1882 or those of Pius IX in 1871 and 1878.) In 1808 Pius VII basically confirmed certain provisions decreed by Pius VI in 1782 and 1789. It has not been easy, one infers, to tie up all loose ends and forestall all possible abuses. [Pope Francis has made his own adjustments.]

Important though these documents from the last several centuries are, they do not challenge two basic elements that emerged between the eleventh and thirteenth centuries and that have persisted up to the present: cardinals and conclave. Those are the two pillars on which the system rests. The election process retains, however, vestiges that are even older. The fundamental tradition going back to the earliest centuries of Christianity is, as already mentioned, that bishops are elected by the clergy and the people of their city. In a symbolic way, that is what will happen shortly in Rome. The new pope will be elected by members of the clergy of the diocese of Rome—by cardinals of "the Holy Roman Church." When he appears afterward on the balcony of St. Peter's, loud cheers will rise from the people, who, whether they realize it or not, will be acquiescing in the results of the election. Here we have a clear instance of how the familiar French maxim must sometimes be turned around: the more things remain the same, the more they have changed.

4

REFORM OF THE ROMAN CURIA

Historical and Theological Perspectives

The reform of the Roman Curia has been a recurring problem in the church since at least the fourteenth century. It is closely related to the phenomenon of papalization. During the scandal of the Vatican Bank in 2013 and just after the election of Pope Francis, Il Regno, *a highly respected Catholic journal in Italy, asked me for this article. It appears here for the first time in English.*

Amid all the current publicity about the faults and failings of the Roman Curia and the cries for its reform, we need to step back for a moment and put the situation into a larger context. We need to remember that the reform of the curia has been a recurring and sometimes an insistent issue in the history of the church. What have changed over the centuries have been the problems that need remedy. As the curia changed, the problems changed.

The institution originated modestly in the early centuries. The bishop of Rome, like other bishops, needed assistance in keeping records, tending to correspondence, and similar tasks. As he in time claimed ever more oversight and jurisdiction beyond Rome, so did the number and authority of his assistants grow. A major turning point came in 1059, with the decree establishing cardinal bishops as the electors of the pope, which was also the point when papal claims over the church began to escalate.

Bit by bit the cardinals in the papal *famiglia* began to consider themselves the "senate" of the Holy Roman Church, which the pope was required to consult on important matters. Their meetings ("consistories") with the pope gradually took over the function earlier performed by the Roman synods in which the pope met with his clergy. The cardinals' wealth and their ability to manipulate canon law in their favor increased accordingly.

In 1588 Pope Sixtus V took the drastic step of displacing the consistorial system with a bureaucracy—that is, fifteen congregations, each with a specific area of competence. Although subsequent popes have reshuffled these bureaus or departments many times, they have not changed the bureaucratic structure Sixtus set in place. From 1588 forward, therefore, the curia enjoyed all the advantages and suffered all the disadvantages that a bureaucracy entails.

Another turning point—subtle, gradual, and undeclared—occurred after the solemn declarations of papal primacy and infallibility at Vatican Council I in 1870. With those declarations, not only the pope but also those who assist him in the governance of the church achieved a degree of authority and a claim to unquestionable acquiescence in their decisions never known before.

What were the grievances at each stage in this development? In the twelfth century St. Bernard complained about the curia's practice of "giving judgment in the absence of the accused, simply as its members wish," and he warned his fellow Cistercian Pope Eugene III about the worldliness of Rome. In the fourteenth century the wealth and luxury the cardinals enjoyed in Avignon during the papacy's residence there excited calls for its reform. Only in the fifteenth and early sixteenth centuries, however, did cries against venality and corruption find urgent expression at the highest level of ecclesiastical authority—in the Councils of Constance, Basel, and Lateran V.

Reformers now complained also about the quid-pro-quo patronage system that rewarded family and friends, who were often unworthy of the positions bestowed on them. Even more irritating to many bishops and rulers was the growing centralization of authority in the Holy See and the imposition by the papacy of ever more taxes and other financial exactions to fund an ever more ostentatious papal court. Reformers called for the elimination of simony in the curia that occurred through the buying and selling of offices and services. Luther's "Appeal to the Nobility of the

German Nation" in 1520 contained a long catalog of abuses perpetrated by the curia. It was a catalog more remarkable for its stridency and comprehensiveness than for any originality in the complaints.

The decrees of the Council of Trent (1545–1563) give no hint that bishops at the council found the curia the major obstacle to the measure they felt essential for the reform of the church—namely, obliging bishops to reside in their dioceses and to perform there their traditional pastoral duties. The curia's practice of granting dispensations from this obligation in return for cash to finance the court (and thus itself) had for centuries consistently undercut every attempt to change the situation.

The issue brought the council to such a crisis that for ten months between September 1562 and July 1563, it could not pass a single decree. Only the solemn promise of Pope Pius IV to undertake the necessary reform broke the deadlock and enabled the council to conclude its business. Pius and some of his successors made changes, but changes less thorough than reformers called for. Nonetheless, the popes could not altogether ignore Trent's decree requiring residence even of the cardinal bishops in the curia.

After a period of relative quiescence during the long post-Trent era, reform of the curia bounded to the surface during the first period of Vatican Council II in 1962. Nobody at that time accused the cardinals of the curia of an extravagant lifestyle. The problem was, rather, the attempt of some of them to control the council and, indeed, to force their own agenda on the bishops. The chair of the Doctrinal Commission of the council was Cardinal Alfredo Ottaviani, who was at the same time the secretary (head) of the "Supreme Congregation of the Holy Office of the Roman Inquisition."

Suprema! The word not only indicated the congregation's ranking among the other congregations but also suggested a prerogative of even correcting the council itself. Against this arrogance, as many bishops characterized it, the council reacted vigorously. As the first period drew to a close, reform of the curia—indeed, a radical reform—seemed almost certain to appear prominently on the agenda when the council reconvened the next year.

Just before it reconvened, however, Pope Paul VI, elected a few months earlier, spoke to the members of the curia, impressed on them the urgency of the issue, and informed them that together—he and they—would take the needed steps. The pope thus defused the tension by effectively removing the issue from the agenda. Even so, the issue simmered beneath the surface for the rest of the council and sometimes burst onto the floor. The intrepid Melchite patriarch, Maximos IV Saïgh, at one point proposed, for instance, that the curia report directly to a rotating commission of bishops established to aid the pope in the government of the church. The commission would be the *Suprema.*

Just as the council was ending, Paul VI published *Integrae Servandae,* which gave the *Suprema* the new name of the Congregation for the Doctrine of the Faith and also assigned it the new task of promoting good teachings as well as condemning bad. He later made other adjustments, such as increasing the international composition of the curia's personnel. The changes were far from radical.

The same can be said of Pope John Paul II's apostolic constitution, *Pastor Bonus* (1989). However, in 1995 he issued the encyclical *Ut Unum Sint* and invited dialog about how the successor of Peter might better perform his ministry. In so doing, he at least implicitly invited dialog on further, presumably more radical, reform of the curia, as Archbishop John R. Quinn saw and elaborated on so well in his book, *The Reform of the Papacy.*

What conclusions can we draw from this history? The first is that the curia is a fact of life; the Roman pontiff needs assistance, and the curia has traditionally been the instrument to provide it. (Whether he needs assistance to the degree and in the extensive and elaborate form currently at his disposal is another question altogether.) The second is that, like every bureaucracy, this one needs to be monitored and from time to time undergo reforms that are more than mere tinkering. *Ecclesia semper reformanda* here means specifically *curia semper reformanda.* Reform of the curia is a task that must be done over and over again. Third, reform meets the resistance of an entrenched system.

Who is to do the reforming? For bureaucracies, self-reform invariably means no reform. If the reform is to be effective, it must be done by a disinterested outside agency. It must be done by an agency not enmeshed in the system. It must be done by an agency, that is to say, that has a critical distance from the system and is familiar with other systems that operate more effectively. The Commission of Cardinals that Pope Francis has appointed for this task, as well as for broader church issues, is a step in the right direction, but the cardinals are themselves churchmen working inside the system, even though not inside the curia. Is it unthinkable to supplement their work with a secular agency that is completely outside the church orbit? Such an agency is much more likely to ask questions that do not even occur to church members.

What needs reform today? That is a question far beyond my competence to answer. There are in fact two problems so profound that they seem beyond almost everyone's competence. First is the fact that men and women today do not easily accept the idea that a distant and faceless body of elites claims the right to tell them what to think and how to behave. Second, there is the difficulty today of finding a theological justification for the curia—or, put more concretely, there is the difficulty of finding a theologically credible connection between Peter, the simple fisherman of Galilee, and Peter, prince of the apostles, heading a large bureaucratic central office.

If we descend from the heights of those two problems to others seemingly more tractable, several things seem fairly obvious. Some remedy needs to be found for the well-publicized lack of communication among the congregations, tribunals, secretariats, and other offices within the curia, which results in their sometimes working at cross-purposes and creating the impression of a system that is profoundly disorganized and dysfunctional.

Further, a remedy needs to be found for the process of recruiting the personnel of the curia, which sometimes seems to function more as system of patronage than a system based on merit—a long-standing problem in the curia. *Promoveatur ut amoveatur*—prelates called to Rome because they have failed on their home turf—is an especially troubling aspect of the recruitment problem. Finally, a mechanism needs to be devised to ensure that the heads of the different bureaus are held accountable for fulfilling their duties.

There are surely other problems. But what is above all needed is a clarification of the ecclesiological framework in which the curia functions. In the decades before Vatican II, textbooks on ecclesiology described the governance of the church as an unqualified monarchy. The pope was the absolute head of a hierarchical pyramid, from which all authority flowed downward from him to the rest of the church. The triumph of this idea was the result of a long process that accelerated in the nineteenth and early twentieth centuries and reached its apogee on the eve of the council. The very word *Suprema* suggests the mentality that was operative.

Vatican II tried to modify that ecclesiology by recovering the early synodal and collegial tradition of the church of the first millennium. The result was the doctrine of collegiality. That doctrine became the lightning rod of the council. No other doctrine met with more unrelenting opposition. Its enemies grasped its radical character and implications. The council eventually ratified the doctrine but only after "a higher authority" attached a "preliminary note" (*nota praevia*) that has ever since confounded interpreters of it and therefore blunted the doctrine's sharpness. Moreover, the council's attempts to give collegiality a form to make it operative in the church were preempted when, at the beginning of the fourth period, Paul VI instituted the Synod of Bishops, which he defined as a purely consultative body.

Collegiality holds immense implications for the curia. It means operating not as agencies in charge of the church but as agencies that serve lower agencies by helping them do what they are supposed to do. It means, in other words, strictly observing the Catholic rule of subsidiarity: the higher authority intervenes only when a problem exceeds the ability of a lower authority to deal with it. More basically, it means seeing the church itself as a collegial body, which imposes even on the *prima sedes*, the obligation to function in a collegial fashion regarding other bishops, who, as Vatican II stated, have authority in their own right and are not vicars of the pope.

Even in the few months he has been pope, Francis has given evidence that he intends to function in a collegial fashion. He has, moreover, provided a wonderful example of the servant-leader, which is another theme of the council and a corollary to the doctrine of collegiality. The challenge now is to translate that example into structural changes and then somehow to ensure that the personnel responsible for the effective functioning of the *prima sedes* subscribe to it wholeheartedly and perform their duties in accord with it.

5

THE BEATIFICATION OF POPE PIUS IX

The beatification on the same day, 3 September 2000, of two former popes—Pius IX and John XXIII—was unprecedented. That fact alone would have been enough to persuade an editor that he needed a commentary on its significance. But the fact that one of the popes was Pius IX made a comment even more imperative because of the highly politicized context of his pontificate and the questions it raises for today. No surprise, therefore, that then editor of America, *Thomas Reese, requested this article of me.*

Pope John Paul II has beatified and canonized more individuals than all his predecessors put together. Since these solemnities occur with such frequency, they receive at most perfunctory mention in the American press. The beatifications taking place in Rome on 3 September, however, have excited notice because, though they include Pope John XXIII, they also include Pius IX, who reigned from 1846 to 1878. Some Jewish organizations, Catholic columnists, and others have made their shock, even indignation, known because of the so-called Mortara incident during Pius's pontificate, almost forgotten until David L. Kertzer published *The Kidnapping of Edgardo Mortara* three years ago. In Bologna, after nightfall on 23 June 1858, the papal police arrived unannounced at the Mortara home and removed from this Jewish family one of their sons, six-year-old Edgardo, because he had been secretly baptized by a Christian maid when he was dangerously sick as an infant. Despite the anguished pleas of

Edgardo's parents and international indignation, the boy was never returned to his family. He became almost a personal ward of Pius IX and eventually was ordained a priest.

But there are misgivings in other quarters and on other scores. On 8 July 2000 the *Tablet*, the well-regarded English Catholic weekly, carried an editorial, "A Beatification Too Far," that was uncommonly sharp in its criticism of the Holy See. "It can only be seen as a political move, designed to provide a conservative and reactionary counterweight to the beatification of John XXIII. . . . The conclusion is surely inescapable that the beatification of Pius IX is the work of a small group of ultra-conservatives." In Italy, I am informed, the political left is howling with feigned indignation, which masks its genuine glee that the Catholic Church has through this action once again manifested its true, fascist character.

The focus on Pius has thrown into the shadows Pope John XXIII (and three others) who will be beatified in the same ceremony. Nonetheless, almost as if in anticipation of the *Tablet*'s inference, Msgr. Brunero Gherardini, postulator of Pius IX's cause, has publicly denied that the beatification together of the two popes is a political juggling act. They were both great saints, he claims, although very different human beings. The beatification of Pius IX is an act of justice delayed for too many decades by objections from circles outside the church.

The controversy, such as it is, will soon die down, and the event will be forgotten. Not many Catholics care one way or the other, for they have never heard of *Pio Nono*. Even in the Marches, the region of Italy from which he came, he is today scarcely remembered and has there today no cult among the faithful, which does raise the question of where the recent impetus for the beatification came from. Although Pius IX may become an icon for militant traditionalists, for the devotional life of the faithful he will almost certainly continue, even if later canonized, in his present state of oblivion.

It is important to provide background for understanding how we got to the present point and to examine an issue that goes beyond the event itself. That issue is the problems and ambiguities inherent in trying to define sanctity nowadays and in holding up models of it, especially when the persons are great public figures from times and cultures so different from today. The points discussed will come as no surprise, but they might take on new sharpness when examined with this case in mind, awash as it is in ironies and extremes of various kinds. But first, the background.

The ceremony for Pius on 3 September will be a step on a long and bumpy road that began almost a century ago, when in 1907 the first formal steps were taken in the Roman vicariate. Kenneth Woodward tells the story up to 1990 in great detail in *Making Saints* (1990). Support for the cause waned with the passing of the years. A new phase opened in 1954, and in the early 1960s it entered what seemed to be its final phase before papal approbation. But it languished again. Revived early during the present pontificate, it met a setback when John Paul II, after receiving a long report, seemed persuaded by the arguments of those who opposed it. Then last year the pope asked the Italian episcopal conference if it should go forward, and he received in reply an almost unanimous affirmative. Still, the announcement that the beatification would actually take place caught even many Vatican watchers by surprise.

Causes for beatification and canonization often take a long time, but why has this one dragged on? Not for lack of information. In fact, the overwhelming amount of testimony of various kinds has been as much a hindrance as a help. Pius had the longest pontificate in the history of the church. His definition of the Immaculate Conception, issuance of the *Syllabus of Errors*, and convocation of Vatican Council I make him an extraordinarily important pope and generated even during his lifetime an immense amount of documentation directly or indirectly concerning him. As monarch of the Papal States, his many dealings with leaders of other nations placed him in a major role in the history of the West in the nineteenth century. In Italian history he broods over the century as the most prestigious and most adamant obstacle to the unification of the country that finally took place in 1870 with the seizure of Rome. The amount and diversity of the information concerning him can seem limitless.

The problem has been how to assess this material and move beyond both the vituperation and the adulation in which it has generally been encased. Every historian who has written about him, and the number is legion, divides his life (and pontificate) into two parts: everything up to 1848, when he fled Rome because he believed he was about to be dethroned by revolutionaries, and everything afterward. The conclave that elected him in 1846 chose him over Cardinal Lambruschini because he gave promise of reversing the reactionary and rigidly repressive policies of Gregory XVI.

For the first two years, Pius seemed to respond to those hopes. He had the gates of the Jewish ghetto in Rome dismantled. An ardent patriot, he threatened Metternich of Austria with excommunication when Austrian troops occupied Ferrara. He allowed broader consultation in the administration of Rome. Measures like these assumed a tremendous symbolic meaning that gave birth to the myth of a liberal pope.

In 1848 revolutions against the political restorations of 1815 following Napoleon's defeat spread across the Continent. The restorations had put most of the old monarchs back on their thrones. In Italy the patriots seized the occasion and tried to enlist Pius in their cause, but they envisaged a united Italy in which the pope, though he would have independence as head of the church, would no longer be the ruler of Rome and the Papal States. The political situation was tense and came to a head in the brutal political assassination of Pius's prime minister, Pellegrino Rossi, on the steps of the papal chancery. The pope took fright and, under cover, headed to Gaeta, south of Rome.

When he was finally able, with the help of French troops, to return to Rome two years later, he seemed a changed man. He shed any vestiges of sympathy for the policies of the liberals and set his face against anything modern. Thus was born the familiar image of Pius as the very quintessence of ecclesiastical obscurantism and intransigence.

A few members of the Catholic clergy and laity agreed with this image, but most saw him as a hero, especially after the occupation of Rome in 1870 by the troops of King Victor Emmanuel and the pope's retirement to the Vatican sector of the city as a self-declared prisoner. Sympathy for him, propelled by the Catholic press, surged, along with indignation that the church had been robbed of its sacred, earthly kingdom. Some Catholics argued both before and after the event that the pope and the church would be better off without this temporal monarchy, but Pius condemned the idea as impious.

The pope's distress as the prisoner of the Vatican generated an important and hitherto unheard of virtue—loyalty to the pope. This was not religious faith in doctrines like papal primacy or infallibility but allegiance to an individual and his policies. Thanks to the new means of communication and the drama that so often marked Pius's long pontificate, Catholics knew the pope's name and recognized his portrait. Pius was the first papal megastar.

He was helped in this regard by some nasty enemies, against whom he stood firm. The Catholic clergy and laity in Germany found in him a bulwark against Bismarck's arrogant attack on the church in the Kulturkampf. In Italy itself, the leading liberals were bitterly anticlerical and as out of touch with the religious sentiments of most Italians as Pius was out of touch with political and other realities. The closing of Catholic schools, the exiling of some bishops, and similar moves taken especially before 1870 led many Catholics, even when they felt torn by Pius's policies, to see him a protector of values they deeply treasured. In many parts of the world, moreover, Catholics were a minority oppressed or belittled by progressive regimes, so they could identify emotionally with a pope who seemed to be suffering in a similar way.

Pius promoted devotion to the Sacred Heart and of course to Mary in her Immaculate Conception. Although Jansenism as an organized movement had by then spent its force, it had left an impact on Catholic life almost everywhere. Through these devotions, through declaring Francis de Sales a doctor of the church, and through other means, Pius helped turn piety in a more heartfelt direction. After his death Catholics began calling for his canonization. Then he rather quickly slipped from their minds.

For decades practically every assessment of him was tendentious, one way or the other. In 1952 came the first sign of change. Canon Roger Aubert, then professor in the seminary at Malines, Belgium, published in French a book on his pontificate that employed a more dispassionate and methodologically sound approach, which he followed in 1962 with one on the First Vatican Council. But then came the three-volume biography, *Pio Nono* (1974, 1986, 1990), by Giacomo Martina, a Jesuit professor of ecclesiastical history at the Gregorian University. The work of a lifetime of research and reflection, Martina's *Pio Nono* is a masterly accomplishment, a balanced critical and painstakingly thorough account. None of these works has been translated into English.

With that background we can move to the second point: this beatification raises in a particularly sharp way intriguing questions about sanctity and models of sanctity, questions that would not have been so acute for earlier generations. There are a number of them, all interrelated, so that dealing with one invariably entails dealing with others. We are today psychologically savvy—or at least we like to think we are. How do we relate sanctity to emotional health? We have a sharper historical consciousness. How do we assess sanctity when manifested in an age whose values and religious sensibilities seem so different from our own? Underlying that question is the question of historicism: Is each age to be judged by its own standards? That is a question about relativity. If each age is so to be judged, how does the relationship between sanctity and orthopraxis/orthodoxy work when standards have shifted with time? The question is acute for Pius, since he left no spiritual writings of note by which we might more directly enter his inner life.

We are suspicious of authority and hold it to high standards. What is the relationship between personal piety and the public actions of persons with grave responsibilities toward others? That question is especially crucial in this case. On 3 September it is not simply Giovanni Maria Mastai-Ferretti, a model Christian man, who is being beatified but also Pius IX, model pope. It is also Pius IX, model monarch, who had troops and police at his service. At issue of course are models of holiness: For whom, to what degree, and with what qualifications is this blessed or saint a model?

Let us pursue those questions with our case. Especially in his early years, Pius, scion of an aristocratic family, impressed everybody with his graceful manners but even more with a serenity of spirit that seemed to radiate from him. The soul of an angel was the reluctant compliment wrung from a liberal Italian politician. Pius, genuinely devoted to the poor, was anything but an ecclesiastical climber, and, unlike Cardinal Antonelli, his long-term secretary of state, he was incapable of duplicity. What you saw was what you got. There is reason to think him holy. In April of this year, when his body was exhumed from the crypt of the Basilica of St. Laurence, the prelates found it almost perfectly preserved.

But saints, with perhaps a few exceptions, have their warts. As the years wore on, Pius's mood swings in public and private became more noticeable and more frequent. In public and private he burst into scoldings of persons present or absent. Intransigent, the adjective so often applied to him by historians who know little about him, is echoed time and again by Martina, the biographer who knows him best. Pius wrote in 1877, the year before his death, "I exclude the possibility of any relation, even indirect, with men who have despoiled the church." As vicar of a crucified God, he would gladly suffer, but never compromise.

Yet he was easily swayed. When in September 1870 the Italian troops had surrounded Rome and were ready to attack, Pius gave orders to his generals that they were to yield at the first gunfire. No blood was to be shed. On the day before the attack, however, the generals pleaded with him that their military honor required that they resist. Pius acquiesced, laying down the condition that firing cease as soon as the enemy made a breach in the defenses. Before the breach was made, some fifty soldiers lost their lives.

The enemies who on that day seized Rome from him did not, for reasons of their own, treat him badly—at least not nearly so badly as they could have. By the Law of Guarantees of 1871 they provided for him almost the same settlement as did the Lateran agreements of 1929 that established Vatican City. Pius had good reason not to trust them, but he also closed his ears to moderating counsel. His *non expedit* policy, forbidding Catholic participation in the politics of the new nation, though of mitigated enforcement, caused anguish and confusion for a half century.

He was a person of modest intelligence. Odo Russell, the British ambassador to the Holy See, fond of Pius, spoke of his amiable but weak mind. Pius's education, innocent of intellectual challenge, was rudimentary in theology and history, which helps account for measures like forbidding women to be members of church choirs because, he affirmed, St. Paul forbade it. Even Monsignor Gherardini admits that from a political point of view, he was not a genius.

Yet we have all known truly holy persons whose education and intelligence were quite modest. Sanctity is an affair of the heart, not the head. The special problem that the beatification of a person with public responsibilities raises is how they try to compensate for such limitations so as to act as judiciously as possible. That means, most obviously, choosing good advisers. This suggests a strange circle: Perspicacity is required to identify the advisers, and yet the advisers are meant to supply for lack of perspicacity. This perspicacity, or wisdom, does not seem, however, unrelated to virtues like humility, the willingness to admit to correction.

Pius surrounded himself with mediocrities, adept principally at telling him what he wanted to hear, a fact commented on by many contemporaries otherwise favorably disposed toward him. As one of his personal chamberlains he chose Monsignor George Talbot, a converted Anglican priest, in whose judgments he placed almost unqualified faith. Talbot, emotionally unstable, fanned Pius's already deep suspicions of Newman and in general offered him the most reactionary advice imaginable. In 1868 he had to be removed from the Roman Curia to a mental institution outside Paris, where he died in 1886.

This raises the issue of Pius's prudence in governing the church, a concern that comes up many times in the official documentation for his cause. This is an aspect of the relationship between sanctity and the public acts of a leader. How prudent, for instance, was Pius during Vatican Council I? Martina maintains that the fundamental freedom of the council was not compromised. But he points out the intrusiveness of Pius's interventions and the emotional pressures he directly and indirectly applied to the bishops, as when he threatened, "If they won't define it [infallibility], I will do it myself." Cardinal Guidi, an ardent infallibilist, proposed to the council that it was the papal magisterium, not the person of the pope, that was infallible and that this magisterium was infallible only when exercised in accord with the episcopacy. Pius, angry, dressed him down that evening with the famous words, "I am the church! I am the tradition!"

Like most ultra-Montanists, Pius saw infallibility as the only bulwark against the moral, doctrinal, social, and political chaos threatening the church and civilization in his times. Liberty, equality, and fraternity summed up the threat. That battle cry of the French Revolution reverberated through Europe in the nineteenth century. For Pius it signified the overturning of the order God had established. It had in fact provided warrant for great atrocities against priests, nuns, and others. Pius saw it expressing the very core of the evils of modern times.

For centuries the phrase "modern times" meant little more than recent times, but particularly in the nineteenth century it assumed an ideology. Modern implied a historical process in which later times were better than former. Modernity meant progress. Progress meant the inevitable march of history away from the superstitions of Christianity or, certainly, of Catholicism. No wonder Pius rejected the construct. He substituted for it its antithesis: modern times were the worst of times, with worse still to come. His vision, apocalyptic, put the papacy at the head of the good in the cataclysmic struggle.

This profound pessimism and sense of siege begot the *Syllabus of Errors* of 1864. Many of the eighty points scored by the syllabus were traditional, but the scathing sweep of the document took people's breath away. Nothing, it seems, was right in the world. The church alone held the truth. The last six points condemned freedom of speech, religious tolerance, the disestablishment of Catholicism as the state religion; it condemned the idea that abrogation of the civil empire of the church would allow it to function more freely and the idea that the pope could and should be reconciled with modern society.

The church has in the meantime been reconciled with modern society in ways and to a degree Pius IX would find utterly incomprehensible and intolerable, which brings us explicitly to the historicist aspect of our issue: Do we judge Pius's conduct against the standards of his day or ours? The forcible taking of the Mortara boy from his parents, who had no legal recourse against the actions of an autocratic state, would be judged by most Catholic theologians today, I believe, as wrong, a violation of a fundamental human right. Yet nothing is clearer than that Pius, basing himself, he said, on the principle that the spiritual takes precedence over the temporal, acted in accord with his conscience. He felt the criticism his action provoked, but he had no choice. In a letter to young Edgardo, he told him how much he had suffered on his account. The governments of Britain and France, for instance, protested and did their best to shake the pope's determination. But the Catholic press and prelates worldwide unflinchingly defended the action as good and right.

Like his papal predecessors, Pius believed in capital punishment. On 12 June 1855, for instance, Cardinal Antonelli saw a disreputable-looking man near him reach into his shirt. Antonelli fled and shouted for the police. The police caught the man, Antonio De Felici, who by then was indeed brandishing a weapon: a large carving fork. De Felici, known as a political subversive, was promptly tried by authorities of the papal government, convicted, and sentenced to death by decapitation. It seems, moreover, that Antonelli intervened with the pope to have the sentence commuted to life imprisonment, but to no avail.

Pius fiercely opposed religious toleration. He contested the extremely modest concessions for worship the Spanish government extended to Protestants and was shocked that the grand duke of Tuscany, yielding to pressure, allowed Jews to attend the university. In all this he was not only following his conscience but also following standard Catholic teaching. Of course, his words and actions helped form that teaching. There is no need to insist on how far they depart from Catholic teaching and a more general moral consensus in place today. To put it crudely, the beatification dramatizes the cultural conditioning, within limits, of what is considered virtue. It dramatizes the historical character of the canon for orthodoxy in moral matters.

I have in these few pages tried to expose issues that the beatification of Pius IX raises. It raises them in a more pointed way than the simultaneous beatification of John XXIII. Although only a century separates these two popes, the former seems almost incomparably further removed from modern sensibilities. Beatifications deal with the past but are actions done in the present and for the present. Pius will, on 3 September, officially become a model of sanctity. For whom is this model meaningful, for whom intended? Popes? Political leaders? Ordinary faithful? No matter what the answer to such questions, the model provided by every saint and blessed must be translated if it is to be meaningful in our lives, but for Pius the translating will be especially tricky and taxing. What kinds of persons, I wonder, will make the effort for themselves? And with what result?

6

TWO POPES

Benedict and Francis

When the Franco-Belgian publishers Lessius recently decided they wanted to translate my History of the Popes *into French, they asked me to bring it up to date by enlarging on the very brief comments I made about Pope Benedict XVI in the original English version (2006) and to add a new chapter on Pope Francis. This text is the result. It has not been published in English before.*

BENEDICT XVI

The long and very public illness of Pope John Paul II provided plenty of time for journalists and others to speculate about possible successors. Speculation took off in earnest when John Paul died on 2 April 2005. Although a number of Italian journalists predicted that Cardinal Joseph Ratzinger would be elected, the field actually seemed to be wide open, with no real front-runners. The Italians turned out to be the best prognosticators.

Joseph Ratzinger's long and close association with Pope John Paul commended him to all those cardinals who owed their position to John Paul and who wanted to continue his legacy. His age, seventy-eight, might be counted against him; yet it was also a point in his favor because it seemed to promise a shorter pontificate after an extremely long one. Moreover, Ratzinger had made a favorable impression by how well he handled the obsequies for John Paul and guided the general congregations held before the conclave.

On 19 April 2005 he was elected on the fourth ballot in a conclave that lasted scarcely twenty-four hours. A relatively unknown cardinal from Argentina, Jorge Mario Bergoglio, received the next largest number of votes. The new pope chose to be called Benedict, which distanced him from his four immediate predecessors and suggested a somewhat new trajectory. Did it suggest a trajectory away from the Second Vatican Council, in which he participated as a young but important theologian, very influential among the German-speaking bishops? In that regard he was destined to be carefully watched by theologians and churchmen, who often disagreed in their assessments.

Joseph Aloysius Ratzinger was born in the small Bavarian town of Marktl on Holy Saturday, 16 April 1927, the youngest of his parents' three children. Although his father, a policeman, was bitterly opposed to the Nazi regime, Joseph was conscripted into the Hitler Youth following his fourteenth birthday in 1941, a membership required by law. Even though he had entered a seminary, he was later drafted into the German anti-aircraft corps and then trained in German infantry. When the Allies arrived in 1945, they interned him in a prisoner-of-war camp until Germany's surrender.

That was in May. In November of that same year, he and his older brother, Georg, entered St. Michael Seminary in Traunstein in southeastern Bavaria close to the Austrian border, and from that moment forward Joseph Ratzinger lived his entire life in either ecclesiastical or academic milieus. In 1951, when he was twenty-four years old, he was ordained a priest by Cardinal Michael von Faulhaber of Munich. Two years later he wrote a dissertation on St. Augustine at the University of Munich and after another two years wrote his *Habilitation* on St. Bonaventure, an achievement that qualified him for a professorship, which he received in 1959 at the University of Bonn. In 1963 he left Bonn to assume a new post at the University of Munich.

During the Second Vatican Council, 1962–1965, he initially served as a *peritus* (theological expert) to Cardinal Joseph Frings of Cologne, and then, beginning in 1963, as a *peritus* appointed by the pope. During the council's first period, the fall of 1962, he, in collaboration with another

German theologian, Karl Rahner, composed an alternative version to the document on "The Sources of Divine Revelation" prepared by the official Doctrinal Commission. Although the venture had the blessing of the German bishops, it was considered a bold move, which placed the young theologian squarely in the camp of the so-called "progressives" at the council.

In the next period, 1963, Cardinal Frings created a sensation when, in a speech before the council that was in part written by Ratzinger, he criticized the whole centralizing tendency of the church but specifically the Holy Office of the Roman Inquisition. He then went on to assert that the procedures of the Holy Office "in many respects are inappropriate to the times in which we live, harm the church, and are for many a scandal." Applause broke out. Not even by that congregation, he went on, should anybody be judged or condemned without being heard. Paradoxically, some twenty years later Ratzinger would become head of the congregation Frings criticized, which by then bore the new name of Congregation for the Doctrine of the Faith. He would find himself on the receiving end of the same criticisms Frings had made long ago.

But those were days in the distant future. Nonetheless, as the council moved on, Ratzinger began to entertain misgivings about the extent of the changes proposed in the council and some of its more fundamental orientations. The matter came to a head with the council's final document, "On the Church in the Modern World," *Gaudium et Spes*. Father Ratzinger led the German-speaking bishops in opposition to the document as not sufficiently theological and not sufficiently cognizant of the pervasiveness of sin in the world. As Cardinal Frings put it, the draft document slighted the "mystery of the cross" and did not sufficiently warn against evil in the world and human propensity to sin. The Germans attributed the document's optimism to undue weight given to views of French-speaking bishops and theologians. In light of the criticism, the council revised the draft, and eventually it won approval. But the debate revealed a significant difference in emphasis among the leaders of the council in their assessment of the human condition and of human achievements.

In 1966, after the council, Father Ratzinger moved from Munich to the University of Tübingen. Two years later, in 1968, student riots and protests exploded almost worldwide, a phenomenon due to a number of factors. Tübingen was not exempt from the unrest, which quickly radicalized. In April and May the disturbances became so disruptive that it was often impossible to hold class or, if class were held, to quell the shouts and taunts of the students. Ratzinger was shocked; he saw these developments as challenges to the almost sacred authority of the professorate and the result of a rejection of traditional Catholic teaching. His theological views increasingly came into conflict with those of colleagues at Tübingen such as Hans Küng. The next year he left Tübingen to take up a position at the more conservative University of Regensburg.

The great turning point in Father Ratzinger's career occurred on 24 March 1977, when Pope Paul VI named him archbishop of Munich. Because the archbishop-elect had had virtually no direct pastoral experience, the appointment came as a surprise. Although he was known as an effective preacher and a supportive mentor to his students, his reputation as a theologian was doubtless the most important factor in determining his appointment. He chose for his motto "Cooperators of the truth" (*Cooperatores veritatis*, 3 John 8). He explained that he chose it because it indicated the relationship between his former life as a professor and his new mission, but also because in today's world truth is neglected, "yet everything collapses if truth is missing." With that explanation he provided an insight into how he would later understand his role as pope, bishop of Rome. He was first and foremost a teacher and a guardian of the truth.

The year following his appointment, Archbishop Ratzinger was made a cardinal and three years later, hardly settled in Munich, he was called to Rome by the new pope, John Paul II, to be the new prefect of the Congregation for the Doctrine of the Faith (CDF). He led the congregation for an unprecedented twenty-four years, during which he forged ever-closer bonds with John Paul and became the most powerful figure in the curia. The pope, formed in the siege situation of the church in Communist Poland, insisted that the church present a united front against those who disagreed with standard teachings or questioned them. His position in this regard certainly affected how Cardinal Ratzinger bore himself as head of the CDF, but the prefect was himself deeply concerned that truth prevail and that the church be purged of misleading or dangerous teachings. The price to be paid for the cleansing was perhaps a smaller but a purer church.

During Ratzinger's tenure as head of the CDF, a number of prominent theologians were censured, such as Leonardo Boff and Jacques Dupuis. Posthumous writings of the Jesuit priest and spiritual writer Anthony de

Mello were the subject of a notification. Catholic journals of opinion, such as *Stimmen der Zeit* (Germany), *Études* (France), and *America* (USA), came under new scrutiny and censorship by the congregation. In the jubilee year of 2000, the congregation published a declaration, *Dominus Jesus*, that affirmed Christ's unique role in human salvation and described followers of other religions as being in a "gravely deficient position." This document offended Protestants by claiming that their institutions were not truly churches but "ecclesial communities," and it created difficulties for relations between the Catholic Church and non-Christian religious.

In 2001, just as the sexual abuse scandal erupted with great publicity in Boston in the United States, Pope John Paul II gave the CDF responsibility for investigating such cases. How well the prefect carried out this responsibility is hotly disputed. The problem would continue to dog Benedict even after he became pope. As time passed and the scandal moved to Europe and elsewhere, he, perforce, became more aware of its breadth and depth and of the severe damage it had done the church. By 2004 he began to make significant changes in the Holy See's procedures and, from some knowledgeable quarters, won praise for his courage in handling difficult cases. As is well known, as pope he moved aggressively against Father Marcial Maciel Degollado, the notorious pedophile, founder of a religious order known as Legionaries of Christ, who had been protected by influential figures in the Vatican. In his visit to the United States in 2008, Pope Benedict met with victims of clerical abuse and won praise for his sensitivity to what they had suffered.

While prefect of the CDF, Cardinal Ratzinger continued to publish books and articles on theological subjects. Of all his writings, the one that created the most comment consisted in a series of interviews he gave in 1985 to an Italian journalist, Vittorio Messori, and published under the title "Report on the Faith" (*Rapporto sulla fede*), or, perhaps better, "Report on the State of the Faith." It was immediately translated into the major European languages. The cardinal deplored the confusion and chaos that, in his opinion, had gripped the Catholic world since Vatican Council II, a situation partially due to misinterpretations of the council as a "rupture" in the tradition of the church, whereas in fact the council was perfectly continuous with that tradition.

He at that moment enunciated an interpretative principle to which he would recur again and again in succeeding years. It was a principle that amounted to a minimizing or even dismissal of discontinuity in the history of Catholic teaching and practice. If pressed to its logical conclusion, the principle means that nothing of significance has happened or changed in the long history of the church. When applied to Vatican II, it implies that the council did little more than ratify the status quo and was far from being the landmark event in Christian history that most historians and other interpreters saw it to be. Ratzinger's appropriation of the principle of seemingly unmitigated continuity in interpreting the council helps to explain many of his decisions as pope, decisions regarding liturgy and other matters that came to be described as "reform of the reforms [of Vatican II]."

As pope he published three encyclicals in his own name and a fourth jointly with his successor, Pope Francis. His first, "God Is Love" (*Deus Caritas Est*), affirmed that human beings, created in the image of God, who is love, were capable of giving themselves to God and to others by receiving and experiencing God's love in contemplation. Thus clearly emerged one of the great themes of his writings, speeches, and homilies: "friendship with Jesus Christ." In the encyclical he stated, "If friendship with God becomes for us something ever more important and decisive, then we will begin to love those whom God loves and who are in need of us. God wants us to be friends of his friends."

He spread this message in his apostolic visitations to different parts of the world. Though a shy man most at home with books, he (especially in the early years of his pontificate) made a favorable impression in his public appearances, and he had notable success during visits to countries where a negative reaction was feared, such as the United States and the United Kingdom. Ever the teacher, he nonetheless showed that he knew how to conduct himself before crowds and in unfamiliar circumstances. Yet, unfortunately, he sometimes made statements that sparked severe criticism and controversy.

He made by far the most explosive of such statements in 2006 in a lecture at his old university in Regensburg. The lecture was titled "Faith, Reason, and the University: Memories and Reflections." During it the pope said, "Show me just what Muhammad brought that was new, and there you will find things only evil and inhuman, such as his command to spread by the sword the faith he preached." Even though the Vatican explained that the pope was quoting from a medieval source, not expressing his own opinion, Muslims reacted with shock and anger. The statement ignited anti-Christian riots in a number of Muslim cities and created an international crisis for the Holy See.

Pope Benedict apologized for any offense he had given and made a point of visiting Turkey, a predominantly Muslim country, and praying in its Blue Mosque. Later he met with Muslim scholars at a Catholic-Muslim seminar in Rome and did his best to reassure them of his esteem. Nonetheless, the damage had been done and seemed almost impossible for him to repair. When he visited Brazil in May 2007, he sparked another controversy when he praised the European missionaries and colonizers, seemingly insensitive to any harm they had done to the native peoples. The then president of Venezuela, Hugo Chávez, demanded an apology. Later in Rome, speaking at a weekly audience, the pope implicitly responded, "It is not possible to forget the suffering and the injustices inflicted by colonizers on the indigenous population, whose fundamental rights were often trampled."

Such embarrassing incidents led even his most ardent admirers to conclude that the pope was not well served by those closest to him in the Roman Curia. Their suspicion was spectacularly confirmed when, in May 2012, Italian journalist Gianluigi Nuzzi published a book titled *His Holiness: Confidential Documents of Benedict XVI* (*Sua Santità: Le carte segrete di Benedetto XVI*). The volume contained correspondence and other sensitive documents. In the book, and then in the reaction of the media to it, the Vatican was portrayed as a hotbed of jealousy, ambition, and intrigue, over which the pope exercised little control. The arrest of the pope's own butler as perpetrator of the crime added an almost Hollywood gloss to the whole affair. At the same time the Vatican Bank kept appearing in the media in unsavory ways, including accusations of money laundering.

Such problems surely took a toll on *Papa Ratzinger*. People began to note how tired and frail he looked. Shortly after his election, the Vatican announced that he had had a mild stroke, and eventually it became known that while he was still a cardinal he had been fitted with a pacemaker. He increasingly seemed to have difficulty walking and mounting steps. Seventy-eight when elected, by 2013 he showed unmistakable signs of age and seemed more and more withdrawn from the day-to-day routines of his office.

Nonetheless, on 11 February 2013 the Vatican utterly surprised the world with the announcement that some two weeks later, 28 February,

Benedict would resign the papacy due to his advanced age. No pope had resigned since Gregory XII did so under duress in 1415 at the time of the Great Western Schism. Although before Gregory other popes had resigned, few, if any, did so voluntarily. In that regard Pope Benedict's resignation may be unique in the annals of the papacy.

After two weeks of ceremonial farewells, the pope left his office on the specified date, and *sede vacante* was officially declared. The machinery moved into action to prepare for a new papal election, a process from which Benedict completely abstained. As he departed, he vowed that he would continue to serve the church "through a life dedicated to prayer." Once his quarters were ready, "the pope emeritus," as he was now officially called, quietly took up residence in a convent on the grounds of Vatican City.

FRANCIS

No one expected Benedict XVI to resign. No one expected Jorge Mario Bergoglio to be elected his successor. (In the speculation before the conclave virtually no one mentioned his name, despite his having received so many votes in the previous conclave.) No one expected Benedict's successor to assume a profile so different from his and to do so from the moment he was elected. No one expected the new pope to ignite an almost manic enthusiasm and to do so not only among Catholics but even among persons from other religious traditions and, still more surprising, from persons without any religious belief whatsoever. All at once a long era seemed to have ended and a new one begun.

Cardinal Bergoglio was elected on the fifth ballot. Why did the cardinals so quickly decide on somebody who in the church at large was an unknown quantity? We can only speculate. During the general congregations preceding the conclave, the cardinals, from all reports, spoke frankly about what seemed to be a widespread malaise in the church as manifested especially in a dysfunctional central administration. Bergoglio had a reputation as an excellent administrator and, as a person, not afraid to make difficult decisions. When he addressed the cardinals, as did many others during the congregations, he made a powerful impression by his insistence that the church had to move out of its self-referential mode and more resolutely undertake its mission to bring the joy of the Gospel to the world.

A change was needed. To elect Bergoglio would be to elect a man who would be "a first" in several important ways—a fact that suggests he might have the perspective and the critical distance to undertake changes more than cosmetic. Of course, many popes have been "firsts." Pope John XXIII was the first pope in five hundred years to choose the name John. Pope John Paul II was the first pope ever to come from Poland and the first non-Italian in over four hundred years. Benedict XVI was the first German pope since the Middle Ages. However, no pope in modern times has been first in so many and such significant ways as Francis. He is the first pope from the Americas, the first Jesuit, the first to take the name Francis, and the first pope in fifty years not to have participated in Vatican Council II. Each of these firsts is significant.

Jorge was born in Buenos Aires on 17 December 1936, the eldest of five children. His father was an Italian immigrant who left Italy largely to escape Mussolini's fascism. As a young teenager Jorge received his secondary education in a technical school, where he earned a diploma as a chemical technician. After graduation he worked for several years in the laboratory of a commercial firm in Buenos Aires and, to make a little extra money, worked in the evenings as a janitor and briefly as a bouncer in a bar. After he entered the Jesuits, he, as part of his formation in the order before ordination, taught literature and psychology at a Jesuit secondary school. Later, as provincial of the Jesuits, he had to negotiate the difficult years of his country's "dirty war," when even Jesuits had bitterly divided allegiances. Finally, as archbishop of Buenos Aires, he served as president of the episcopal conference of Argentina and heard from his fellow bishops the challenges they faced in their ministry.

These experiences of his native land formed this "first pope from the Americas" and gave him background unique for a successor of St. Peter. Buenos Aires is a stunningly sophisticated city, with all the challenges to the church such sophistication implies. But it is no more sophisticated than many other cities around the world, and it would be difficult to ascertain just how being an South American city makes its sophistication distinctive. Perhaps more pertinent for Francis than being from South America is his being immersed in such a secular environment on so many different levels. In that regard he is different from his predecessors. Even Pope John Paul II, whose early life as an aspiring actor might seem to put him in the same category, appropriated a straightforward us-them mindset in confrontation with a totalitarian regime, an experience altogether different from Francis's experience of all the virtues and vices of a modern democratic state.

The election of this first Jesuit pope surprised the Jesuits as much as it did anybody else, and for a moment it caused them considerable consternation. Memories were still tender in the order of Bergoglio's controversial term as provincial superior of the Argentinian Jesuits, when, among other problems, he was perceived as opposed to the "promotion of justice" that the Jesuits at that time formally declared a dimension of all their ministries. But within days after Francis's election, the Jesuits were able to put their misgivings behind them and were through his words and deeds able recognize him as genuinely one of their own. Pope Francis himself has confessed to being rigid and authoritarian while he served as the provincial superior of the Jesuits of Argentina. He made clear by his actions as archbishop that, if he earlier had misgivings about the direction the order took, he later fully appropriated it, and still later, as pope, he made it integral to his understanding of his service to the church.

A facet of Pope Francis's Jesuit background that is extremely important but rarely commented on is that his first important assignment after ordination was master of novices to young men who had just entered the order. By virtue of that office, he met with his novices individually at least once or twice a month for the two years they were under his care. The principal task of the master of novices is to help the novices deepen their spiritual lives, a task that usually helps the helper in his own spiritual life as much as it does those he is called on to help.

Most important, the master of novices leads the novices through the "long retreat," the thirty days of prayer and meditation according to the *Spiritual Exercises* that St. Ignatius prescribed for novices in the order. The whole purpose of the exercises is to assist the individual into a heartfelt commitment to the Lord that goes beyond ritual, routine, and the practice of "good works." Of course, it is impossible to chart the effect Pope Francis's years as master of novices had on him, but the long hours he as pope spends alone in the chapel every day suggests an intimacy with the Lord that gives him energy and the courage in addressing institutional problems he displayed from the first days of his pontificate.

There are a few more palpable Jesuit markers. When Francis tells us that the church must go "to the peripheries"—that is, to the marginalized, the neglected, and the nonbeliever—he draws on vocabulary found in Jesuit documents, both ancient and contemporary. According to his own account, he has long found inspiration in Pierre Favre, one of the first companions of St. Ignatius. His announcement in December 2013 that he intended to canonize Favre came, therefore, as no surprise. Francis praised Favre for his "dialogue with all, even the most remote and even with his opponents, his simple piety, a certain naïveté perhaps, his being available to others straightaway, his careful discernment, the fact that he was a man capable of great and strong decisions but also capable of being so gentle and loving." In praising the Jesuit Favre, Pope Francis revealed his ideals for himself.

In choosing the name Francis, he made another of his ideals for himself and for the church clear even before he appeared on the balcony of St. Peter's the night of his election. As he himself explained, he chose the name of the great saint of Assisi because of Francis's mission of promoting peace, his dedication to the poor, and his love of nature and the environment. It was thus in a gesture more powerful than the words of an encyclical that he set those priorities. They are, moreover, not priorities born in a sacristy. They are priorities consonant with the long Catholic tradition, but priorities that in the first instance look to the good of the world in which we live, priorities espoused by many persons who are not Catholics or Christians, priorities widely recognized as among the most urgent facing the human race. They are, to say the least, "substantive" priorities.

Like St. Francis, therefore, *Papa Bergoglio* communicates as effectively by gestures as by words. When, on 13 March 2013, he appeared on the balcony of St. Peter's and asked the thousands gathered there to bless him before he blessed them, he by that very gesture made a significant statement. By refusing to live in the Apostolic Palace, he made another. When on Holy Thursday 2013 he washed the feet of a Muslim woman, a convicted criminal, he sent the church and the world an unforgettable image that conveyed an unmistakable and extraordinarily powerful message.

Yet he also has a gift for expressions and striking metaphors that impress themselves on the memory and make them ideals, as when he told priests and bishops "never to be afraid of tenderness." Even more unforgettable was his declaration that they must dirty themselves with the "smell of the sheep"—that is, they must not stand apart and above their flocks but immerse themselves in the real problems and struggles members of their flocks daily face. The heartrending scene that met him on 8 July 2013 on his visit to the African refugees on the island of Lampedusa wrought from him his anguished cry against the "globalization of indifference" that dulls the world's conscience and renders it impervious to human misery. When he spoke of the church as a "field hospital" where the task, immediate and urgent, is to tend to the wounds, he taught a vivid lesson in ecclesiology by reminding Catholics that the church is first and foremost a place of refuge and solace for those bloodied and brought low by the struggles, moral and other, of life as it is really lived. Already in the first months of his pontificate, the mercy of God, boundless and ever ready, had become a recurrent theme in his speeches and homilies.

On the day Vatican Council II opened, 11 October 1962, Pope John XXIII told the assembled prelates that the aim of the council was to show the church to be "the loving mother of all, benign, patient, full of mercy and goodness," a metaphor more positive than field hospital but consonant with it. *Papa Bergoglio*, the first pope in fifty years not to have participated in the council, is also the first pope to have grown up in the postcouncil church and thus to have accepted the council as a fact of life. His immediate predecessors often seemed incapable of forgetting the battles of the council in which they had been engaged, but Pope Francis has no such memories. He was still a student of theology while the council was in session and was schooled in its documents as the substance of his theological training. Paradoxically, his not having participated in the council has given him an advantage by providing the critical distance to see with clear eyes the council's major orientations.

The council was an exceedingly complex event and cannot be reduced to a slogan. Nonetheless, *dialog*, a word that for some people became almost synonymous with the council, captures the council's determination to seek reconciliation and common ground within the church and with those outside it. The word indicates both an ideal and a method. There can be no doubt that as archbishop Bergoglio understood what the term involved and that he did his best to put it into practice.

In Buenos Aires he, as archbishop, carried on a series of meetings with Rabbi Abraham Skorka in which they exchanged their positions on a wide range of topics, with seemingly nothing excluded as out of bounds. In 2010 their dialog was published more or less verbatim in a volume titled *Sobre el Cielo y la Tierra*. After Pope Francis's election, the book, translated into a large number of languages, became an international "best seller." For an archbishop to sit down with a rabbi for such an exchange would have been utterly unthinkable before Vatican II. Even in the half century since the council, no other high-ranking prelate has ever dared go so far. No pope in history has ever had such an experience or had an experience even remotely equivalent to it.

Within the church dialog finds its institutional equivalent in what the council called "collegiality." At Vatican II the prelates intended to revive the old synodal tradition of the church by which bishops on the local level, working together with other bishops of the same country or province, made decisions binding on their churches. The prelates at the council insisted at the same time that bishops had a responsibility not only for their own diocese but also, in union with the pope, for the universal church. Pope Paul VI created the Synod of Bishops as a way of dealing with the council's teaching.

Pope Francis seems determined to put this teaching into practice, as is suggested by his naming nine cardinals from around the world to advise him on problems affecting the church, especially those affecting the Roman Curia. He has indicated that he wants to make the Synod of Bishops operate more effectively than up to now and to do the same for the local episcopal conferences. These institutions give substance to Vatican II's intention to make cooperation and more widespread participation the mode in which the church operates both internally and externally. John XXIII implicitly commended this mode when he told the council to present the church as the loving mother, benign and patient, an ideal Francis has obviously interiorized as his own. According to a reliable report, had Cardinal Bergoglio been elected in the conclave in 2005, he would have chosen to be called John XXIV because of the deep inspiration he derived from "the good pope," *il papa buono*.

Pope Francis projects the image of a person not unlike Pope John, to whom he is often compared—a person genuinely kind and good, a person ready to listen to what you have to say, a person who will not judge you rashly, a person you would enjoy having dinner with. These are some of the qualities that in the first months of his pontificate made him such a world figure of unprecedented popularity. Over three million people gathered on the beach at Rio de Janeiro to see and hear him. He has appeared on the cover of some of the world's most secular journals. Presidents and prime ministers vie to identify themselves with him.

But his appeal is based on something more profound than personality. It is based most profoundly on his message, which is essentially an implicit or explicit invitation for people to be their best selves. Since becoming pope he has issued that invitation in virtually everything he has said and done. It is an invitation desperately needed in today's world and, perhaps for that very reason, it has evoked such a huge response. Francis is far from being the first pope to issue such an invitation. He has managed, however, to touch people's hearts and make achieving their best selves seem within reach. Only time will tell what the outcome will be in this new page in the history of the oldest living institution in the Western world.

Part II

Two Councils: Trent and Vatican II

7

THE COUNCIL OF TRENT

Myths, Misunderstandings, and Unintended Consequences

This piece was originally a lecture at the Pontifical Gregorian University, Rome, on 12 March 2013. It was later published as issue number 4 of Gregoriana. *It summarizes some of the highlights of my monograph on the council published that year, the 450th anniversary of the closing of the council in 1563.*

In the course of the 450 years since its close, the Council of Trent, perhaps more than many other important historical events, has suffered from myths and misunderstandings. I say "perhaps more than many other" for a number of reasons. Among these was the fact that the council was an object of vicious controversy and polemic even before it opened—by Catholics as well as by Protestants. The Catholic kings of France, for instance, threw obstacle after obstacle in its way and in effect boycotted it until the last moment. The fact, moreover, that the council dragged on for an interminable eighteen years made it an object of derision and satire by both Catholics and Protestants. Contributing to the problem was the fact that its final documents are dense with theological and canonical technicalities that make them extraordinarily susceptible to misunderstanding except by specialists skilled in the subtleties of canon law and medieval Scholasticism.

There is a further problem. Shortly after the council concluded in 1563, Pope Pius IV confirmed its decrees, but he forbade the printing of commentaries or notes on them without the explicit permission of the Holy See. That decree was never formally rescinded. Then in the early seventeenth century, Pope Paul V collected into fifty volumes all the materials related to the council that were available to him and stored them in the Vatican archives under the heading *fondo concilio*. Those archives were private, closed to scholars. The restrictions on access and on commentary made comprehensive scholarship and research on the Council of Trent impossible.

The situation changed only in 1880 when Pope Leo XIII opened the Vatican archives. Shortly thereafter, the Görres Gesellschaft, the learned society founded in 1876 by German Catholic scholars, went to work to produce a critical edition of the documents pertinent to the council. The first volume appeared in 1901. The final volume did not appear until 2001, precisely a century after the first. Those huge eighteen tomes, some of which run to nine hundred pages, principally in Latin and Italian but with a sprinkling of other languages, finally provided the basis for dispelling the myths and misunderstandings that have enshrouded the Council of Trent. What they revealed, however, was how complex the council was and how many skills were needed to untangle the sources that were now finally accessible.

The hero of the story is Hubert Jedin, a Görres Gesellschaft member, who in 1949 published in German the first volume of his history of the council, *Geschichte des Konzils von Trient*. He published the fourth and final volume some twenty-five years later, in 1975. Everybody today who writes on the council is heavily indebted to him, not only for the history but also for his many other writings on the council. In the course of almost a century that has elapsed since the 1930s, when Jedin first began to write, his work, not surprisingly, has shown its limitations. Still, the large corpus of his writings on the council, especially the history, has held up remarkably well.

Jedin's writings are, however, all in German. The four volumes of his history were translated into both Italian and Spanish, but only the first two into English and only the first into French. There are no translations into any other languages, as best I have been able to ascertain. Moreover, Jedin's many and extremely important articles on the council remain locked away in their original language. Jedin dispelled many of the myths and misunderstandings, but for much of the world, even much of the scholarly world, he did so to little avail.

With full acknowledgment of my debt to Jedin, I will this evening try to dispel a few of the myths and misunderstandings. I divide what I have to say into three parts, as promised in my title. I will first address some major myths, then some common misunderstandings, and, finally, describe three major consequences of the council that it did not intend.

Before I go any further, I perhaps first need to recall for you some basic facts about the council. Only after contentious negotiations did the interested parties settle on the then small city of Trent as the council's location, a compromise fully agreeable to none of them. Contention over the location presaged many other disagreements and conflicts of priorities that plagued the council from its first moment to its last.

The Council of Trent met over the course of five pontificates in three distinct periods: 1545–1547, 1551–1552, and 1562–1563. This long trajectory meant that very few of the bishops and theologians who opened the council in 1545 were still alive or well enough to participate in the final period that opened seventeen years later. As in previous councils, secular monarchs were present at Trent through their ambassadors, who made the concerns of their sovereigns known and operative in the council's deliberations. The Council of Trent was not a sacristy affair. Its outcome held serious political, as well as religious, consequences for all concerned.

With that very brief setting of the scene we can begin with the first of the three myths. By *myth* I mean here simply a widely held but misleading belief or opinion. It is different from a simple mistake or misinterpretation in that it tends to have an overarching significance and to rise to a high level of generalization.

MYTHS

1. The Council Was Essentially Aimed at Repression and Social Discipline

There is evidence that supports this myth. Exhibit number one is the fact that during the third period a committee of the council worked at elaborating a new *Index of Forbidden Books*. Exhibit number two is the famous decree of the council titled *Tametsi* that for the first time required Catholic marriages to be witnessed by a priest, an incursion into the spouses' freedom to exchange vows when and how they wanted. The third exhibit is the fact that during the so-called Counter-Reformation the Spanish, papal, and other inquisitions launched campaigns of surveillance and imposed restrictions to a degree unknown before the council. The council must be responsible.

Before addressing those issues, I must put the council into perspective. First of all, from the very beginning until Vatican II, councils conducted their business as legislative and judicial bodies—that is, they made laws and they heard criminal cases. The laws had to do with public conduct, and they were usually, but not exclusively, aimed at the clergy and were intended in most cases to correct abuses. Laws are by definition a restriction of freedom, which is justified in view of a greater good. Trent passed a lot of laws because the council deemed them necessary for the badly needed reform of the church.

What is peculiar about Trent and seldom commented on is that the bishops at Trent aimed their reform principally at themselves. There were two glaring abuses in the episcopacy. The first was absenteeism. Before the council, for instance, Milan—the largest, richest, and most important archdiocese in Italy—had not had a resident archbishop for forty years. The second was holding more than one bishopric at a time, so as to collect more revenue than one bishopric yielded.

The great struggle at Trent was to enact the most stringent legislation possible to correct these blatant abuses. The aim was more pastorally responsive bishops. The disciplinary decrees of the Council of Trent in the aggregate deal almost exclusively with this problem and with its correlate, making sure pastors of parishes also reside in their parishes and do their traditional jobs. Very little of Tridentine legislation deals directly with the laity.

What about the *Index of Forbidden Books* that the council tried to elaborate? In 1559, the year of his death, Pope Paul IV issued the first papal index. It was so extreme that his successor, Pius IV, felt obliged to set up a commission to mitigate it. In the meantime, Pius convoked the council for its third period. For reasons too complicated to go into here, the council could not immediately take up its agenda from where it had left off ten years earlier. It needed to spin its wheels for a while until a crucial procedural question could be resolved.

The pope hit on the idea of transferring the revision of the index from the commission he had originally established and of giving the job to the council—almost as work to keep it busy until it could address the real issues. Many members of the council objected to the idea—revision of the index was a waste of the council's time, the council did not have the resources to do it properly, and so forth. Nonetheless, the council had little choice. In any case, we must remember the revision was undertaken to mitigate the index, not in any way to make it stronger.

The committee of the council, in fact, was unable to complete its work on the index and therefore never submitted its draft to the bishops at the council for discussion and debate. Given this situation, the council at the last minute consigned the task of completing its work to the pope himself. What was published after the council as the *Tridentine Index of Forbidden Books* was, therefore, never discussed or approved by the council, even though a committee of the council had provided the basic materials for it.

The decree *Tametsi* ("Even though"), requiring a priest witness for the validity of a marriage entered into by Catholics, was the one decree of Trent that had immediate impact on the laity. Was it a typical power grab by the church, as it is sometimes portrayed, and an instance of Trent's unwarranted disciplining of the laity? The answer to both those questions is a negative.

Everyone at Trent—indeed, all Christian theologians, Protestant and Catholic alike—agreed that the essence of marriage was the exchange of vows between the two partners. Why, then, did Trent think it necessary to issue a decree on the matter? It did so to try to solve the problem of so-called clandestine marriages—that is, the exchange of vows between the two partners without any witnesses present whatsoever. What this meant was that a few years or a few babies later, one of the partners, usually the man, could deny that the marriage had ever taken place and move on to take a new spouse. Trent's decree was meant to protect the innocent spouse, usually the woman, so that the other spouse could not without further ado abandon the marriage. It was to put a stop to this abuse that the council, after heated debate, decided on *Tametsi*.

What about inquisitions? The first thing to note is that in their Spanish, Roman, and Venetian forms, they all antedate the Council of Trent. The Spanish Inquisition does so by a half century. The second thing to note is that the Council of Trent neither commended nor condemned them. It said not a word about them. If the council was somehow responsible for their greater stringency after the council, that responsibility was indirect and, as far as our evidence goes, unintended.

2. The Council Exacerbated the Religious Division

As with all myths, this one contains more than a grain of truth. With hindsight we see clearly that in its doctrinal decrees the council drew a sharp line of demarcation on the contested issues, especially on the sacraments. To deal adequately with this myth, we must make the crucial distinction between what the council intended to do or thought it was doing and how it was interpreted or employed after the council. We tend to forget that the council was meant to be and hoped to be a council of reconciliation with the Lutherans. That was the primary purpose that Emperor Charles V had in mind as he for a full decade tried to persuade first Pope Clement VII and then Pope Paul III to convoke the council.

Although Paul III and his successors were skeptical that such a reconciliation could be effected by the council, they nonetheless subscribed to that goal. As a gesture of goodwill, Paul III, at the very beginning of the council, directed that no one was to be condemned by name. This was contrary to the practice of every council up to that time. Moreover, strenuous efforts were made to have representative Lutherans and others come to the council to defend their positions, and, in fact, a few Lutherans did appear toward the end of the second period, 1551–1552. By then, however, it was decades too late. Lutheranism had by that time become a full religious system, and it was a system incompatible with Catholicism.

Even with this setback, Pius IV, when he years later convoked the third period, still made efforts that today we might even call ecumenical. On 1 December 1560 he sent a letter to the Lutheran princes in Germany inviting them to send envoys to the council, and in early February two papal legates appeared before them in Naumburg to ask their support for the council. In May 1561 the papal nuncio Girolamo Martinengo, bearing an invitation to the council for Queen Elizabeth of England, was denied entrance to the kingdom on the grounds that the presence of a nuncio in England was illegal and could give rise to unrest.

Most surprisingly, Pius dispatched legates to the Coptic patriarch in Alexandria, to the Greek Orthodox patriarch in Constantinople (Istanbul), and to the Armenian patriarch in Antioch. His several attempts to reach the Russian patriarch in Moscow were obstructed by the Poles. You will not be surprised to learn that none of these efforts bore fruit.

3. The Council of Trent Was a Single-Minded Meeting That Legislated on Every Important Aspect of Catholicism

Jedin's writings showed how contrary to fact this myth was, but, despite his efforts, it persists to the present. From its opening days the bishops showed their independence and continued to challenge every effort to make them conform to some preconceived program. The bishops and theologians participating in the council reflected the wide and diverse range of positions on almost every aspect of Catholic teaching and practice that characterized European Catholicism at the time. The council was, therefore, a contentious and extraordinarily difficult undertaking. It lurched from major crisis to major crisis. For a period of ten months, from September 1562 to July 1563, it was so paralyzed that it could not issue a single decree.

Nor did the council try to legislate on every important aspect of Catholicism at the time. I have already mentioned that it abstained from any mention of inquisitions. More surprising from a twenty-first-century perspective, it had not a word to say about foreign missions, even though the evangelization of the newly discovered lands had already become one of Catholicism's most distinctive and defining features and without doubt an enterprise of immense import for the future of the church. Nor did the council say anything about war, Renaissance humanism, or many other things. The Council of Trent had a very straightforward and clearly focused agenda: affirmation of Catholic doctrine on the contested issues and reform of three offices in the church—the papacy, the episcopacy, and the pastorate.

There are, surely, other myths concerning the council, but we must move on to misunderstandings, misinterpretations, or misinformation about it. These differ from myths in that they are very specific and, as single issues, lack the overarching range that is peculiar to myth. They are not for that reason less important for understanding certain issues that are lively within Catholicism today. In fact, in that regard they may be more important than the myths.

MISUNDERSTANDINGS, MISINTERPRETATIONS, AND MISINFORMATION

1. The Council Forbade the Use of the Vernacular in the Liturgy

The council issued only a single line on the issue: "It is wrong to say that the liturgy must always be celebrated in the vernacular." If we turn it around, the text says Latin is legitimate but not required. Surprisingly, from our perspective today, the council spent little time on this issue. The possibility of vernacular liturgy sparked virtually no controversy in the council. The bishops seemed to agree with one of their colleagues, who reminded them that in the church of the Holy Sepulcher in Jerusalem liturgies were celebrated, as he said, "in every language under the sun." As far as the legislation of Trent was concerned, vernacular liturgy was not a problem. Long before the council ended, however, the Latin liturgy had become such a sign of Catholic identity vis-à-vis the Protestants that the council's decree never had a chance to become operative.

2. The Council Forbade the Printing, Selling, and Reading of Bibles in the Vernacular

The invention of the printing press in the fifteenth century resulted almost immediately in the diffusion of Bibles in the vernacular. Luther's brilliant translation into German was just the most famous but far from being the first, and the council members' opinions differed sharply about what to do in the face of this relatively new reality. For some bishops vernacular Bibles were the root of all heresies, whereas for others they were the essential nourishment for the godly life.

For the council the problem had political ramifications. In France and Spain (as well as England) such translations had long been forbidden, even though they circulated in those places rather freely. If the council advocated them, the episcopacy and probably the crown would countermand the decree. If it forbade them, Germany, Italy, Poland, and other places where they were allowed would react just as negatively, but for the opposite reason. The council decided not to decide and left the question open.

That was in 1546. But, as mentioned, during the third period the council undertook a revision of the index of Pope Paul IV. In the committee's recommendations, it provided norms for episcopal surveillance of vernacular translations and restrictions on reading them. These rules were incorporated into the index issued after the council in the council's name. Remember, however, that the council itself never saw these rules, nor did it ever discuss and approve them.

3. The Council Forbade All Latin Translations of the Bible Except the Vulgate

As you know, the Vulgate was the Latin translation done principally by St. Jerome in the early fifth century that eventually became the standard version in the West. As you also know, the Council of Trent declared that version "authentic." What did the council intend by that declaration?

By the time the council met, the Vulgate had come under scathing criticism from scholars newly schooled in critical philology, beginning with Lorenzo Valla (1407–1457) a good century before Trent met. As a result, several new translations were in circulation, of which the best known was Erasmus's translation of the New Testament. Many of the bishops at Trent were keenly aware of the problems with the Vulgate and were favorable toward one or other of the new translations.

But the council needed to settle the practical question of what version to use in its own deliberations. If they were to choose a text other than the Vulgate, which would it be? Were the problems with the Vulgate so serious as to prevent its use in the council and in the church at large? The council in the end decided, almost as a practical measure, to use the Vulgate, which it deemed "authentic"—that is, reliable (or even "reliable enough"). The council also decreed that the Vulgate be thoroughly revised so as to make it conform with the best philological standards.

The crucial intervention at the council on this issue was made by Bishop Pietro Bertano, a member of the commission who drafted the decree. In the name of the commission, he explained:

> We do not consider it an abuse that there are various and different translations of the Bible because this was tolerated in ancient times and should be tolerated today. . . . We wish the Vulgate edition to be accepted as authentic . . . [but] we do not reject other versions because we do not want to restrict Christian liberty. Moreover, we do not want even to reject the translations of the heretics, in conformity with the example of the ancient church.

At the time of the decree, Pope Paul III and his advisers were dismayed by the council's statement on the Vulgate and let the legates know they thought the council was too soft on it. After the council, however, the decree was taken as warrant for outlawing other translations, and the definite article "the" became attached to the Vulgate. It became "the authentic version," but of course Latin has neither definite nor indefinite articles. The council said simply that the Vulgate was authentic—that is, sufficiently reliable.

4. There Is Such a Thing as a "Tridentine Liturgy," Sanctioned by the Council

Today there is much confusion on the question of "Tridentine liturgy" and the role of the council in that regard. The truth is that there is no such thing as a "Tridentine liturgy" in the sense that the council created a liturgy, substantially revised the traditional liturgy of the Roman Rite, or even issued anything that we today would recognize as a "decree on the liturgy." The bishops and theologians at Trent simply accepted the different liturgies in use at the time of the council, of which by far the most prevalent in the West since the thirteenth century was the Roman Rite, which was originally the rite used by the Roman Curia.

What the bishops were concerned about was the sad state of that rite's liturgical books. They were concerned, in particular, about the textual discrepancies in the many editions of the missal that were then in circulation. Since the invention of printing publishers had turned out missals in large numbers in which local interpolations and typographical errors were rife. In some cases this might mean failing to include important parts of the text. This, in turn, meant that priests out of ignorance sometimes went so far as to omit the Our Father, other important prayers, or even the entire central Eucharistic prayer, the Canon of the Mass.

The council briefly debated the problem but took no action on it until the very last moment of the council, 4 December 1563, when it recommended, almost as a two-word tag onto a larger decree, that the missal and breviary be corrected. Those few words constituted "the liturgical reform" of the Council of Trent. After the council the pope confided supervision of the revision to the capable hands of Cardinal Guglielmo Sirleto, who produced just what the council intended—a reliable text that conformed to the best and oldest manuscripts and printed editions. The text itself is perhaps less important than the bull of Pius V promulgating it, which ordered the universal adoption of the Roman Rite unless another rite had prevailed in a given region or institution for over two hundred years. Missing from the bull is any intimation that a vernacular adaptation might be possible.

5. The Council Decreed That Priests Must Be Celibate

In the Western Church, celibacy of the clergy early became an ideal, and it soon began to be required of everybody in major orders—from deacon through priesthood and episcopacy. Observance of that discipline was always far from perfect. The issue erupted into open controversy in the eleventh century with the Gregorian Reform and then again in the sixteenth with the Reformation. Luther declared celibacy unwarranted by the Bible and an instance of papal tyranny over consciences. Other Protestant reformers followed his lead.

It was almost inevitable that the issue be raised at the council, especially when in the third period it debated the sacraments of matrimony and holy orders. Responsible, however, for explicitly raising the matter was the Holy Roman emperor, Ferdinand I, the successor to Charles V. He was seconded by Duke Albrecht V of Bavaria. Early in the third period of the council, Ferdinand's ambassadors to the council handed the papal legates a memorandum from him. In it the emperor recommended a number of things. Among the more urgent of them was mitigation of celibacy. The legates took no action on the memorandum at that time.

Some weeks later, however, Sigismund Baumgartner, a layman, arrived at the council as the ambassador of Duke Albrecht. According to standard protocol for such occasions, the ambassador addressed the council to convey to it the concerns of his sovereign. Citing information gathered from an extensive visitation of Bavaria in 1558, Baumgartner painted a dark picture. The vast majority of the clergy was ignorant and infected with heresy. Out of a hundred only three or four were not secretly married or keeping concubines, to the great scandal of the faithful.

Baumgartner pleaded on behalf of Albrecht for permission for the clergy to marry. He made the point that in German-speaking lands devout and faithful Catholics had come to the conclusion that "a chaste marriage is preferable to a tainted celibacy"—*castum matrimonium contaminato coelibatui praeferendum*. The situation would deteriorate further, he predicted, unless, in accordance with the custom of the early church, well-educated men who were married were admitted to holy orders. He added, "It is, after all, not a divine law that requires priests to be celibate. As is clear from the historical record, married men were admitted to holy orders in past ages—and not only to the dignity of priesthood but even to the exalted heights of the episcopacy."

As was its practice, the council issued a formal acknowledgment of the address but then moved on to the business at hand. Some months later Duke Albrecht, through the envoys he sent to Rome, asked Pius IV directly for permission for "upright and learned married men to perform certain ecclesiastical duties, especially preaching the divine word." The pope replied that he would refer the matter to the legates at the council. When the legates received the pope's inquiry, they consulted four theologians at the council, who replied that the request was against the tradition of the church and, in their opinion, inexpedient "even for these calamitous times." For the time being the matter rested there.

Many months later, Georg Draskovich, Emperor Ferdinand's ambassador, addressed the council on the issue. He reminded the bishops of the grave scandal priests caused by their sexual misconduct and said, "If you want young priests, let them get married first." Strange to say, this intervention sparked virtually no discussion. For better or for worse, celibacy lacked urgency for bishops from Italy and Spain, who made up the vast majority of the bishops at Trent. The same was true for the theologians. When they presented their views to the bishops on the sacrament of matrimony, only in a few instances did they touch on this question.

In the final document on the sacrament, celibacy is neither commended nor condemned. It simply is not mentioned. The council decided not to decide. Two canons, however, danced around the issue. Canon 10 condemned the view that marriage was a more blessed state than virginity or celibacy. Canon 9 condemned the view that clerics in holy orders or members of a religious order who had taken a solemn vow of chastity could validly contract marriage. This was a minimal statement, more juridical than theological, and it sidestepped the real issue.

After the council the matter landed on the desk of Pope Pius IV. The emperor and the duke continued their quest for a mitigation of celibacy at least for German-speaking lands. Ferdinand, for instance, wrote to a number of cardinals who he thought might influence Pius in his favor. After Ferdinand's death, his son Maximilian II continued the effort, as did

Albrecht. Pius, undecided, in early January 1565, about a year after the conclusion of the council, created a deputation of cardinals to deliberate on the matter.

Two months later King Philip II of Spain let the pope know that he was utterly opposed to any concession. He argued that if a change were made for Bavaria and the empire, other nations would demand it, which would result in the destruction of the church's hierarchical structure. In the few months left to him before his death, Pius procrastinated. But when his successor, Pius V, let it be known immediately on his election that he was determined to grant no concession or to admit any change, the issue died.

UNINTENDED CONSEQUENCES

I am sure that all of you in this room have experienced the law of unintended consequences in your own lives as a result of decisions you have made. Here is how it works: You are faced with a decision. You weigh the reasons for choosing one alternative over another. Finally, you make your decision. Even when it turns out to have been the right decision, you soon realize that it entails consequences, good or bad, that you did not foresee and certainly did not intend. What is true for decisions in our personal lives is true for decisions taken by institutions. It was certainly true for the Council of Trent. I will describe three of them. The first two were consequences for Catholic culture in the broad sense of that term. The last was a consequence that directly affected the papacy but then deeply affected the trajectory of the history of the Catholic Church from that point forward.

1. Catholicism and Historical Continuity

The Council of Trent unwittingly gave powerful impetus to a distinctively Catholic bias regarding the past that had, in fact, begun to emerge even before the council. The Protestant reformers, beginning with Luther, accused the Catholic Church of having completely broken with the Gospel. For Luther, the fact that the church did not preach justification by faith alone, as he understood it, meant that continuity with the true teaching of the New Testament had been ruptured. Moreover, by its exaltation of the papacy and the sanction of papal tyranny, the church had broken even more radically with the teaching of Christ and the apostles.

Catholic apologists immediately rushed to counter that charge, insisting on the church's unbroken continuity with the apostolic era. By the way Trent spoke, especially of the sacraments, it seconded the point the apologists made. In canon 6 of its decree on the sacrament of penance, for instance, the council asserted that "from the beginning" the church had required the secret confession of one's sins to a priest, in conformity with the command of Christ. As we know, however, that practice developed centuries later in monasteries and became widespread in the West only in the eleventh and twelfth centuries.

When the council affirmed that in the Catholic Church "the ancient, absolute, and in every respect perfect faith and doctrine of the Eucharist had been retained," it was only making fully explicit for one aspect of its teaching what generally underlay its doctrinal pronouncements. What Christ and the apostles handed on, the church retained and has always retained unchanged. No previous council ever insisted so often and so explicitly on its teaching's continuity with the authentic Christian past. In so doing, the council helped develop the Catholic mindset, reluctant to admit change in the course of church tradition. Although there is certainly a sense in which believing Catholics can and must subscribe to the church's claim of continuity, in its undifferentiated form it flies in the face of incontestable evidence.

In any case, a peculiarly Catholic mindset in that regard became more fully crystallized some decades after the council with the publication of works like Cardinal Cesare Baronio's *Ecclesiastical Annals*, which was a response to Lutheran histories that tried to prove Catholicism represented a break with the apostolic era and with the primitive church. That mindset is with us today, in places high and low.

2. After the Council, Catholicism Emerged as the Most Sensuous of the Churches

Long before the Reformation, devout Christians reacted against the crass superstition, even carnal character, of many religious practices of the day and sought a more genuine religious experience. That is to say, they sought a religion that was more spiritual than what they saw around them. The collection of devout axioms and musings that became known as *The*

Imitation of Christ, which was in circulation from the early fifteenth century onward, quickly became popular. The call it issued in the first chapter, traditional though it was, assumed a new urgency: "Withdraw your heart from the love of visible things and turn it to the love of things invisible."

Erasmus, the great humanist of the early sixteenth century, contributed to this movement with his satires about phony relics, credulous pilgrims, and questionable apparitions of the Virgin Mary and other saints. He, and other humanists like him, sought a more spiritual religion that distanced itself from the sensuous, especially in its grosser and more ostentatious forms. Largely through Erasmus's influence, the Latin word *caerimoniae* acquired the pejorative meaning of "trivial little rituals" that were more of a distraction than an aid to true devotion. Statues of the saints were just as likely to lead to idolatry as to emulation, which, according to Erasmus, was the only correct aspect of the cult of the saints.

Only with the Reformation, however, did this trend take a destructive turn. It began in Wittenberg with Andreas Karlstadt, one of Luther's disciples. He condemned images of Christ and the saints as a violation of the First Commandment, and he persuaded the city council of Wittenberg to remove all images from the churches of the city. Luther, who was away from Wittenberg at the time, countermanded the order when he returned, and he openly broke with Karlstadt. Not in Lutheranism, therefore, but especially in Calvinism, self-conscious, comprehensively destructive programs of iconoclasm broke out. Those programs were particularly thorough in some cities of Switzerland and in the whole of Scotland. By the third quarter of the sixteenth century, the French Calvinists, the Huguenots, had gained considerable strength in France, and they set about destroying images in churches everywhere they were able.

The Mediterranean world of Italy, Spain, and Portugal was virtually untouched by this movement, which explains why the veneration of sacred images was a nonissue at the Council of Trent until after the arrival of the French during the council's last period. The French brought with them a demand that the council issue a decree declaring sacred images not only legitimate but also useful for instruction and devotion. Because of French insistence, the council at the very last moment complied and produced its famous decree. The decree was so late in coming from the committee responsible for formulating it that the council had time only to rubber-stamp it, without even a moment to discuss or debate it. In any case, the decree is a resolute affirmation of sacred images, allowing the churches and other places to be adorned with them.

In recent decades the decree has been widely discussed by art historians. They have tended to focus on the decree's stipulation that "all lasciviousness and sensual appeal" be avoided in sacred images, and if the images are about biblical persons or events, they should be true to the sacred texts. These provisions are certainly important, and they had an impact on art, artists, and their patrons. The best-known case concerns Michelangelo's *Last Judgment* in the Sistine Chapel. After the council, in an attempt to observe the decree, Pope Pius IV had the frontal nudity in that famous fresco overpainted. That is the *Last Judgment* you see in the chapel today, even after recent restorations. But similar instances of mutilation are few, even in dioceses with bishops zealous to implement the reforms of Trent.

We must remember: despite the decree's warning about possible abuses, which, in fact, consists in only a few words in a long decree, the overall message of the decree is positive. That message, certainly not unexpected, fell sweetly on the ears of artists and their patrons, and it removed from Catholic lands a threat that had devastated others. It was in keeping with the sacramental principle distinctive of Catholicism that the spiritual is mediated to us through material signs.

As the political, military, and religious scene had more or less settled by the late sixteenth century, the two most important centers of art production—Italy and Flanders—were securely in Catholic hands. And by that time, Spain had begun to emerge as another important center, also firmly in Catholic hands. In the early seventeenth century, as artistic taste moved gradually into the baroque era, artists became ever more prone to reveal ever more human flesh. Think of Caravaggio and of the Carracci. No artist of the times revealed more flesh or gloried more in the beauty of the human body than Peter Paul Rubens, the Jesuits' preferred artist in that era, a devout Catholic who attended Mass daily.

In its decree on the Sacrifice of the Mass, the council gave voice to a general principle that undelay its approach to worship. That statement, though less commented on, is perhaps just as important for revealing the council's stance regarding the sensuous. It says, "Since human nature is such that it cannot raise itself up to the meditation of divine realities without material aid, holy mother church has for that reason . . . provided certain things such as symbolic blessings, lights, incense, vestments and many other ritual objects . . . by which the majesty of this great sacrifice is enhanced and the minds of the faithful are aroused by such visible signs of religious devotion to contemplation of the high mysteries hidden in it."

This passage and the decree on images professed a close relationship between the corporal and the spiritual and were thus able to justify and therefore to promote the material enhancements of divine worship, a feature that strikingly set Catholic worship off from most of its Protestant counterparts. They, moreover, promoted profoundly different cultural appreciations in Protestant lands, as distinct from Catholic, that would persist through the centuries. More was at stake, in other words, than theology. Or, perhaps better put, theology in this instance had profound repercussions on culture.

3. The Council Enhanced the Prestige and Authority of the Papacy

The Council of Trent had two principal aims: reform of the church to make it more pastorally effective and affirmation of those Catholic teachings that Protestants rejected. The Protestant Reformation was a complex movement, and different reformers rejected different Catholic doctrines and practices. There was, however, one doctrine they all rejected without exception: papal primacy. Indeed, "No Pope" almost became their battle cry. Top on Trent's agenda, therefore, should have been a decree on the papacy.

But Trent issued no such decree. It did not do so because it could not do so. The bishops and theologians present at Trent disagreed too much about how the papal office was to function. Of course, all those present at Trent believed in papal primacy. Otherwise they would not have come to a council that was convoked by the pope and presided over by the pope's legates. But just how papal primacy functioned, just what its legitimate limits might be, and especially how it related to the council itself were subjects on which there was no agreement at Trent.

Yet it was an issue that simmered beneath the surface almost from the moment the council opened until the moment it closed. It threatened to emerge at a number of different moments and in connection with a number of different problems the council had to deal with. The most serious and sustained of such moments lasted ten months, and it arose in connection with the council's primary reform aim—getting bishops to reside in their dioceses and to hold only one diocese at a time.

There was no lack of clear legislation on the matter. In its first period, Trent itself had passed a strong measure in that regard. But by the time the council met seventeen years later, nothing had changed. The loophole was dispensations from the law granted by the papacy. Popes needed money, and one of their major sources was offerings or stipends offered in return for dispensations. It was the council's attempt to somehow curtail that practice, which was interpreted in Rome as an illegitimate incursion into the authority of the Holy See that divided the council into two diametrically opposed factions. That division brought the council to its most severe crisis in its long history, the crisis I mentioned that lasted ten months.

Moreover, if we focus our attention not on this or that decree of the council but on the entire corpus, especially of Trent's reform legislation, it becomes clear that the fundamental aim of the council was to enhance the authority not of the papacy but of the local bishop. Yet, after the council, the papacy began to enjoy a new prestige among Catholics and began to exert its authority in new areas of church life.

This is remarkable in that before and during the council the three popes who convoked the three periods were often blamed and heavily criticized by Catholics for obstructing the council's progress and, indeed, for being the main obstacle to the reforms of the church the council wanted to establish. Once the council ended, however, Catholics who during the council had ridiculed it now began to rally around it. Pope Pius IV began to get credit for bringing that fractious body to a successful conclusion. Moreover, in its haste to end the council, the bishops had confided certain tasks to the papacy that they had not had time to complete or even to undertake. Inadvertently, the council handed to the papacy a somewhat enlarged job description.

As mentioned, the council confided to the papacy the completion of the new *Index of Forbidden Books*. When Pius IV promulgated the new index a few months after the end of the council, he in effect, and probably unwittingly, not only issued a revision of a document created by his predecessor but also established a new papal institution that from that moment forward would enjoy an uninterrupted life in the church until the middle of the twentieth century.

The council also confided to the papacy the revision of the missal and the breviary. These two tasks bit by bit expanded so as to include other liturgical books, including the *Pontificale* and the *Rituale*. Not surprisingly, therefore, in 1588 Pope Sixtus V moved a significant step forward and founded the Congregation of Rites, an action that implicitly but unmistakably redefined the papacy's role regarding Catholic worship. It, for the first time, provided the papacy with an instrument for ongoing oversight of every possible issue concerning liturgy and the sacraments. That congregation, now with a new name, is still in existence today.

When the council ended, it was unclear who had the primary responsibility for the implementation of its decrees—was it the secular rulers, the local bishops, or the papacy? In the council's documents can be found justification for all three, and, in fact, all three not only claim that authority but actively and effectively pursue it. In this contest, the papacy certainly did not lag behind.

Papal nuncios were ambassadors of the Holy See to monarchs throughout Europe. Long before the council, the papacy had made effective use of them, but after the council, it strengthened and further formalized the institution and used it to press for the implementation of the council in accordance with its own interpretation of it. The nuncios represented the pope and sometimes served as a counterweight to the local hierarchy. This development formed part and parcel of the new shot of energy that the successful end of the council injected into the papal enterprise. As with other institutions in the modern world, the church, too, moved into patterns of ever-greater centralization of authority. The extent to which that development was directly due to the Council of Trent is debatable. Nonetheless, the council certainly contributed to it. Like other developments after the council, this one can in part be described as one of the council's unintended consequences.

8

BISHOPS AND THEOLOGIANS AT THE COUNCIL OF TRENT

A Lesson for Today

While I was writing my book on the Council of Trent, I was struck with the difference between the role the theologians played there and the role they played at Vatican II. Of course, their essential role was the same: to advise the bishops on the theological and doctrinal issues at stake in a given measure. But the way they played that role was notably different in the two councils. I believe understanding that difference throws light on the origins of the sometimes-tense relationship today between theologians and bishops. That is the point of this article, which I published in America *magazine, 31 October 2011.*

The year 2013 will mark the 450th anniversary of the closing of the Council of Trent. I am writing a book about the council to contribute in a modest way to the anniversary's observance. But I am doing so also because I believe that in this case, as in so many others, what happened in the past gives helpful perspectives on the present. What happened at Trent may help Catholics and observers outside the church reflect on the current tension between the magisterium and theologians and suggest better ways to deal with it. The problem is not new in the church, but today it is certainly acute.

Its roots are deep in the past, originating in the twelfth and thirteenth centuries with the founding of the universities. Up to that time, bishops, who almost invariably came from the upper social strata of society, had the same literary style of education as their peers. If all went well, they directed their literary skills to expounding on the text of the Bible and thus became qualified to teach in the church. St. Augustine and St. Ambrose fit this mold. Although these bishops might on their own devote time to the study of philosophy, their culture remained general, indistinguishable in style from that of other leaders in society. They were the equivalent of the "gentlemen scholars" of later ages. They held no university degrees because there were no universities.

This comfortable situation changed drastically in the High Middle Ages, when Greek science, newly imported, challenged the Bible as the source of all knowledge. Reflection on the "sacred page" would never again be so easy, as the relationship between "reason and revelation" moved into a new and direct confrontation. That confrontation has continued into the present—in different forms, surely, but in forms even more exacerbated. There are no easy answers to how to reconcile issues arising from the confrontation, most especially not in the intellectually and technologically complicated twenty-first century.

Just at the time the confrontation first took place, and to some extent because of it, the university came into being. The purpose of the new institution was to train professionals, including professionals in the sacred page. At the University of Paris, the faculty of theology was one of the three professional schools, along with law and medicine. To complete the full course in theology might require some fifteen years. It was in that faculty that the many problems arising from the new problematic of reason and revelation intruded into the more serene scenario of contemplation of the sacred page. Disputation, not contemplation, was the standard university exercise.

Note that these new professionals in theology were not bishops. For the most part bishops and future bishops continued to be educated in the old ways; some, however, earned university degrees in canon law, a discipline soon considered more appropriate for them than theology. Thus it happened that bishops, the traditional teachers of the faith, generally did not have the technical expertise required to deal with the ever-more-challenging questions raised in discourse about "sacred doctrine." They had to rely on professionals.

In a rough sketch, that is the origin of the tension between magisterium and theologians that we experience today. The relationship between these two classes of teachers has not, of course, always been tense. That is where the Council of Trent can be instructive. It stands as an important instance of cooperation. The Second Vatican Council also provides an example of cooperation, but at Trent the theologians played a more formally recognized role and had fewer limitations imposed on them.

At Vatican II the pope directly appointed all official periti, the theological experts, even though bishops were free to bring their own. The theologians sat with the bishops on the commissions that prepared the documents. Although they had considerable influence in the commissions, they were officially admonished that they were to speak only when spoken to. They never addressed the bishops in the plenary sessions in St. Peter's Basilica. That was reserved exclusively for the bishops.

The procedures at Trent were different in two significant ways. First, the pope appointed only two or three of the council's theologians. The rest were appointed by the bishops, by monarchs, and by the religious orders. During the second period of the council, 1551–1552, for instance, the pope appointed two; the bishops, fifteen; the Holy Roman emperor, seven; Queen Mary of Hungary (the emperor's sister), nine; and the religious orders, twenty-two.

Second, the role the theologians played in the preparation of the doctrinal decrees differed. The procedure was as follows:

To start, one or more theologians, designated for the task by the papal legates who presided at the council, sorted out the principal points at issue in the doctrine under discussion. These points, brief and pointed, usually amounting to only a sentence or two, were then given to the other theologians and to the bishops.

Second, in the presence of the full assembly of bishops, the theologians in turn, one by one, presented their views on the articles. Individual presentations might last two or three hours. These meetings, called congregations of theologians, were held morning and afternoon and sometimes went on for several weeks at a time. Although bishops were not strictly required to attend these sessions, most did so. They listened in silence and heard a wide spectrum of views.

An example will illustrate the difference between the two councils. The concept of Tradition (the Second Vatican Council) or traditions (Trent) was treated in both. At the Second Vatican Council, the Doctrinal

Preparatory Commission, made up of bishops, composed a draft decree that was then submitted to the other bishops gathered in St. Peter's. Two theologians—Karl Rahner, SJ, and Joseph Ratzinger—were convinced that a whole school of thought on the matter had been a priori excluded from consideration. They therefore felt compelled to create an alternative text, which they circulated on an unofficial basis among the bishops. At Trent the first action was in reverse order: theologians vetted the problem, while prelates listened silently.

Third, only then did the bishops, now well informed about the theological options available to them, in similarly serial fashion address the articles. When they finished, a deputation of bishops together with theologian consultants drew up a draft document, which was then debated by the bishops, amended as needed, and finally approved by them. It was a long, often tedious procedure, but it resulted in decrees that were fully informed and well thought out.

The bishops at Trent were typical of the Catholic episcopacy at the time. They had little formal training in theology, even though they otherwise might be well educated according to the standards of the day. If they had university degrees, those decrees tended to be in canon law. The theologians at Trent, however, came exclusively from universities or comparable institutions, and some were men of great distinction. They were not hand-chosen to promote a particular perspective but represented a random sampling of theological "schools." The bishops did well to hear them out before proceeding to their own deliberations.

Since the beginning of the twentieth century, virtually all bishops have attended seminaries. In that respect they are different from the bishops who participated at Trent. Nonetheless, few have advanced degrees in theology at a time when the Christian situation has become complex to an extent unimaginable in an earlier age. Now, as never before, cooperation and mutual respect are important. In that regard, I believe, the Council of Trent may hold a lesson for both parties.

9

THE COUNCIL OF TRENT AND MICHELANGELO'S *LAST JUDGMENT*

The Council of Trent's decree on sacred images has in recent decades attracted considerable interest from art historians. Immediately after the close of the council, the male frontal nudity in Michelangelo's Last Judgment *in the Sistine Chapel was overpainted. In this article, I explain the relationship between the council document and the overpainting. The article was originally a lecture delivered in Philadelphia at the autumn meeting of the American Philosophical Society, 18 November 2011.*

Michelangelo's *Last Judgment* is one of the world's most famous paintings, by one of the world's most famous artists, and located in one of the world's most famous rooms, the Sistine Chapel. It was Pope Clement VII (1523–1534) who commissioned Michelangelo to paint "the resurrection" for the rear wall of the chapel, behind the altar. By *resurrection*, he did not mean the resurrection of Christ, but rather the resurrection of the blessed on "the last day," as professed in the Creed, which concludes, "I believe in the holy Ghost, the holy Catholic church, the communion of saints, the forgiveness of sins, the resurrection of the body, and life everlasting."

Clement died before Michelangelo could begin the project, but his successor, Pope Paul III (1534–1549), renewed the commission. The artist completed the fresco in 1541 to great acclaim. It was admired for its religious power. Paul III allegedly fell on his knees when he first saw it and exclaimed, "O Lord, charge me not with my sins when you come on the day of Judgment." It was equally admired for the genius Michelangelo showed in rethinking and executing a standard subject in medieval painting. Cardinal Francesco Coronaro wrote that if Michelangelo gave him a painting of even one of the figures, he would pay him whatever he asked.

Although commissioned as "the resurrection," the painting has always been known as *The Last Judgment*, which is appropriate because the resurrection and the judgment are in Christian tradition but two aspects of the same reality. You will remember that the painting displays plenty of naked flesh, which is, of course, a hallmark of Michelangelo's work. The display here is, however, appropriate according to the Latin version of the Creed that Michelangelo and all associated with the papal court would have known: not "resurrection of the body," as the English has it, but "resurrection of the flesh," *carnis resurrectionem*. But the painting as we see it today is not quite what was seen in 1541, when it displayed even more flesh, including full frontal nudity of some male figures. We have a good idea of what the painting originally looked like from a contemporary engraving by Giulio Bonasone. Although much praised the moment the public was allowed to view it, it was also heavily criticized for the nudity. Critics found especially distressing the configuration of the figures of St. Catherine of Alexandria and St. Blaise, off to the left in the painting below Christ's left hand. Catherine seemed to be looking warily over her shoulder, as if intuiting that Blaise was contemplating something naughty regarding her.

Among the critics was the papal master of ceremonies, Biaggio da Cesena, who supposedly remarked to Paul III that the painting was more fitting for a tavern or a bathhouse than the pope's chapel. Pietro Aretino, the poet and satirist, was another. He pronounced a well-publicized criticism of the painting's indecency in "the most sacred chapel in all the world." Nonetheless, the *Judgment* remained untouched for more than two decades, through the pontificates of Paul III, Julius III, Marcellus II, and Paul IV, and most of the pontificate of Pius IV.

That changed in 1564, when Pius IV employed Daniele da Volterra, an important painter and disciple of Michelangelo, to address the problem. In the process, the genitals were discreetly covered and the Catherine/Blaise group was reconfigured. The result was the painting more or less as we see it today.

The Council of Trent ended in 1563, the year before the overpainting. What is the connection between these two events? Answering that question is the burden of my talk today. I am certainly not the first to address it. In fact, discussion of the relationship is a staple of art-historical literature.

Influential in that regard has been the judgment of the Italian historian Romeo De Maio, who, in his *Michelangelo e la Controriforma* (1978), said, "The Judgment was discussed during the debate on sacred images, which took place at Trent during the Twenty-Fifth Session of the council, November 11 until December 3 [1563]. . . . The fact that just after the council was concluded the 'revision' of the Judgment was ordered . . . shows that at Trent discussion of the painting was lively" (p. 39, my translation).

De Maio's book reflected and gave powerful impetus to the idea that Michelangelo's painting got singled out at the council for special criticism, and it even suggested that the painting incited the council to issue its decree on images. That idea became received wisdom in much of the literature about the painting and has persisted down to the present. I will now try to show that scarcely a single word in De Maio's statement is true, which does not mean, however, that there is no connection between the council and the painting.

The Council of Trent was convoked by Pope Paul III in 1545 at the insistence of Emperor Charles V. It called together the Catholic bishops of Europe to respond to the Protestant Reformation and met over the course of eighteen years in three distinct periods: 1545–1547, 1551–1552, and 1562–1563. Three different popes convoked each of the three periods, but none of them ever set foot in Trent. They instead appointed legates to preside in their names.

The council had an extraordinarily troubled history, suggested by the fractures into three periods, and it lurched from major crisis to major crisis. Popes, kings and queens, the Holy Roman emperors, bishops, and Protestants threw obstacles of every kind in its way, including war and the threat of war. The choice of the then small city of Trent as the meeting place was itself the result of a difficult compromise, satisfactory to none of the parties involved. (The Latin name for Trent is *Tridentinum*—hence the English adjective Tridentine.)

Regarding Trent's decree on sacred images, the first thing to note is that it was occasioned not by a desire to regulate the quality or decorum of the art in question but to affirm the legitimacy of such art in the face of severe outbursts of iconoclasm. The second thing to note is that the council, though it passed a decree on sacred images, never in plenary session discussed it. Why was this the case? In brief, the council was occupied with other business that it deemed more important—namely, the great doctrinal issues raised especially by Luther and the urgent problem of reform of the church, especially of the episcopacy (which meant, basically, getting bishops to reside in their dioceses and do their jobs).

Moreover, the vast majority of prelates at the council were from Italy, more than two-thirds during the last period of the council, followed at great distance by prelates from Spain and then Portugal. In these countries iconoclasm was virtually unknown. Contrary to what art-historical literature sometimes suggests, not only were images an unimportant issue at the council, but until the final hour they were not an issue at all for the vast majority of the council's participants.

The same was not true for France, where iconoclasm had broken out as early as the 1520s. That outburst was little more than a symptom of the more general and early infiltration of Protestant ideas into France and especially into the capital. In response to the situation, Antoine Duprat, cardinal archbishop of Sens, convoked in 1527 the most important local synod (or council) of the sixteenth century before Trent. Although its decrees were binding only in the local environs, they were broadly known and respected by Catholic reformers, as is confirmed by their invocation at Trent even by Italian and Spanish prelates when it served their purpose.

Held in Paris, the Council of Sens, as it is known, issued a large number of decrees on a wide range of subjects. Two of the decrees pertained to sacred images. The first was a long but traditional justification of them as useful for instruction and devotion. The second, much shorter, dealt with their quality: "So that nothing improper take place in the church of God, it seemed right and reasonable [to decree] that, because of the sensuality of some images [lascivas] and their deviation from the truth of Scripture, in the future none be placed in the churches unless the bishop or his vicar approve beforehand and visit the church." This was the first time in the period that this issue was raised in an influential way in an official, though local, ecclesiastical document.

Despite the religious unrest in the kingdom, the French had tried from the very beginning to prevent the convocation of Trent and virtually boycotted it once it finally opened in 1545. King Francis I saw the council as strengthening the hand of his enemy, Emperor Charles V. His son and successor, Henry II, saw it the same way and boycotted the second period, 1551–1552. But ten years later, in November 1562, following the death of Henry, and after the third period of the council had already been under way for ten months, a relatively small but important delegation led by Cardinal Charles de Guise finally arrived at Trent.

The religious situation in the kingdom had become desperate, and even Henry II's widow, the regent Queen Catherine de' Medici, realized that recourse to the council was unavoidable. Iconoclasm had meanwhile broken out once again as the French Calvinists, the Huguenots, grew stronger.

Even in the rapidly deteriorating religious and political situation in France, the queen regent had earlier unrealistically hoped to calm the waters by bringing leaders of the Huguenot and Catholic parties together so that, through conversation, they might resolve their differences at the Colloquy of Poissy, 31 July to 9 October 1561. Among many other issues, image veneration was hotly debated. The colloquy resolved nothing.

In desperation Catherine called another colloquy, which met in her own quarters at the Château de Saint-Germain a few months later. The first item on the agenda was the veneration of images, for which the theologians of the faculty of theology of the University of Paris had prepared a *sententia* (an "opinion" or "position paper"). The *sententia* was fundamentally a long justification of sacred images. However, it included the following caveat, possibly or probably in echo of Sens: "It is also by no means a small abuse if images are painted and depicted in an indecent and sensually alluring form [*impudica et lasciva*] and one at odds with the chastity and upright character of the holy men and women the images represent."

The château colloquy was, however, an utter and immediate failure, breaking down on the first item on the agenda, the veneration of images, which Catherine had considered among the easier issues to resolve. As mentioned, a new rash of iconoclasm then broke out as France headed for thirty years of civil war, the "French Wars of Religion." Catherine was now convinced that she had no alternative but to support French participation in the council.

On 13 November 1562, therefore, "the cardinal of Lorraine," Charles de Guise, arrived at Trent with twelve bishops, three abbots, and eighteen theologians. This small delegation, which was later somewhat enlarged, proved extremely influential, due largely to the forceful personality of de Guise, who from this point forward played a role at the council second only to that of the papal legates themselves.

On 3 January 1563, little more than six weeks after the French arrived, they presented the legates with a memorandum of thirty-four articles on reform, one of which (number 29) dealt, not surprisingly, with images:

> 29. Because iconoclasts have arisen in our times, men who believe images must be destroyed, which has resulted in grave public disturbances in many places, the council must take measures to ensure that the faithful are properly instructed in church teaching regarding the veneration of images. The council should likewise take measures to eliminate the abuses and superstitious practices that have grown up in that regard.

The legates took the French proposals extremely seriously and in early February sent to Rome an article-by-article report drawn up by an eleven-person committee as their own considered response. On number 29, the committee said simply, "Let the matter be treated in the catechism." That is, the council should not take it up. It would be difficult to minimize an issue more effectively than that.

The pope, Pius IV, responded to the legates as quickly as they could have desired. On 13 February his reply to each of the thirty-four articles arrived in Trent. The comment on some of them was lengthy, but on number 29 it was simply, "The most reverend legates responded well." That is, they relegated the matter to the catechism. One thing is clear: neither the legates at Trent nor the pope in Rome saw "images" as a concern.

The French proposals, like similar documents from the Spanish bishops and from Emperor Ferdinand I, Charles V's brother and successor, never made it to the floor of the council, nor were they distributed to the bishops for their perusal. Images, therefore, were still not on the agenda of the council. Other matters took precedence through the rest of the year and absorbed everybody's attention.

As the months dragged on, Pius urged the legates to bring the council swiftly to conclusion. Even though many issues still had to be resolved, the legates succeeded in the middle of November in setting 9 December as the terminal date for the council, which meant that in only three weeks all business had to be completed, a goal that to many at the council seemed highly unrealistic. But still no action was taken on images.

Finally, on Sunday morning, 28 November, Cardinal Charles de Guise, seeing that time was fast running out, appeared in legates' quarters and categorically demanded that the council enact a decree on the veneration of images. The next morning, 29 November, the legates established a committee under the chairmanship of de Guise to deal with that subject as well as a number of other matters, such as indulgences, fasting, and the veneration of saints and relics. At that point only eight working days remained if the council were to finish on 9 December. During those days, the council had much other business to handle besides the matters committed to the new deputation. The agenda was overloaded almost to the point of absurdity.

Late in the evening of the next day, 30 November, however, news arrived from Rome that Pope Pius IV was so seriously ill that his life was in question. On the following morning, 1 December, the legates insisted that the council be concluded immediately; that the next day, 2 December, be the council's last working day; and that the final solemnities of the council be held on 3 and 4 December, known as Session Twenty-Five. ("Session" designated a day or, in this extraordinary case, two days, principally ceremonial, when documents already debated, amended, and in principle approved were formally accepted. It was not the long period De Maio designated.)

This change in closing date meant that the deputation had only a day to complete its many tasks. For the decree on images, however, de Guise had with him the *sententia* the Paris theologians had prepared for the colloquy at Saint-Germain. Had it not been for him, it is not at all certain the council would have taken up the issue, or, if it did, that the decree would have been formulated the way it was—that is, that it would have included a provision about removing from images all "sensual allurement" [*lascivia*]. The long decree the committee formulated and the council later approved is, however, in substance a resounding validation of images. It reads in part:

> And they [the bishops] must also teach that images of Christ, the virgin Mary, and the other saints should be set up and kept, particularly in churches, and that due honor and reverence be shown to them, not because some divinity or power is believed to lie in them . . . but because honor showed to them is referred to the persons they repre-

sent. . . . All superstition must be removed from the invocation of the saints, the veneration of relics, and the use of sacred images. All aiming at base profit must be eliminated. All lasciviousness [*lascivia*] must be avoided, so that images are not painted or adorned with seductive charm [*procaci venustate*].

No record survives of the deliberation of the committee that formulated the decree. But when the decree is examined in its totality, its textual dependence on the *sententia* of Saint-Germain is clear. In particular, the *lascivia* ("sensual allurement") in the Tridentine text, a word much discussed in art-historical literature, is a simple reworking of *impudica et lasciva* in the Saint-Germain text, which itself was probably an echo of the *lascivas* in the decree from the Council of Sens.

On the afternoon of 2 December, the council in a plenary working session received the decree along with so many others that no time could be allowed for comment on any of them. Nonetheless, it deemed them all worthy of final approval.

Thus, all we know about the construction of a text that had such influence on artists and patrons and has in the past hundred years generated so much scholarly comment is that it was virtually the exclusive product of French concern; that Charles de Guise was the principal agent in its evolution; that it was in a general way based on the *sententia* of Saint-Germain; that it was put together in almost desperate haste; that it was passed by the council without examination or debate; that iconoclasm, not a desire to regulate artistic decorum, was the motivating force behind it; and that in the records of the council there is not a single mention of a painter or a painting—not even of Michelangelo and his *Last Judgment.*

After 4 December the bishops left Trent for home with the self-imposed mandate to implement the council's decrees. Pope Pius IV, as bishop of Rome, felt himself under the same mandate, of course, but perhaps in an even more urgent way because of the preeminence of his bishopric and because of the need he surely felt to reassure the world that the harsh criticism the papacy had received at the council and especially the bitter criticism he himself had received for being the major obstacle to reform was not justified. Now fully recovered from his illness, he, on 30 December 1563, created a deputation of cardinals to review the council's many decrees to see what could and should be put immediately into practice in Rome. The deputation met three times between 18 and 21 January and dealt with a wide spectrum of issues.

In its final meeting, 21 January 1564, it, among many other matters, issued a short recommendation about images: "The pictures in the Apostolic Chapel are to be covered, as [is to be done] in other churches [of Rome] if they display anything obscene or obviously false, according to the decree of the council."

What followed was basically what we saw, the painting over of some of the figures in *The Last Judgment* and the more drastic refashioning of Saints Catherine and Blaise. In the literature about the relationship between the council and those actions, there has been considerable confusion. Some scholars have mistakenly identified the action of the Roman deputation as an action of the council itself. Others up to the present follow De Maio by asserting that the *Judgment* was discussed by name at the council. Mistakes like these unfortunately became established verities in scholarship about the painting and have been passed on to innumerable tourists who visit the Sistine Chapel. Aside from article 29 in the French memorandum on reform and the correspondence between Trent and Rome concerning it, sacred images and art in general were a nonissue at Trent until the curtain was already descending on the council.

The notoriety of the *Judgment* easily accounts for the Roman deputation's action after the council. From the moment of its unveiling twenty-three years earlier, it had, though much admired, been harshly criticized for its nude figures and been the object of public controversy at least since the publication of Pietro Aretino's letter of 1545 deploring the indecency of the images "in the most sacred chapel upon the earth." The offending painting in the Sistine Chapel was the *Judgment*, even though there were, of course, other nudes in the chapel. In the ceiling not only Michelangelo's enigmatic ignudi but also the frontal nudity in his *Drunkenness of Noah* escaped such criticism and escaped overpainting.

Not until 21 January 1564, a month and a half after the council ended, do we have a document that relates the council's decree to the *Judgment.* That is the moment, moreover, that the more general application of the decree to the diocese of Rome got officially set into motion. Although artists and patrons there were made to feel the pressure of the regulation, there is no instance of any other painting in Rome being defaced as a result of it.

At about the same time, other conscientious bishops set to work implementing the new duties the council imposed on them. The bishops in Italy acted in accordance with the decree on sacred art by continuing their enthusiastic patronage for themselves and for the churches over which they presided. There are only a few isolated instances of any defacing of art already in place. That is far from saying, however, that the warning in the decree about "sensuous images" remained a dead letter, or that it did not provide the grounding for the important cultural phenomenon known as "Tridentine art."

10

TEN SUREFIRE WAYS TO MIX UP THE TEACHING OF VATICAN II

As every good historian knows, interpreting documents is never easy, a point I made in chapter 7 on the myths and misinterpretations of the Council of Trent. Here I call attention to ten common assumptions about Vatican II that have led to serious misunderstandings of the council. I published the article in America, *4 February 2013, at the very end of the pontificate of Pope Benedict XVI, a time when the most basic orientations of the council were being questioned.*

It is not easy to interpret any great event, so it is not surprising that today there is disagreement about how to interpret the Second Vatican Council. Here, I want to turn the issue around to indicate how not to interpret it. (Of course, astute readers will see that this is just a sneaky way of making positive points.) Some of these principles are, in fact, of direct concern only to historians or theologians. The issues that underlie them, however, should be of concern to all Catholics who cherish the heritage of the council. These ten negative principles are simply a back-handed way of reminding ourselves of what is at stake in the controversies over the council's interpretation.

1. Insist Vatican II was only a pastoral council.

This principle is wrong on two counts. First, it ignores the fact that the council taught many things—the doctrine of episcopal collegiality, for instance, which is no small matter. It was thus a doctrinal as well as a pastoral council, even though it taught in a style different from previous councils. Second, the term can be used to suggest an ephemeral quality because pastoral methods change according to circumstance. Wittingly or unwittingly, therefore, "pastoral" consigns the council to a second-rate status.

2. Insist it was an occurrence in the life of the church, not an event.

This distinction has currency in certain circles. Its import is best demonstrated by an example: A teacher is given a year's sabbatical, which she spends in France. The experience broadens her perspective. She returns home enriched, but she again takes up her previous routines. Her sabbatical was an occurrence. But suppose she, instead, is offered a position as dean at an institution other than her own. She pulls up stakes, moves, gives up teaching, and in her new job learns new skills and makes new friends. That is an event, a significant turn in the road.

3. Banish the expression "spirit of the council."

Sure, the expression is easily manipulated, but we need to recall that the distinction between spirit and letter is venerable in the Christian tradition. We should therefore be loath to toss it in the dustbin. More important, spirit, rightly understood, indicates themes and orientations that imbue the council with its identity, because they are found not in one document but in all or almost all of them. Thus, the "spirit of the council," while based solidly on the "letter" of the council's documents, transcends any specific one of them. It enables us to see the bigger message of the council and the direction in which it pointed the church, which was in many regards different from the direction before the council.

4. Study the documents individually, without considering them part of an integral corpus.

I cannot name anyone who insists on this principle, but it has been the standard approach to the documents ever since the council ended. Of course, to understand the corpus, one must first understand the component parts. Hence, study of individual documents is indispensable and the first step in understanding the corpus. Too often, however, even commentators have stopped at that point and not gone on to investigate just how a specific text contributed to the dynamics of the council as a whole—that is, to its "spirit." Without too much effort, it is easy (and imperative) to see the relationship in themes and mindset, for instance, between the document on religious liberty and the document on the church in the modern world.

5. Study the final sixteen documents in the order of hierarchical authority, not in the chronological order in which they were approved in the council.

The documents, of course, have varying degrees of authority (constitutions before decrees, decrees before declarations). But this principle, when treated as exclusive, ignores the intertextual nature of the council's documents—that is, their interdependence—one building on the other in the order in which they made their journey through the council. The document on the bishops, for instance, could not be introduced into the council until the document on the church was fundamentally in place, especially because of the crucial importance of the doctrine of collegiality being debated in the "Dogmatic Constitution on the Church." The documents, therefore, paraphrased, borrowed from, and adapted from one another as the council moved along. Thus, they form a coherent and integral whole and need to be studied that way. They are not a grab bag of discrete units. To toy with one of the documents, therefore, is to toy with all of them. (Unfortunately, the latest edition of the widely used translation of the council's documents, edited by Austin Flannery, OP, prints them in hierarchical, not chronological, order.)

6. Pay no attention to the documents' literary form.

A feature that most obviously distinguishes Vatican II from all previous councils is the new style in which it formulated its enactments. Unlike previous councils, Vatican II did not operate as a legislative and judicial body in the traditional sense of those terms. It laid down certain principles but did not, like previous councils, produce a body of ordinances prescribing or proscribing modes of behavior, with penalties attached for nonobservance. It tried no ecclesiastical criminals and issued no verdicts of guilty or not guilty. It most characteristically employed a vocabulary new for councils, a vocabulary filled with words implying collegiality, reciprocity, tolerance, friendship, and the search for common ground. Instead of ignoring this distinctive feature, explanation and analysis of the documents' literary form seem to be indispensable for understanding the council.

7. Stick to the final sixteen documents and pay no attention to the historical context, the history of the texts, or the controversies concerning them during the council.

This principle allows the documents to be treated as if they float somewhere outside time and place and can be interpreted accordingly. Only by examining the travail that the decree on religious liberty, for instance, experienced during the council, to the point that it seemed it could not be approved, can we understand its path-breaking character and its significance for the church's role in the world today. Moreover, there are official documents beyond the sixteen that are crucial for understanding the direction the council took, such as Pope John XXIII's address opening the council, "Mother Church Rejoices," and the "Message to the World," that the council itself published just as it was getting under way. These two documents opened the council, for instance, to the possibility of producing "The Church in the Modern World."

8. Outlaw the use of any "unofficial" sources, such as the diaries or correspondence of participants.

No doubt, the official sources—the final texts and the multivolume *Acta Synodalia*, published by the Vatican Press—are and must remain the first and most authoritative point of reference for interpreting the council. But the diaries and letters of participants provide information lacking in the official sources and sometimes better explain the often-sudden turns the council took. Making use of such documents is not an innovation in scholarship. The editors of the magnificent collection of documents concerning the Council of Trent, the *Concilium Tridentinum*, did not hesitate to include diaries and correspondence, which have proved indispensable for understanding that council and are used by all its interpreters.

9. Interpret the documents as expressions of continuity with the Catholic tradition.

As an emphasis in interpreting the documents of the council, this is correct and needs to be insisted on. The problem arises when this principle is applied in a way that excludes all discontinuity—that is, all change. It is an absurdity to believe that nothing changed, nothing happened. On 22 December 2005, Pope Benedict XVI provided a correction to such exclusivity when he said in his address to the Roman Curia that what was required for Vatican II was a "hermeneutic of reform," which he defined as a "combination of continuity and discontinuity at different levels."

10. Make your assessment of the council into a self-fulfilling prophecy.

This principle is not so much about misinterpreting the council as it is about employing assessments to determine how the council will now be implemented and received. The principle is dangerous in anyone's hands but especially dangerous in the hands of those who have the authority to make their assessment operative. In this regard "the party slogan" in George Orwell's novel *Nineteen Eighty-Four* hits the nail on the head: "Who controls the past controls the future; who controls the present controls the past."

11

WHAT HAPPENED AND DID NOT HAPPEN AT VATICAN II

As with the Council of Trent, myths and misunderstandings about Vatican II began even while the council was in progress. The interest of the media in the council was aggressive, and journalists translated the council into terms their readers might understand. Although their reports tended to be accurate as far as they went, they often missed the deeper issues and the more profound implications of what the council was attempting. This article, published in Theological Digest, *was originally a lecture I gave at Saint Louis University, 28 April 2008, just before my book on the council was published.*

Lots of things happened—and did not happen—at Vatican II, as was to be expected from the biggest meeting in the history of the world. Four crucial things did not happen because they were explicitly withheld from the agenda by Pope Paul VI: consideration of priestly celibacy, consideration of birth control, the reform of the Roman Curia, and establishment of an institution that grounded within the social reality of the church the doctrine of episcopal collegiality that the council had laid out. None of these four had appeared in the recommendations for the agenda that bishops sent to the Vatican before the council, even though bishops spoke about the last two during the council, sometimes even on the floor of St. Peter's.

There was another thing that did not happen: the council did not confer on the Virgin Mary a new title, such as coredemptrix or mediatrix of all graces, as many bishops had asked. Marian piety was at its highest peak in the history of the church on the eve of Vatican II. One of the original seventy documents the bishops were to deal with when the council opened was on Mary. What to do with it? Some bishops wanted to incorporate the material into the Dogmatic Constitution on the Church to show Mary as the ideal member, whereas others wanted to honor her with her own document. This was an explosive and divisive issue. In the closest vote of the council, with only a forty-vote margin, the council decided to incorporate the statement into the church document, where it forms the last chapter. In that chapter the council neither conferred on her a new title nor defined any new Marian dogma.

There is something else of extreme importance that sort of "half happened." In 1979, five years before his death, the German Jesuit theologian Karl Rahner spoke of Vatican II as opening a third epoch in Christian history. The first epoch was the brief period of Jewish Christianity, which began to end as early as Paul's preaching to the Gentiles. The second ran from then until Vatican II, the period of Hellenism and the European church. The third period, the postcouncil present, is the period of the world church.

Did the council really initiate this new period? At first glance, it would seem not. What is striking about Vatican II is not any prominent role played by "the new churches" of former colonies but how dominated it was by Europeans. The leading figures were almost exclusively from the Continent, and those few that were not, like the American Jesuit John Courtney Murray and Archbishop Paul-Émile Léger of Montreal, were European in the broad sense. The council was even more deeply Eurocentric in that the issues it dealt with originated in the history of Western Europe.

Europe, its concerns, and the legacy of its history provided the framework within which Vatican II operated. The colorful and astute bishops from the ancient churches of the Middle East, especially the Melkites, sometimes prodded and sometimes shamed the council fathers into a broader perspective and pointed out how parochial the general frame of reference was.

Even so, as the council revisited the history and traditions of the Western Church, it was sometimes engaged, not necessarily wittingly, in transcending its European determinations. The debate over Latin was a revisiting of the debates of the Reformation era, but the outcome would have world-church repercussions. The softening of the role of Aquinas in the curriculum of seminaries—and in philosophical discourse more generally—revisited the nineteenth century's exaltation of Thomas and had principally in view a greater openness to other European philosophies. But it also opened a window to non-European philosophies and approaches.

Of direct import, of course, were the council's specific recommendations for adaptation to local customs and cultures. In the Constitution on the Sacred Liturgy, the first document the council approved, occurs the crucial line: "The art of our times from every race and country shall be given free scope in the church." Such explicit openness and adaptation were not quite leitmotifs of the council, but they occurred just often enough to signal that a wider vista was trying to break through.

If those are some important nonhappenings or half happenings, what did happen? A great deal! Distinctive of the council was the broad scope of the matters it addressed. It pronounced on scores of particulars, such as the use of the organ during Mass; priests' salaries; the relationship of the church to the arts; the geographical boundaries of dioceses; married deacons; the legitimacy of worshiping with non-Catholics; the legitimacy of stockpiling nuclear weapons; the proper time for blessing the water used in baptisms; translations of the Bible; and so on—almost, it might seem, into infinity.

All the matters the council dealt with must, of course, be taken seriously. Nonetheless, some are certainly of greater significance. Where to begin? The best place is with the general topics dealt with in the sixteen final documents of the council. They right off indicate sixteen areas where the council was engaged and on which it made decisions. That is both obvious and important. Nonetheless, during and after the council nobody thought that what the council said about the mass media (in a document that, even when it was being discussed, many bishops found lackluster) compared in importance with what it said about the church's relationship to Muslims and Jews.

There seems to be a consensus among scholars on what those more important issues were. They were the ones that usually, but not always, generated the most heated debate during the council. These issues are contained in the document on the liturgy, with the kinds of changes it mandated that immediately impacted on the ordinary believer in the pews; in the document on the word of God (or Revelation), with its promotion of the new role for the Bible in Catholic piety and its validation of modern methods of exegesis; in the document on the church, with its description of the church as "the people of God" and its affirmation of the doctrine of episcopal collegiality; in the document on ecumenism, with its emphasis on what Catholics and other Christians have in common and its encouragement of cordial relationships in the hope of accomplishing a new Christian unity (touted as the end of the Counter-Reformation); in the document on non-Christian religions, especially Islam and Judaism, with its deploring of religious bigotry in all its forms; in the document on religious liberty, which affirmed the right of every human being to embrace the religion the person's conscience dictates as best (touted as the end of the Constantinian era); and in the document on the church in the modern world, where human dignity is extolled and the responsibility of every person on the planet to work for a better world is laid out in detail.

The council thus wrestled with profound problems that affect us still and came up with decisions and directions that, for the most part, have lost none of their relevance to the lives we live. But if we want to understand the council, we need to go deeper, to three issues-under-the-issues. These are across-the-board issues, lurking beneath the surface of many of the up-front issues: (1) Under what circumstances is change appropriate in the church, and with what arguments can it be justified? (2) What is the relationship of center to periphery, which, put in its most concrete form, is the relationship between the papacy (including the curia) and the rest of the church, especially the bishops? (3) No matter how authority is distributed, what is the style or model according to which it should be exercised?

THE PROBLEM OF CHANGE

The first issue, appropriate change, became acute in the nineteenth century because of the new historical consciousness characteristic of that century (i.e., the new awareness of discrepancies between past and present) and the debates over what those discrepancies meant, especially for the church. The leading voices at the council were much more aware than were their counterparts in earlier councils of the profound changes that had taken place in the history of the church. Moreover, Vatican II made some decisions that seemed to contravene accepted teaching, as in the church-state issue.

The keener sense of historical change that was operative at the council can be captured by three words current at the time—*aggiornamento* (Italian for updating or modernizing), development (an unfolding—in context, sometimes almost the equivalent of progress or evolution), and *ressourcement* (French for, literally, return to the sources). One basic, absolutely crucial assumption underlay all three of these terms as they were used in the council: the Catholic tradition is richer, broader, and more malleable than the way in which it had in the past often been interpreted and presented, especially during the nineteenth and early twentieth centuries. The three terms overlap in meaning, and one is often used when another is meant. But in general they look to the present (*aggiornamento*), to the future (development), and to the past (*ressourcement*). They are all concerned with change and, in the context of a church reluctant to admit change, operate as a soft synonym for it.

Aggiornamento, attributed to Pope John XXIII as an aim he had for the council, was, of the three terms, the most invoked to describe what Vatican II was all about. In a number of decrees, Vatican II determined that some expressions of religious practice should be changed to conform them to the "new era" the council saw opening up.

On one level this was nothing new. Lateran IV (1215), for instance, legitimated changes made for reasons of "urgent necessity or evident utility"—*urgens necessitas vel evidens utilitas*. But the *aggiornamento* of Vatican II was special in several ways, particularly in that no previous council had ever taken the equivalent of *aggiornamento* as a leitmotif, as a broad principle rather than as a rare exception.

Nonetheless, although *aggiornamento* was the most widely invoked term to explain what happened at Vatican II, it was the least radical of the three, had long been accepted as a principle, and, as such, ran into no resistance at the council. Disagreement arose only about the extent and the appropriateness of the updating in particular cases.

What about development? This term reflects a nineteenth-century phenomenon. (It was the age of Darwin, after all.) John Henry Newman's *Essay on the Development of Christian Doctrine* (1846) was the classic statement on the subject. Received with suspicion in Catholic circles when first published, the book was by 1962 widely accepted as almost the definitive exposition of the subject. By the time of the council, just about every bishop had a generic familiarity with the concept and, in principle, accepted its legitimacy.

Development is usually understood as moving further along a given path, as happened when the definition of Mary's Assumption (1950) followed on the earlier definition of her Immaculate Conception (1854), a move that led to the widespread hope for a further Marian definition at the council. The idea of development is congenial to progress, especially as a further clarification or greater efflorescence. It was used to explain the Marian definitions in 1854 and 1950 and, particularly, to justify the growth of papal authority from earliest times until its culmination with the definitions of papal primacy and infallibility in Vatican Council I, as from the acorn comes the oak. It took the present as the norm for understanding the past, and it searched the past for evidence to confirm the present.

Bishops often invoked the idea—or at least used the term—in the debates in St. Peter's. We find an explicit and crucial adoption of it in the Constitution on Divine Revelation, *Dei Verbum*: "The Tradition that comes to us from the apostles makes progress in the church with the help of the Holy Spirit. There is a growth in insight into the realities and words that are being passed on." Tradition in this sense is not inert but dynamic.

The Declaration on Religious Liberty, *Dignitatis Humanae* (church-state), justifies its position by saying it is evolving or developing (*evolvere*) the teaching of previous popes on the matter. Perhaps the biggest problem the document ran into on the floor of the council, however, was that its teaching seemed not to be a further step along the path but the abandonment of the traditional path for a different (and indeed forbidden) path. The popes of the nineteenth century had repeatedly condemned separation of church and state—it was a "madness" for Gregory XVI—and now the council proposed such separation as a legitimate development of Catholic and papal teaching. To critics this seemed like legerdemain, if not downright dishonesty. Hence the vigorous and sustained opposition that almost shipwrecked the document.

If development takes the present as its starting point and looks to the future for more of the same, *ressourcement* is skeptical of the present because of what it has discovered in the past. It entails a return to the sources with a view not of confirming the present but of making changes to conform the present to a more authentic or more appropriate past, a return to a more profound tradition. It takes the past as the norm for judging and correcting the present. While development is understood as moving things along a given path, *ressourcement* implicitly says that we are no longer going to move along path X. We are going back to the fork in the road and now, instead, are taking path Y, a better path. Or *ressourcement* may mean that we're just going to take a little rest on the path or even settle down permanently at this point on the path and not go any further, declaring a dead end—which is what happened at the council with the impetus to define more doctrines about Mary.

The word *ressourcement* was a neologism, coined by the French poet Charles Péguy early in the twentieth century and adopted in the middle of the century by scholars in France associated with *la nouvelle théologie*, a theological movement extremely important for the shape Vatican II took. But unlike the development theory that first got straightforwardly proposed only in the nineteenth century, *ressourcement*, under different names, had enjoyed a truly venerable history in the Western Church, and in Western culture more generally. (Ever hear of the Renaissance?) It made its first dramatic appearance in the eleventh century with the Gregorian Reform. At the midpoint of that century, a series of reforming popes spearheaded a vigorous campaign of change in the name of restoring a more ancient canonical discipline regarding clerical celibacy and the free election of bishops.

A return to the sources is what drove the Protestant reformers as they sought to restore the authentic Gospel that, in their opinion, the papal church had obscured and perverted. In Catholicism, *ressourcement* lay behind Prosper Guéranger's efforts in the nineteenth century to restore the liturgy, and it lay behind Pope Leo XIII's revival of the study of Thomas Aquinas. On the eve of Vatican II, *ressourcement* drove the surge in biblical, patristic, and liturgical studies.

Of the three ways of dealing with the past, *ressourcement* was the most traditional but also the most radical. It was also the most pervasive in the council. It undergirded the Constitution on the Sacred Liturgy. The fundamental principle of the liturgical reform was the participation of the whole assembly in the sacred action, a principle derived from ancient liturgical practice. Restoring the dignity of the first part of the Mass, the Liturgy of the Word, was similarly derived. The application and accommodation of such principles to the present, the *aggiornamento*, was a consequence, not a starting point. In other words, the council did not set out to "modernize" the Mass.

Other examples abound. In the Declaration on Religious Liberty, the council leapt over the nineteenth-century condemnations of separation of church and state to delve more deeply into the tradition by applying the absolutely fundamental principle that a true act of faith had to be free, not the result of coercion, and by emphasizing the ancient and uncontested principle that individuals must follow their own consciences in moral and religious choices.

No instance of *ressourcement* was more central to the drama of Vatican II and its aspirations than was the turn to episcopal collegiality (i.e., the teaching that the bishops as a collectivity have a responsibility along with the pope for the general governance of the church). Proponents saw collegiality as a recovery of a traditional aspect of church life that had been increasingly sidelined in the West since the late Middle Ages and practically pushed off the ecclesiastical map by Vatican I's definition of papal primacy. Although the church had never officially defined collegiality as constitutive of the church, it for centuries took collegiality for granted as its mode of operation. Especially in the first millennium, the church functioned collegially in literally hundreds of local synods or councils and, of course, in the great ecumenical councils.

CENTER-PERIPHERY RELATIONS

Collegiality brings us to the heart of the second issue-under-the-issues at Vatican II, the relationship between center and periphery—here, between papal primacy and the authority of residential bishops at the periphery (that is, at their local sees). Yet it is impossible adequately to speak of collegiality without at the same time speaking of *ressourcement*. To speak of collegiality, moreover, is implicitly to raise the third issue-under-the-issues, the style in which the church operates—a monarchical style or a collegial style. Collegiality, the lightning-rod issue at the council, manifests the intimate relationship among the three issues-under-the-issues.

Collegiality's claim to legitimacy at Vatican II certainly did not surface altogether independently of postwar political developments in Europe. Christian democracy in its parliamentary forms flourished, with the blessing of both Pius XII and John XXIII. Both popes spoke eloquently about how participation in the political process accorded with human dignity and was now a moral responsibility. European and North American bishops came to Vatican II with direct experience of politics by participation. However, collegiality had much better claims on the bishops than the fact that it was a species of *aggiornamento* in tune with the political correctness of the contemporary West, in tune with "the signs of the times."

Ressourcement and development locked horns over collegiality. In the West, papal primacy "developed" incrementally in a steady and almost continuous line up until the nineteenth century, which is when it accelerated at almost breathtaking speed (for the church!) and resulted in papal definitions of the Immaculate Conception and the Assumption; in the growth and increasing authority exercised by the congregations of the Roman Curia; in the devolution of the appointment of bishops almost exclusively into the hands of the popes; and, of course, in 1870, in the definitions of primacy and infallibility.

Through the centuries in the West, collegiality, on the contrary, had not "developed." It survived but had entered a slow process of atrophy. It was operative even into the twentieth century in provincial and national synods such as the various Councils of Baltimore in the United States, and it was acknowledged in the fact that the popes addressed their encyclicals to their "venerable brothers," the bishops. But the starch was out of it. Now at Vatican II a process of *ressourcement* or renaissance had retrieved it. Its proponents placed collegiality side by side with papal primacy as defined in Vatican I and packaged the two as compatible, as to a large extent they had been in a much earlier era. In the view of these proponents, which was the view of the vast majority of bishops at the council, collegiality was an enhancement of the primacy and an aid to its proper functioning.

A tiny but unyielding minority at the council did not buy that view. This kind of *ressourcement*, despite all the fine words of the speakers for the majority, seemed to them to limit the solemn definitions of Vatican I and threaten the way the church operated at the center. Collegiality, in the view of the council minority (we're talking here about 10 percent or less), was unworkable, unacceptable, dangerous, and now, after the definitions of 1870, perhaps even heretical. Primacy and collegiality were irreconcilable. The minority understanding of primacy sometimes seemed, to put it crudely, to be identified with absolute monarchy possessing all authority in the church, which it bled out or recalled at will. The council fathers who thought and spoke in this way opposed collegiality on sincerely held theological and logical grounds, yet it is no accident that leaders among them were from the curia or associated with it. They worked in and for the center.

The majority at the council certainly did not press for a statement on collegiality merely to make a theological point. They brought it to the fore, like other *ressourcement*, because it had practical repercussions in how the church operated. They wanted to redress what they saw as the imbalance between the authority exercised especially by the Vatican and their own authority as successors of the apostles. Agitation for collegiality was the supreme instance in the council of the effort to moderate—to put the brakes on, or to reverse—the centralizing drive of the ecclesiastical institution. It sought to give those from the periphery a more authoritative voice not only back home but also in the center.

Although the statements in various council documents insisting on the authority of national or regional episcopal conferences to regulate affairs on the national or regional levels validated an institution already functioning in most parts of the church (somewhat pale reflections of the former national councils or synods), those statements also tried to strengthen that authority. They represented, therefore, another effort to counter centripetal forces. The Constitution on the Sacred Liturgy, for example, stated that, while oversight of the liturgy belongs in the last instance to the Holy See, it belongs in the first instances to episcopal conferences in various parts of the world. Making the same point in blunt terms, the Dogmatic Constitution on the Church asserted that bishops "are not to be regarded as vicars of the Roman Pontiff, for they exercise the powers they possess in their own right." The bishops, that is to say, are not branch managers or local offices of the Vatican. Their exercise of power out of authority intrinsic to their office is a corollary to the doctrine of episcopal ordination that the council affirmed, and that corollary explains in large measure why the minority at the council so fiercely opposed the doctrine.

The documents of the council tend, however, to be soft-spoken on the center-periphery relationship. In them the relationship between bishops and the Holy See is developed only once, in a short paragraph in the Decree on the Pastoral Office of Bishops. The passage gives no hint of the intensity of the bishops' feelings on this topic, and it is a good instance of how deceptive the placid surface the documents present to the world is. It is not the documents, therefore, that reveal how hot the issue was but the narrative of the battles for control of the council itself—as you will be able to read beginning in September in the exciting new book by John O'Malley, *What Happened at Vatican II*.

But collegiality was not merely a teaching geared to modify the church's central operating mechanisms. It was also a specific instance that grounded and pointed to a more general trend—measures to promote more collegial relationships throughout the church, as found, for instance, in the Decree on the Pastoral Office of Bishops and the Decree on the Life and Ministry of Priests that called for the creation by bishops of diocesan councils in which priests would cooperate in the government of the diocese. While the documents insisted that the relationship between the bishop and his priests was hierarchical, the priests are still consistently described as the bishops' collaborators. The bishop should regard them "as brothers and friends." Pius X had in 1907 forbidden priests to meet together except with the bishop's explicit (and rarely to be given) permission, whereas the council's decree on priests encouraged precisely the opposite. This decree, as well as the Decree on the Apostolate of the Laity, encouraged participation of the laity, priests, and religious, in councils of various kinds on the parish, diocesan, and national levels.

STYLES OF AUTHORITY

The center-periphery issue thus blends into the third issue-under-the-issues, the issue of church style. With what style does the church communicate and operate? How does it present itself, and how does it "do business"? What is its personality? The literary style of the documents of Vatican II is what, at first glance as well as most profoundly, sets this council apart from all other councils. The bishops at Vatican II, following the orientation from John XXIII, consistently and repeatedly described the council as pastoral in nature, and they sought a style for the documents in conformity with that aim. The leaders of the majority came with a clear idea that the style was, as far as possible, to be biblical and reminiscent of the literary mode of the fathers of the church, and by the second period they had, after a struggle, won their point. If collegiality is the first great *ressourcement* of the council, the second is the recovery of a style of discourse. These two *ressourcements* are in fact intimately related.

The adoption of a new style, which was really a renaissance of an old style (Bible and the Fathers), was the most far-reaching of the many *ressourcements* in which the council engaged. It was at the same time a repudiation of other styles and of the Roman Senate as the implicit model for what a council is and does. Repudiation of the Roman Senate model was thus another instance of how the council was "the end of the Constantinian era."

Through the centuries, councils have made use of a range of literary genres, but practically all of them evince characteristics derived from the legislative and judicial traditions of discourse developed in the legal traditions of Roman antiquity. The genres in large measure were, or closely resembled, laws and judicial sentences. While ensuring correct belief and enforcing appropriate behavior, especially of the clergy, decisions of the council were not and could not be separated from securing public order in society at large, and for that reason secular authorities undertook enforcement of those decisions. The decisions were the "law of the land" as well as the law of the church.

Two fundamental assumptions were in play. First, councils were judicial bodies that heard criminal cases and rendered judgment, with anybody found guilty being duly punished. Second, they were legislative bodies that issued ordinances to which, as with any law, were attached penalties for failure to comply. At the first ecumenical council (Nicaea, 325), this pattern got its definitive form.

At Nicaea the model of a council as an ecclesiastical form of the Roman Senate played itself out fully because the council was called by the emperor Constantine, was held in his palace, and followed Roman protocols. Constantine dealt with the council in ways unmistakably similar to the ways he and other late Roman emperors dealt with the Senate, although he gave the bishops greater independence and treated their decisions with greater respect. Even in the later councils of the Latin West, where the emperor played a much-reduced role or even none, the Senate model, though usually unrecognized as such, persisted up until Vatican II. It was this judicial-legislative model that Vatican II radically modified. In so doing, it in considerable measure redefined what a council was. This is, obviously, a change of momentous import but a change whose implications have gone largely unexplored. This inattention has contributed to the confusion and disagreement over how to interpret the council. It has led to an inability to convincingly describe what is sometimes called "the spirit of the council."

Among the many literary forms used by councils through the centuries were confessions of faith, historical narratives, bulls and briefs, judicial sentences against ecclesiastical criminals, and so forth. The form most characteristically employed by Nicaea and by many subsequent councils, however, was the canon, which was usually a relatively short prescriptive ordinance that often carried with it punishment for failure to comply. Canon 27 of the Council of Chalcedon (451) illustrates the point: "The sacred synod declares that those who carry off girls under pretext of cohabitation or who are accomplices or cooperate with those who carry them off, are to lose their rank if they are clerics, and are to be anathematized if they are monks or layfolk."

The Council of Trent in the sixteenth century issued about 135 canons relating to doctrine, to say nothing of its similar prescriptions regarding ecclesiastical discipline. Typical of Trent's doctrinal canons is canon 1 on the Mass: "If anybody says that a true and proper sacrifice is not offered to God in the Mass . . . let him be anathema."

Even such doctrinal canons do not strike directly at what a person might believe or think or feel, but at what he or she "says" or "denies"—that is, at some observable behavior. They are not concerned with inwardness as such. Like any good law, canons and their equivalents were formulated to be as unambiguous as possible, drawing clear lines between "who's in" and "who's out," "who's guilty" and ''who's innocent." They sometimes depict those who are "out" as full-fledged enemies, as did the decree of Lateran V (1512) against the cardinals who had attempted to depose Pope Julius II: "We condemn, reject and detest every one of those sons of perdition." The Council of Constance (1418) denounced the English theologian John Wycliffe as a "profligate enemy" of the faith and a "pseudo-Christian," and it handed over his disciple Jan Hus to be burned at the stake.

These are extreme examples, but they for that reason best illustrate the point. Although allowance must be made for many differences, the councils from Nicaea through Vatican I had a characteristic style of discourse composed of two elements. The first was a literary genre—the canon and its equivalents. The second was the vocabulary typical of the genre and appropriate to it. The vocabulary consisted in words of threat and intimidation, words of sharp demarcation, words of denunciation to a criminal, words of a superior speaking to an inferior—or to an enemy. It consisted in power words. Such vocabulary was not restricted to councils. In the late modern era, it consistently appeared in papal pronouncements, such as Pius IX's *Syllabus of Errors* and Pius X's encyclical *Pascendi*.

Canons and the like deal with the exterior; yet, insofar as they are inspired by religious principles, they must be presumed not devoid of relationship to inner conversion. Changing behavior can sometimes be the first step in a change of heart. Moreover, strict laws and harsh punishment are sometimes required if a long-standing abuse is to be rooted out. The bishops at Trent knew they could not reform the episcopacy (that is, themselves) without strong sanctions. They acted accordingly and to good effect.

There was another language tradition in play in council documents. From the beginning, concepts from Greek philosophy also affected the vocabulary. Especially in the High Middle Ages, when such masters as Peter Lombard and Thomas Aquinas developed the great change in theological method (known as Scholasticism), the dialectical and analytical aspects of the Western philosophical tradition began to play an even greater role in council pronouncements. Dialectics is the art of proving a point, of winning an argument, and of showing how wrong your opponent is. It expresses itself in the syllogism, the debate, and the disputation. Although even when, as is the case in Aquinas, reconciliation is its final goal, it has an adversarial edge to it. It is, further, an appeal to the mind, not to the heart. Its language is abstract, impersonal, and ahistorical. It cannot succeed in its goal without a precise technical vocabulary and the use of unambiguous definitions. In that regard, it is similar to the legislative-judicial tradition. Both are intent on drawing firm, unbridgeable lines of definition.

Vatican I largely eschewed Scholastic language. Vatican II also issued no anathemas and no verdicts of "guilty as charged." The Roman Synod of 1960, two years before Vatican II opened (as supposedly the dress rehearsal for the council), emitted 775 canons; Vatican II, not a single one. The council moved from the dialectic of winning an argument to the dialog of finding common ground. It moved from abstract metaphysics to interpersonal "how to be." Vatican II was a language event. The language event marked, manifested, and promoted a value system that modified the value system in place. It implicitly said, for instance, that it is better to work together as neighbors than to fight over differences, as we have up to now been doing.

The style of discourse the council adopted was, like the discourse of previous councils, also made up of two essential elements—a genre and a vocabulary appropriate to and expressive of that genre. The genre can be precisely identified. It is a genre known and practiced in many cultures from time immemorial but clearly analyzed and its features carefully codified by classical authors such as Aristotle, Cicero, and Quintilian. It is panegyric—the painting of an idealized portrait in order to excite admiration and appropriation. It was an old genre in religious discourse, used extensively by the Fathers of the Church and then revisited in the twentieth century by "the new theology" (*la nouvelle théologie*). It was a literary or rhetorical, not philosophical or legal, genre, and hence it had altogether different aims and rested on different presuppositions. Its purpose was not so much to clarify concepts as to heighten appreciation for a person, an event, an institution, or an ideal. Its goal was not winning an argument but winning an internal assent. If most Fourth of July speeches are secular examples of the genre at its worst, Lincoln's Gettysburg Address and his Second Inaugural Address are examples of it at its best. At Gettysburg, Lincoln tried simply to hold up for appreciation what was at stake in the war and, by implication, to praise it as noble and worthy of the great cost.

Although the documents of the council, having been drafted by committees, are far from being literary masterpieces and are not stylistically consistent, they in their general orientation fit the panegyric model. That is their style. They hold up ideals, from which they then draw conclusions and often spell out practical consequences. This is a soft style, compared with the hard-hitting style of canons and dialectical discourse. It is a style geared to persuasion, and persuasion looks to reconciliation. Persuaders and reconcilers do not command from on high but, to some extent, put themselves on the same level as those being persuaded or reconciled.

Those are some of the traits of the genre, and those are the traits characteristic of the discourse of Vatican II. As with the traditional genres used by councils, the most concrete manifestation of the character of the genre is the vocabulary Vatican II adopted and fostered. Nowhere is the contrast between Vatican II and the preceding councils more manifest than in vocabulary—in the words Vatican II most characteristically employed and in the words it eschewed.

What kind of words did it eschew? Words of alienation, exclusion, enmity; words of threat and intimidation; words of surveillance and punishment. Although the hierarchical character of the church is repeatedly stressed and the prerogatives of the pope reiterated almost obsessively, the church is never once described as a monarchy or the members of the church as subjects—a significant departure from previous ecclesiastical discourse.

What kind of words does it employ? Words untypical of the vocabulary of previous councils. They occur too consistently and insistently to be mere window dressing. They do not occur here and there but are an across-the-board phenomenon. They can be divided into categories, but the categories are imperfectly distinct from one another. They overlap and crisscross, making the same or related points.

There are horizontal words like "collegiality," which blend into equality words like "people of God" and "priesthood of all believers." Collegiality is particularly important because, although it can be taken, as here, as an image representing a general orientation, in the council it also had a specific content. It well exemplifies the illegitimacy of separating style from content. Style is, after all, the ultimate vehicle of meaning. It does not adorn meaning but is intrinsic to it. Dare I say the medium is the message? Style, in its two component parts of genre and vocabulary, is the interpretative key par excellence. A poem is read differently than is a medical treatise.

Reciprocity words abound—cooperation, partnership, collaboration, dialog, and conversation. Striking in the Pastoral Constitution on the Church in the Modern World is the unprecedented admission that, just as the world learns from the church, the church learns from the world—in a relationship of mutuality. Humility words recur, beginning with the description of the church as a pilgrim and perhaps ending with the consistent redefinition of ruling to equate serving. Even though the word "change" scarcely appears as such in the council documents, other words that imply historical movement make a notable appearance in a council for the first time in Vatican II—words like development, progress, and even evolution.

The final category is interiority words, such as "charism," "inspiration," "joy and hope, grief and anguish," which are the well-known opening words of the Pastoral Constitution on the Church in the Modern World. Few words occur more frequently than "dignity"—dignity of the human person, of human aspirations, of human culture. Particularly impressive among inward-looking words is "conscience." I quote that same constitution: "Deep within their consciences, individuals discover a law that they did not make for themselves but that they are bound to obey, whose voice, ever summoning them to love and to do what is good and avoid what is evil, rings in their hearts" (no. 16).

Vatican II was about the inward journey.

For me, perhaps the most remarkable aspect of *Lumen Gentium*, the Dogmatic Constitution on the Church, is chapter 5, "The Universal Call to Holiness." No previous council ever spoke of this call, in large measure because the genre and vocabulary inhibited such discussion. *Lumen Gentium*, however, set the agenda for the council, leading the way for the call to holiness to become one of the great themes running through the documents of the council, thus helping to make the documents *religious* documents in ways notably different from previous councils. Holiness is something more than external conformity to enforceable codes of conduct. Holiness: among the most inward of words!

The values the new vocabulary expresses are anything but new to the Christian tradition and Christian discourse. They are in fact more common than their opposite numbers, but they are new to councils. In promoting the values they express, the council did not deny the validity of the contrasting values. If Vatican II is distinctive for the pervasive emphasis it put on horizontal relationships, for instance, it is also noteworthy for its correlative insistence on the vertical. It sought not displacement but modulation.

Nonetheless, when both genre and vocabulary are taken into account in Vatican II, they convey a remarkably consistent message. The message is that a model shift and, with it, a value shift has occurred, or, more accurately, is struggling to occur. Genre, together with its appropriate vocabulary, also imbues Vatican II with an internal coherence that was groundbreaking for ecclesiastical assemblies. The documents of Vatican II play off one another, respond to one another, and were shaped to be consistent with one another in principles, and in style. They are remarkably intertextual.

This coherence, immediately recognized by participants in the council and by commentators on it, was often expressed in the vague expression "spirit of the council." By "spirit" was meant a guiding vision and an across-the-board orientation that transcended particulars and was thus a key to understanding and properly interpreting them. The vagueness of "spirit" is brought down to earth and made palpable and verifiable by paying attention to the style of the council, by paying attention to its unique literary form and vocabulary, and by drawing out the implications of the form and vocabulary. Through an examination of "the letter" (form and vocabulary), it is possible to arrive at "the spirit."

In its general orientation, in its vision, in its spirit, as articulated especially in its most characteristic vocabulary, the council taught how the church should in the future do business. In so doing, it devised a profile of the ideal Christian, a profile for each one of us. It also set an extraordinarily high standard and ideal of the kind of world for which we are all called to work.

The council was about much more, then, than a handful of superficial adjustments of the Catholic Church to the so-called modern world, about much more than changes in liturgical forms, and certainly about much more than power plays among high churchmen. It had a message. The message was traditional while at the same time radical, prophetic while at the same time gentle. The message speaks, I believe, to our world today—a world wracked with discord, retaliations, hatred, bombs, preemptive attacks, wars, threats of wars, as if never to end. The message of the council is profoundly countercultural while at the same time responding to the deepest yearnings of the human heart: Peace on earth. Goodwill to men.

12

DIALOG AND THE
IDENTITY OF VATICAN II

On the occasion of the fiftieth anniversary of the opening of Vatican II, Georgetown University sponsored a three-day conference on the council. As the keynote opening the conference, 11 October 2012, I gave this lecture, which was later published in Origins. *In the meantime, the topic has become even timelier with the election of Pope Francis, who while archbishop of Buenos Aires carried on his famous dialog with Rabbi Abraham Skorka, an absolutely unprecedented initiative on the part of a Catholic prelate. Their dialog was published and after the election of Francis became somewhat of a best seller. The title of the English trans-lation is* On Heaven and Earth.

In the year 1525, Martin Luther published his tract titled *The Enslaved Will*. It was a vitriolic response to Erasmus's *The Free Will*, which had appeared the previous year. Erasmus's work was an irenic attempt to put an end to the controversy already raging on the relationship between grace and freedom that threatened to tear Europe apart. Erasmus con-cluded his piece with a compromise he hoped would bring all parties in the great uproar into agreement: attribute virtually everything in justifica-tion to grace, and just a little bit to free will. In proposing this solution, Erasmus went on to say that in such complex matters he believed asser-tions, the apodictic and uncompromising pronouncements Luther seemed to be slamming around everywhere on every topic, did more harm than good. Erasmus most tellingly stated that in such crucial matters as justification, he "favored moderation."

In Luther's eyes Erasmus could not have spoken in more damning terms than these. One could not be moderate in such life-and-death matters. One had to speak boldly, not daintily. For Luther, Erasmus's approach was that of a skeptic, of a person uncertain of his beliefs. Against that approach Luther let fly the full fury of his contempt. Peace at any price—that was what Erasmus was really about. If Erasmus's compromise on justification, which conceded something, however small to free will, did not make him ungodly, his mealymouthed dislike of assertions certainly did.

Luther in his own words: "Not to delight in assertions is not the mark of a Christian heart. Indeed, one must delight in assertions to be a Christian at all. . . . Take away assertions and you take away Christianity." The Holy Spirit, no skeptic, has written not doubts and opinions in our hearts but "assertions, more sure and certain than life itself and all experience. We neither accept nor approve Erasmus's moderate, middle way."

Today we dainty postmoderns probably feel more kinship with Erasmus than with Luther, but what is to be said of Luther's insistence that assertion is the proper mode of Christian discourse? I think that if we examine the language of the patriarchs and the prophets, including the prophet Jesus, we find a discourse apodictic and assertive. Prophets proclaim their message. They do not suggest it. They do not present reasons for it, nor do they call for discussion of it. Take it or leave it—but leave it at your own peril.

"Thou shall not commit adultery." No discussion. "Love your neighbor as yourself." No discussion. "Blessed are the poor in spirit." No discussion. "Repent." No discussion. "Thou art Peter." No discussion. "You have heard it said, but *I say unto you* . . ." No discussion. This is prophetic discourse in its rawest and most powerful form, the absolute and uncompromising proclamation. It is quintessentially top-down discourse. The underlying paradigm is uncompromisingly vertical.

We postmoderns know that this mode of discourse is not restricted to the Bible, nor is it a thing of the past. We meet it every day in almost innumerable ways, of which advertising slogans are the most obvious. For generations now Coca-Cola has proclaimed that it is "the pause that refreshes." Really? Who says? Why? These are questions we do not even think to ask. We often meet more serious but similarly uncompromising slogans such as "Support our troops."

Religious discourse, to its credit, at least lets us know what is going on—lets us know we are dealing with raw assertions. Do we not speak at Mass of "proclaiming [asserting] the Gospel"? In so doing, we say that we act as "heralds of the good news," and heralds shout the truth, pure and simple. They do not ask for discussion of it. After I finish my homily at Mass, I don't smile at the congregation and ask, "Do you think I'm on the right track? Any questions?"

Religious discourse can legitimately use apodictic assertions because it bases itself on a higher, unquestionable authority: the authority of God himself. From that authority, there is no appeal. That authority is above and beyond what our poor human faculties can fathom and therefore must be accepted in its stark, sometimes counterintuitive claims. "Blessed are the poor in spirit." "Forgive seventy times seven."

Since Jesus promised to be with his church for all ages, and further promised the Holy Spirit to keep the church from error, we should not be surprised that the church has appropriated features of prophetic discourse as properly its own. Pope Pius IX, for instance, *proclaimed* the doctrine of the Immaculate Conception, and Pius XII *proclaimed* the doctrine of Mary's bodily Assumption. They were not putting the dogmas up for discussion.

Even the decrees of councils prior to Vatican II evince this same trait. Those councils saw themselves as essentially legislative and judicial bodies. They made laws, and they rendered verdicts of guilty or not guilty in criminal cases. Neither of those two kinds of pronouncements are invitations to dialog. They assert. In their canons, which were short ordinances and the councils' most characteristic form of discourse, they laid down the law. The formula goes this way: "If anybody should say such and such, let him be anathema." "If anybody should do such and such, let him be anathema." Out you go! No discussion!

If assertion is such a characteristic form of Christian discourse—perhaps even the authentic form—how can Vatican II make such a big deal of dialog, which seems to be the very opposite of assertion and proclamation? Dialog is a synonym for conversation. Its first purpose is simply to understand the Other—to know where he or she is "coming from," to use the vulgar expression. Dialog consists in speaking and listening. And, after listening, letting what one has heard sink in. While dialog implies that each of the partners begins the conversation holding certain positions and even convictions, it also seems to imply a willingness to be affected by the conversation—to learn from the other, to be enriched by the other, and in some measure to rethink one's positions or convictions.

In the history of Christian discourse, are there examples of such a style of discourse, of such conversations? In the Hebrew Scriptures there are several examples of Moses conversing with the Lord, even as "a man speaks to his friend" (Ex. 33:11). But the best-known instance of such a conversation is Abraham bargaining with the Lord as he tried to persuade the Lord not to destroy Sodom and Gomorrah. "Suppose there are fifty righteous within the city; wilt Thou destroy the place and not spare it for the righteous fifty?" The Lord replies that he would not destroy it if there were fifty righteous. Then Abraham asks about forty-five righteous, and so forth until Abraham gets the Lord all the way down to ten righteous (Gen. 18).

In Luke's Gospel, Jesus, after his resurrection, dialogs with the disciples on the way to Emmaus. In John's Gospel, Jesus dialogs with Nicodemus, for instance, and with the woman at the well. These dialogs, however, do not correspond to what dialog meant in the twentieth century, because they are teaching moments for Jesus, geared to vindicate his position. Thus, although the Bible evinces a wide variety of literary forms, examples of dialog in the modern sense are hard to come by.

For Catholics, as well as for some other mainline Christian churches, however, the Bible does not stand alone, as if outside the wide arc of human culture. When in the early third century the fierce Christian apologist Tertullian asked, "What does Athens have to do with Jerusalem?"— that is, what do the transcendent claims of the Bible have to do with the human culture of classical antiquity—he replied categorically that Jerusalem had nothing to do with Athens. Down through the centuries other Christian thinkers followed him, in what perhaps can be called forms of "cultural Augustinianism." Luther certainly fits into this tradition, as do the Jansenists and many others. Complex though this tradition is, and instantiated in multiple forms in the long history of Christianity, it can nonetheless be characterized as a tradition or culture of alienation. It will stand apart and seek to create a place, howsoever small, that is pure and undefiled.

From the very beginning, however, Athens and Jerusalem were, perforce, on speaking terms. The New Testament was written not in Hebrew or Aramaic but in Greek, the language of Athens. As Christianity spread throughout the Hellenistic world, its converts came to it from the culture of Athens, which they could no more shed that we can shed living in the culture of the twenty-first century. The Fathers of the Church—such as Ambrose, Jerome, Gregory the Great, and, yes, Augustine—were steeped in that culture, and it was through the lenses of that culture that they understood and defended the faith of Jerusalem.

Their education was the literary and rhetorical education that dominated the Mediterranean world from the third century before Christ until the early Middle Ages. That education culminated in rhetoric, the art of persuasion. The art of persuasion is very different from the practice of assertion, and that art was in principle bewildered by such a practice. The Fathers and the other Christians of those centuries, however, were able, as Christians, somehow to put the two together and make them work as partners.

Here is the point: That partnership can be understood as a form of dialog, an exchange in which each of the partners is affected by the other, in different ways and in different degrees. It seems to me that that phenomenon is dialog on a mega basis. It was a cultural dialog that for Christians was by no means restricted to the patristic era. It took on a more explicit and straightforward form with medieval Scholasticism.

The central intellectual problem of the Scholastic enterprise was how to reconcile the Bible with Greek learning, most particularly with the philosophy of Aristotle, which was virtually unknown in the West until the late twelfth century. That philosophy challenged fundamental doctrines the Christian church had derived from the Bible. Aristotle knew neither Creation nor grace; yet he seemed to have something to say worth listening to and, indeed, learning from. From that point of view, the Scholastic enterprise was radically dialogic. It was, further, despite the vicious criticism the Scholastic theologians often directed to one another, fundamentally a reconciling enterprise. It refused to dismiss the Other as in principle ignorant and ungodly. It, on the contrary, wanted to make the Other a partner—perhaps a junior partner, but a partner nonetheless. If the Augustinian tradition can be called a tradition of alienation, this tradition can be called a tradition of reconciliation.

Now we move to the Renaissance, which is defined as the artistic and literary rebirth that occurred in the fifteenth and sixteenth centuries, beginning in Italy but fast moving to the rest of Europe. An artistic revival:

Many of you have been to the Sistine Chapel and seen Michelangelo's ceiling. You surely recall the panels depicting scenes from the early chapters of the book of Genesis, such as the creation of Adam. Did you pay attention to the large portraits of the prophets who predicted the coming of Christ, such as Isaiah and Jeremiah, that frame those Genesis scenes? Did you notice as well that alternating with the portraits of the prophets were portraits of the Sibyls, those mantic priestesses of obscure origin from pagan antiquity? The belief was ancient and strong that somehow, by some mysterious means, the Sibyls also predicted the coming of the Savior, though in more veiled ways than the Hebrew prophets. Think of it! In the pope's own chapel! Saving truth outside the canonical Scriptures!

But more pertinent for our purposes is the literary revival of the Renaissance known as humanism. In it we find another culture of reconciliation, most consistently embodied of course in Erasmus, justly known as "the prince of the humanists." Erasmus despised the Scholastic system. Like them, however, he too was engaged in a dialogic enterprise. Humanism was an attempt to leap backward in time over the medieval Scholastics, with their barbarous Latin style, and to replace that style with the "good style" of the writers of Greek and Roman antiquity—to replace it with precisely those authors whom the Fathers of the Church had studied and been formed by. On the surface what Erasmus and the others wanted to recover was good style, but for them good style could not be divorced from good morals. Indeed, the ancients were worth recovering because they held up high moral standards, which, moreover, they were able to promote through their attractive style of speaking and writing.

In recovering good style—that is, in causing the rebirth or the Renaissance of good style—the humanists also recovered from antiquity a specific literary form that was unknown in the Middle Ages. They recovered the dialog or the colloquy. In 1448 Lorenzo Valla published his book *On the True and False Good*, a three-way dialog among a Stoic, an Epicurean, and a Christian. It was important work for the era and helped promote the genre.

But the master of the dialog was Erasmus. He wrote dozens of them, many of which were delightfully satirical. But he also wrote serious ones, of which the most sublime is titled "The Godly Feast," *Convivium Religiosum*. In it a group of friends, all devout believers, gather at a villa for a meal and conversation—a conversation about their faith and about their literary interests, which of course center on the classics and the Fathers of the Church. "The Godly Feast" not only is an example of interpersonal dialog at its best but also exemplifies an underlying cultural dialog, as the friends reflect on the relationship between their Christian faith and the classical authors they so much esteem.

At a certain point the friends discuss a text of St. Paul. One of them asks if he can interject something from "a profane writer" (in this case, Cicero) into "such a religious conversation." Another replies to him, "Ah, whatever is devout and contributes to godly living cannot be called profane." And then he goes on to say, "And perhaps the spirit of Christ is more widespread than we understand and the company of saints includes many not in our calendar. I cannot read Cicero's essays on friendship and old age without blessing that pure heart, inspired as it was from on high."

Later on another friend commented on Socrates's words before he drank the hemlock, as recorded in Plato's *Phaedo*. He reflected that because in his life Socrates had tried hard to please God, he said he could face death serenely. A friend then joins in: "An admirable spirit, surely, in one who had not known Christ and the Sacred Scriptures. And so, when I read such things of such men, I can hardly help exclaiming, 'O, Saint Socrates, pray for us.'"

I mention Erasmus because he provides us with such a clear example of what we might call the dialogic mindset. In "The Godly Feast" the discussion is among a group of Christians, but they betray that they as Christians are engaged at a deep level in dialog with the Other, with the non-Christian, to whom they are listening intently. By the time Erasmus died in 1536, however, the dialog form as religious discourse was doomed not to catch on. It was too fragile, urbane, and open ended to survive the bitter polemics of Reformation and Counter-Reformation. As a form of religious discourse, dialog would not come back in favor until the twentieth century.

Thus, different though Scholasticism and Renaissance humanism were from each other and, indeed, often bitterly antagonistic to each another, they shared one important trait: they were both powered by a reconciling dynamic. They both looked on the Other with curious, sometimes admiring eyes, and they sought to learn from an encounter with that Other.

Erasmus, however, is important for the twentieth century and for Vatican II for another, closely related reason. His intellectual enterprise bears a striking resemblance to the enterprise in mid-twentieth-century France known as *la nouvelle théologie*—an enterprise that had such a big impact on the council.

Erasmus worked to accomplish three interlocking goals: (1) He wanted to put Christian discourse into the language of Scripture and the Fathers—that is, to displace Scholastic jargon with a language that was comprehensible to ordinary persons and that was immediately directed to living a devout life. (2) As a closely related undertaking, he wanted to reform theological method to derive it more directly from Scripture— Scripture as understood by him and his humanist colleagues, not as a database of proof texts from which to build a cathedral in the mind but as historically bounded texts that had to be understood in their historical context and in the integrity of their literary forms. In that regard he and his fellow humanists were the great forerunners of the critical-historical method that reached a maturity in the twentieth century. (3) He, thus, wanted to restore practices of piety to models prevalent in the early church, which entailed promoting the reading of the Bible as one of the premier such practices. It is no accident that Henri de Lubac, one of the architects of *la nouvelle théologie*, esteemed Erasmus so highly.

It seems, however, that only in the cultural context of the early and mid-twentieth century could religious dialog emerge again as a viable, or even as an indispensable, model for Christian discourse. In that regard, two features of the twentieth-century context stand out. The first is multiculturalism and the second, multiculturalism's cousin, religious pluralism. The world had always been multicultural, of course, but only with the ease of travel and communication of the twentieth century did it become an unavoidable fact of life.

Moreover, especially with the end of World War II, the cultural imperialism practiced by the great Western powers was at an end and "the white man's burden" despised as a form of oppression. Unfortunately, in the nineteenth and early twentieth centuries, missionaries, both Protestant and Catholic, had not been innocent of promoting the culture of their native lands almost as ardently as they promoted the Gospel. In that regard the churches were now at a point of crisis. Missionaries realized they had to divest themselves of their cultural prejudices and take benign account of the cultures where they were evangelizing. They had to learn from the Other.

By that same date, religious pluralism had similarly become a fact of life. The religious ghettos that had sometimes encompassed even great nations had for the most part dissolved. People rubbed elbows on a daily basis with persons from other Christian churches, as well as from synagogues and, in some places, from mosques. In this context, absolute assertions of exclusive rights to God's grace lost credibility. Were the Jews truly a race cursed by God? Were the Muslims, as Pope Paul III said in 1542, "our eternal and godless enemy"?

Was it really true that there was "no salvation outside the church"? Did that mean that my beloved Lutheran husband was destined to hell? Although the axiom of no salvation had long been the subject of debate and qualification, it was still maintained by some in its most literal and unqualified meaning, as became clear in the 1940s in the famous "Feeney Case." Father Leonard Feeney, a Jesuit of the New England Province, ran a Catholic Center in Cambridge, Massachusetts, just about thirty yards from the entrance to Harvard University. Feeney preached the doctrine of no salvation loud and clear in the unadulterated sense. Unless a person was a de facto member of the Catholic Church, he or she was destined to hell. The president of Harvard University was not amused by the thought that he and virtually everybody associated with Harvard in those days were eternally lost.

He appealed to the archbishop. The archbishop referred the case to the Vatican. The Holy Office finally had to intervene. It decreed that, however the axiom was to be understood, it was not to be understood in the absolute sense Feeney attributed to it: namely, unless a person was a member of the Catholic Church, he or she could not be saved. The Holy Office further taught that a person could be a member of the church, and therefore saved, *voto et desiderio*—by some mysterious way known only to God.

Related to the phenomenon of religious pluralism was the growing and more widespread awareness at the end of World War II of the horror of the Holocaust—that indescribably wicked crime against humanity that occurred in Christian Germany, where over 40 percent of the population were churchgoing Catholics and another 40 percent churchgoing Protestants. How could this have happened? What responsibility for it did the churches bear? Maybe the practice of denigrating other religions and of treating them as enemies by definition and as outside the mantle of God's saving grace had something to do with it.

The cultural milieu was, therefore, ready. But dialog needed a voice. That voice was supplied most notably by the religious thinker and philosopher Martin Buber. Early on Buber published two works that radically challenged the objective and impersonal frame of reference in which Western philosophy traditionally addressed human issues. The first, published in 1923, was titled *I and Thou*. The second was an essay titled *Dialogue*, published in 1929. In later works Buber went on to criticize Aristotle and Aquinas for the abstract character of their systems, which removed individuals from real-life situations where they had to make decisions.

For the abstractions of the great philosophical systems, Buber substituted relationships, in which mutuality and sharing of experience and beliefs were the hallmarks. In such relationships the privileged form of communication was dialog. He defined dialog in different ways but most effectively as "conversation . . . from one open-hearted person to another open-hearted person." Dialog for Buber was not a ploy, not a technique, but the surface expression of the core values of honesty, curiosity, and humility. These values are different from those found in dialog's contrary, monolog.

Buber's works attracted a wide readership, and they directly and indirectly influenced Christian thinkers. The year before the council opened, the young Catholic theologian Hans Ur von Balthasar published *Martin Buber and Christianity*, in which he praised Buber as "one of the most creative minds of our age" and as "the originator of the dialogical principle." But the idea and ideal of dialog was by then in wide circulation. In fact, the year before von Balthasar published his book, the American Jesuit theologian Gustave Weigel noted that dialog appeared so frequently in journals and even newspapers that it was beginning to seem "cultish and faddish." Weigel could not possibly have foreseen the prominent role dialog would play in Vatican II, along with its related ideals of partnership, cooperation, and, of course, its synonym, conversation, to the point that we can—as we do so here this afternoon—speak of it in terms of the very identity of the council.

That having been said, it is important to note that the word as such made a relatively late appearance in the documents of the council. Vatican II was already at the halfway mark. Only after the publication of Pope Paul VI's first encyclical, *Ecclesiam Suam*, on 6 August 1964, just before the third period of the council opened, did dialog appear and immediately become one of the council's most characteristic categories, appearing in ten of the sixteen final documents, in some of which, such as the Pastoral Constitution on the Church in the Modern World, it is almost a leitmotif.

For dialog, the encyclical was without doubt the great landmark. It validated dialog as a legitimate and needed category in church life. It was a category until then unknown in official church pronouncements, but it now had official and, indeed, enthusiastic backing from the Supreme Pontiff himself. This was, wittingly or unwittingly, a bold move from a cautious pope.

Paul VI appropriated the term from Buber, it seems, through the mediation of his friend, the prominent philosopher theologian Jean Guitton, a French layman. Dialog appears a whopping seventy-seven times in the encyclical, and its meaning and application occupy fully two-thirds of that long document.

There can be no doubt that the encyclical infused the word into the council's vocabulary. In the original version of the document, *On Ecumenism*, presented to the council the previous year, for instance, dialog did not appear a single time. In its revised version after the publication of the encyclical, it emerged one of the text's most characteristic words, appearing at least fourteen times. From that point forward, dialog (*dialogus* in Latin) and its precise synonym, colloquy (Latin, *colloquium*), go on to appear some seventy times in the documents of the council. It would be difficult to find a word more characteristic of Vatican II.

Ecclesiam Suam is typical of Paul VI in its care to try to cover all eventualities and especially in its concern not to go too far. At times it seems to see dialog as an instrument of evangelization, but at other times it seems to distance itself from that understanding, especially when it speaks, very briefly, of dialog within the Catholic Church itself.

It is at its best in its description of the first fruits of dialog: "Dialog promotes intimacy and friendship on both sides. It unites the parties in a mutual adherence to the Good, and thus excludes all self-seeking." In another place: "The very fact that persons engage in a dialog of this sort is proof of their consideration and esteem for others, of their understanding and kindness. They detest bigotry and prejudice, malicious and indiscriminate hostility, and empty and boastful speech." And further: "However divergent opinions and beliefs might seem to be, they can often serve to complete one another."

I think it is important to add another fruit of dialog to the pope's list. Dialog, when properly engaged in, results in a deeper grasp of one's own identity. Dialog must not be looked on as resulting in a dissipation of identity but as a means of purifying and clarifying it. I think it is a law of life that it is only through interaction with the Other that we come to understand ourselves. Only after I spent a full year in a Jesuit community in Austria, my first time living outside the United States, did I come to grasp with a new depth what it meant for me to be an American. That knowledge was not simply intellectual. It touched me more deeply than that, in ways I find difficult to describe. In any case, when I came home I said to myself, "You will never be the same again."

Important though Paul's encyclical was, it could not have made the headway it did if the council had not already adopted a reconciling orientation that made it immediately receptive to dialog. Because of that orientation, one can say, I believe, dialog was present in the council before the word itself appeared. That orientation had been given it by Pope John XXIII in his intention that the council be an instrument of reconciliation among the churches and his inviting leaders from non-Catholic churches to come to the council and, perforce, it seems, to engage in dialog at least on an informal basis with the members of the council. In his opening address to the council on 11 October 1962, he wanted the council to distance itself from a spirit of condemnation and to let the church show itself to be "the loving mother of all, benign, patient, full of goodness and mercy."

Yes, dialog was present in the council before the word itself appeared. In the council's very first and orienting document, the Constitution on the Sacred Liturgy, the council called the church to respect the traditions, symbols, and rituals of cultures other than Western, to the point that they could be incorporated into the liturgy itself, insofar as they were free of superstition. This is a gesture of reconciliation with non-Western cultures and an implicit call for dialog with them related to the most intimate and sacred expression of Christian life, the Eucharistic sacrifice.

By the second period of the council, 1963, the revised version of the document on the church, *Lumen Gentium*, was ready for discussion. It differed from the version originally presented to the council the previous year in notable ways, but perhaps the most noticeable was in its vocabulary and its very style, which was an important and often underestimated innovation in the council. The new style of the document was at the time considered an implementation of what Cardinal Joseph Frings of Cologne the previous year had called for as debate opened on the council's first document, the Constitution on the Sacred Liturgy. Frings commended the text for its "truly pastoral literary style, full of the spirit of Holy Scripture and the Fathers of the Church," and he implied that was the style the council should adopt as its own.

In *Lumen Gentium* the change from the earlier version was remarkable. Instead of the steadily juridical style of that document, the style of the revision was filled with biblical images and patristic allusions. Except for its juridical third chapter on the hierarchy, the document almost overflows with images of the church and its members that suggest fecundity, dignity, abundance, charism, goodness, safe haven, welcome, communion, tenderness, and warmth.

That style did not come out of nowhere. In the decades before the council, it had been promoted and exemplified by proponents of *la nouvelle théologie*. If we want to reach further back, it was the style promoted and exemplified by Erasmus, who himself believed he was replicating the style of his beloved Fathers of the Church, both Greek and Latin. As instantiated in *Lumen Gentium* and then in subsequent documents, the style avoided using language of alienation and condemnation and favored words suggesting reconciliation and mutuality. Such words provided the context and the horizon that assured dialog of a warm welcome once Paul VI brought it to the fore.

In other words, though dialog is certainly important in itself for understanding the council, it is simply one word that fits into it and helps create a new language for defining how the church is to operate. As the council moved on, the number of such words continued to grow—friendship, brotherhood, sisterhood, partnership, reciprocity, respect, freedom, conscience, holiness, and the innate dignity of every human person. With special prominence, the list included and honored collegiality. As I said, taken together, the words suggest and promote reconciliation and mutuality. Dialog is the preferred instrument for accomplishing those ends. These words and expressions are not casual asides. They recur with the insistence of a drumbeat. They are not new in Christian vocabulary, but they are strikingly new for a council. They bear a kinship with one another in that they express not top-down, vertical relationships but horizontal ones. As we try to assess Vatican II, we must include in the reckoning the fact that it was a major language event in the history of the church. It represents a language reversal, from monolog to dialog. For it to be honest and genuine, for it to be something more than a ploy or a tactic, this new style of discourse requires a new style of being—a conversion—which then results in a new style of relationships to just about everybody and everything.

The council wanted to promote dialog especially in four specific areas. First, a dialog with non-Western cultures, as I mentioned earlier. Second, and most famously, a dialog with other Christian churches, and to do so with the recognition that the old practice of belittling and denigrating them produced no good fruit. Indeed, in past ages it had led to the slaughter of Christians by Christians in wars fought in the name of the God of love.

In the third place, the dialog with non-Christian religions, especially dialog with Jews and Muslims, as outlined in the document *Nostra Aetate*. This document provided the Catholic Church with a new mission, with a new role in the world—a mission of mediation in a divided world. Today with the tensions between the so-called Muslim world and the West, I cannot think of a more urgent or more exalted mission for the church. It is a mission Pope John Paul II took on with great vigor and courage. His many meetings with Jewish leaders and his extending a hand in friendship to them are well known. Less well known, but at the present moment perhaps more urgent, were his many meetings with Muslim groups throughout the world.

Finally, the dialog with "the modern world" as proposed in *Gaudium et Spes*. In that document the relationship between the church and the world is described precisely as "a dialog." In the document, which is addressed to all men and women of goodwill, occurs the remarkable and unprecedented statement that, while the church teaches the world, it also learns from the world. That is a statement of dialog, again, of cultural dialog and of cultural dialog on the megascale.

The title of the document deserves comment. It is, as you know, "The Church in the Modern World"—*in* the modern world, not the church *for* the modern world, nor certainly the church *against* the modern world. The very neutrality of the title is remarkable given the alienation from the modern world that especially Catholic officialdom felt and promoted among Catholics from the time of the French Revolution even to the eve of Vatican II. *Gaudium et Spes* is a quintessentially dialogic and reconciling document.

But what about the subject Pope Paul VI briefly touched on in his encyclical—dialog within the church? Although in that regard dialog (*di-*

alogus) does not appear a single time, its synonym, colloquy (*colloquium*), appears often and is usually and correctly translated into English as "dialog." In the decree on bishops, for instance, the bishop is told to "initiate and promote dialog (*colloquium*) with his people" (no. 13). Later he is told to "engage in dialog with his priests, both individually and collectively" (no. 28). In the decree on the training of priests, the seminarians are to be trained so that they are equipped to "dialog with the people of these times" (no. 15). The same idea appears in the decree on the life and ministry of priests (no. 18). Just as important is the many times words like "friendship," "brother," and "sister" recur to describe all of the above relationships. The council, therefore, did not limit dialog to those outside the church but saw it as a style of discourse appropriate to the church's internal functioning. Episcopal collegiality is dialog at the highest level functioning within the church.

But a word of caution: The council never intended to diminish in the least degree the authority of the pope and the bishops. The buck stops with them, as the council insisted almost obsessively. Moreover, the council never intended to compromise the church's first and most essential ministry, the proclamation of the Gospel. It could not have done that without utter betrayal of the transcendent message of which it is the herald. Dialog cannot replace proclamation. However, it can, the council seems to say, coexist with it, to the advantage of proclamation. It can play a role in how the church bears itself, in how, as a body made up of human beings, the church deals with human beings in accordance with their intelligence and dignity.

The title of my talk this afternoon is "Dialog and the Identity of the Council." Dialog does not exhaust the meaning of the council. If it did, it would utterly displace proclamation, which would be a betrayal. But dialog is an essential and distinctive characteristic of the council. It is a characteristic absolutely unique to Vatican II and the surface manifestation of a deep, corporate shift in mindset. To take it seriously is to undergo a kind of conversion, for it entails a shift from one style of behavior to another and even from one set of values to another. Maybe the following set of contrasting points will help grasp the manifold dimensions of the shift.

From laws to ideals
From commands to invitations
From threats to persuasion

From rivalry to partnership
From exclusion to inclusion
From hostility to friendship
From pettiness to magnanimity
From suspicion to trust
From fault-finding to appreciation
From intransigence to seeking common ground
From behavior modification to conversion of heart
From top-down (vertical) to horizontal
From alienation to reconciliation
From monolog to dialog

13

TWO COUNCILS COMPARED
Trent and Vatican II

In January 2013 a three-day international conference was held at the Catholic University, Leuven, one of several such conferences around the world on the 450th anniversary of the closure of the Council of Trent in 1563. At Leuven I gave the concluding lecture, which was this comparison of Trent and Vatican II. It seems a fitting way to conclude the second part of this volume. It will also be published with a slightly different title in the three-volume collection of papers from the conference, edited by Wim François and Violet Soen, tentatively titled The Council of Trent: Reform and Controversy in Europe and Beyond (1545–1700).

By a strange coincidence, the year of our conference on the occasion of the 450th anniversary of the closing of the Council of Trent coincided with the fiftieth anniversary of Vatican Council II. The coincidence offers an opportunity to compare the two councils that are so often contrasted with each other. In so doing, we will find that each throws light on the other and thereby enables us to understand both of them better. We are, of course, particularly concerned with seeing how the contrast with Vatican II helps us better understand the Council of Trent and provide sharper perspectives on it.

The two councils differ in so many and such important ways that a comparison may seem unlikely to yield anything of substance. Sometimes, when I try putting them side by side, I feel as if I am comparing the merits and demerits of apples against the merits and demerits of lasagna. Moreover, prejudices have in the past fifty years obstructed clear vision. Some Catholics, for instance, assert confidently that Trent created all the bad things that Vatican II rescued them from, whereas others just as confidently assert it created all the good things Vatican II robbed them of.

The grain of truth in such assertions is that the councils are so different that one wonders if they have anything at all in common. Of course, they were both councils of the Catholic Church, which means they fit the basic definition of a church council—a meeting principally of bishops gathered in Christ's name who, by virtue of that name and the presence of the Holy Spirit, are empowered to make decisions binding on the church. Beyond that, is there anything they share?

There certainly is, as I will attempt to show. But first we need to examine ways they differ from each other. The most immediately obvious way is the places where they were held. Not only is that an obvious fact, but it is also a clue pointing to a crucial difference in their dynamics. Trent is hundreds of kilometers from Rome. The popes agreed to the city only with the greatest reluctance. With the Councils of Constance and Basel, they had learned the sorry lesson of the danger to themselves of councils distant from Rome.

Trent meant they would not have the immediate oversight they desired and that Julius II and Leo X had had for the Fifth Lateran Council a few decades earlier. None of the three popes who convoked the three periods of the Council of Trent ever set foot in the city, though Pius IV came under pressure to do so. The popes tried, with some success, to control the direction of the council through their legates. But that was certainly not the same thing as having the council meet right under their noses in Rome. Communication between Rome and Trent through couriers was reliable, but even with special couriers at least six or seven days were required for an exchange of letters.

The contrast with Vatican II is striking. Although neither Pope John XXIII nor Pope Paul VI attended the working sessions of the council, they had immediate communication with what was happening in the Basilica of St. Peter through radio and closed-circuit television in the papal apartments and through almost daily meetings with individual bishops. Because of the complicated, cumbersome, and almost unintelligible mix of entities working on the floor of the council that shared responsibility for moving the agenda forward, it was impossible to know who was in charge there. The solution was to run to the pope for the resolution of conflicts that arose.

John XXIII tended to let the council sort out its problems on its own, but Paul VI directly intervened time after time. He did so to a degree and with a frequency, immediacy, and impact that was unprecedented for a council. One of the paradoxes that arises through this comparison of the modes of papal oversight is that, much as the modes differed, in both instances they provoked the bishops to ask the same question: Is the council free?

A second immediately obvious difference between the councils is the number and origins of the participants. When the Council of Trent opened on 13 December 1545, only twenty-nine prelates, including the three papal legates, had showed up. The number for this first period eventually climbed to about a hundred. At the opening of the second period, only fifteen showed up. The third period was the best attended, usually a little over two hundred prelates, but over two-thirds were from Italy and most of the rest from Spain and Portugal. Even the arrival of the small but important French delegation toward the end of 1562 did not change the proportions significantly. Unlike Lateran V, there was not a single bishop from "the New World." Trent was essentially a council of the Western Mediterranean.

At most of the working sessions of Vatican II, the bishops numbered about 2,100, some ten times larger than the peak number at Trent. They came from 116 different countries from around the world, to make Vatican II truly ecumenical in the sense of church-wide or worldwide and to do so to a degree that dwarfed even Vatican I, its only rival in that regard. Many of the bishops from former European colonies were natives of those countries and brought to the council a new sense of the catholicity of the Catholic Church.

There were other important differences in the membership of the two councils. At Trent the secular powers—that is, the laity—were present through their ambassadors (technically, "orators"), and their influence on the direction of the council was considerable. Although some of the ambassadors were prelates, others were laymen, who had the right to speak to the council when they presented their credentials. They used the occasion to further the agenda of their monarchs. They tended to be strong supporters of the reform impulses of the council, except of course when those impulses turned in the direction of their sponsors.

Of all the monarchs, Emperor Charles V exercised the most decisive influence on the council even before it opened. He insisted that the council make reform of the church its top agenda item in the face of Pope Paul III's insistence that the council deal primarily, if not exclusively, with doctrine. Pressure from the emperor helped determine the council's decision to deal with both issues simultaneously and not privilege one of them over the other. To some extent, "doctrine and reform" were perhaps inevitable as twin agenda items; yet Charles V's insistence on the primacy of reform cannot be discounted. During the third period, his brother and successor, Emperor Ferdinand I, continued, especially in the spring of 1563, to press the agenda Charles had initiated, to the great discomfort of Pope Pius IV.

Vatican II followed the precedent set by Vatican I, which was the first council in the history of the church to exclude the laity from participation. True, Vatican II eventually invited a few laymen and then, to its great credit, a few women, but they were essentially tokens. To look on these actions of the Vatican II as a breakthrough for the laity is to forget the large role the laity traditionally played in councils, beginning with Nicaea and Emperor Constantine in the fourth century. The best that can be said of Vatican II in this regard is that it was an improvement over Vatican I and implicitly reopened the question.

In another way, however, Vatican II accomplished what Trent was unable to do. At Vatican II members of other Christian churches—Protestant and Orthodox—were present as so-called "observers" from the moment the council opened until the moment it closed. By the end of the council, the number of observers and non-Catholic "guests" rose to close to two hundred. Although they could not speak at the working sessions of the council, they made their influence felt in informal ways. The bishops and theologians formulated their decisions with the keen awareness that they were being scrutinized by scholars and churchmen who did not share many of the basic assumptions on which Catholic doctrine and practice were based, and they adjusted them accordingly.

In both councils theologians played a crucial role, but in ways that were considerably different. At Trent the theologians at times outnumbered the bishops. Of them, the pope chose only two or three. The rest were chosen either by their monarch or by their religious order. For the second period, for instance, Pope Julius III sent only two, whereas Emperor Charles V sent seven and his sister, Queen Mary of Hungary, Governess of the Low Countries, sent eight. At Vatican II, although bishops were free to bring their own theological advisers, only the pope chose official theologians for the council. Only those theologians could sit on the commissions formulating the decrees. Although the number of such officially designated theologians eventually rose to almost five hundred, it was proportionately much less than the number at Trent.

The theologians functioned differently at the two councils. At Trent they opened the discussion of every doctrinal issue by commenting on it in serial fashion, one theologian at a time, until all had spoken. Each of them might speak for a few minutes or for as long as two hours or more. The bishops listened in silence, and only after all the lectures were completed did they themselves set to work. Sometimes for weeks on end, therefore, the bishops sat as students to listen to the theologians. Once commissions were formed to construct the actual decrees, the theologians again entered the process as advisers to the bishops.

Even though theologians played an absolutely major role at Vatican II, the role was less immediately determinative than at Trent and, on an official level, much reduced. Both before and during Vatican II, the formulation of every document rested from beginning to end exclusively in the hands of the bishops working in the various commissions of the council. The bishops, of course, relied on the theologians the pope had named to the commissions. But the theologians knew and were reminded that they were present in a strictly advisory capacity and were allowed to speak only when the bishops asked their opinions. Although they had a big impact on the direction of Vatican II, they were not as closely integrated into the operating procedures of the council as they were at Trent.

When the bishops arrived at Trent in 1545, nothing had been prepared for them to help them formulate their agenda. Even so, they soon hit on the focused agenda of doctrine and reform with which we are familiar. They proposed for themselves what was essentially a narrow agenda, which meant they left many aspects of Catholic life and practice untouched. Under doctrine they would deal only with beliefs challenged by the Protestants. Under reform, they would deal only with the reform of the three traditional offices—papacy, episcopate, and pastorate.

If the agenda of Trent was limited and quite specific, the agenda of Vatican II was just the opposite. In Pope John XXIII's letter to the bishops of the world shortly after he announced the council, he asked them to send for the agenda anything they thought the council should treat. Thus the agenda was from the beginning wide open. The council itself then developed an agenda beyond the topics the bishops initially supplied. As a result, there is scarcely any aspect of church life that the final sixteen documents of Vatican II do not at least touch on.

Unlike the bishops arriving at Trent, the bishops arriving at Vatican II found some seventy-five documents or pieces of documents prepared for them and calling for action. Vatican II was the most extensively prepared council in the history of the church. It was not, however, prepared in a coordinated and coherent way. Nor was it prepared in a widely collaborative way. The reaction of the bishops once they arrived at the council was twofold: first, confusion and dismay—they felt there were drowning in a flood of paper and an infinitude of issues screaming for their attention; second, resentment—many bishops soon came to believe they were being manipulated into rubber-stamping documents they did not altogether agree with. Despite the extensive preparation, the bishops at Vatican II had a more difficult task in finding their focus than did the bishops at Trent. They began to get their bearings only at the end of the first period, December 1962.

The most profound difference between the two councils is this: they spoke in two different forms of discourse. Trent followed the pattern basically set at the first ecumenical council, Nicaea, 325. It is fair to say that when Emperor Constantine convoked Nicaea, he saw it as in some measure the ecclesiastical equivalent of the Roman Senate. The Roman Senate made laws and rendered verdicts in high-level criminal cases. It was concerned with public order in the empire. Nicaea was concerned with public order in the church, whether regarding proper teaching or proper discipline. It therefore issued laws prescribing or proscribing certain behaviors, and it heard the case against Arius, accused of the high ecclesiastical crime of spreading heresy. Laws invariably carry penalties for nonobservance, and negative verdicts in criminal cases carry even heavier penalties. Although Nicaea and later councils adopted a number of literary forms, the most prevalent was the canon, a short ordinance prescribing or proscribing some behavior. Canons commonly ended with an anathema—that is, a sentence of excommunication.

Trent followed unquestioningly in this pattern, as the number of both its doctrinal and disciplinary canons testifies. It modified considerably the traditional form of the doctrinal canons in that they did not condemn persons but only teachings. Strictly speaking, Luther, Calvin, and the other reformers were not condemned at Trent, even though in a general way it was obvious who was being condemned. Moreover, the council prefaced most of its doctrinal canons with so-called chapters—positive expositions of Catholic teaching related to the positions condemned in the canons. The council was clear, however, that the canons were the form that bore the burden of the council's teaching.

I have written extensively on the form of discourse Vatican II came to adopt. It is a subject far too complex for me to develop adequately in these few pages. Suffice it to say that when John XXIII addressed the council on its opening day, he stressed in his gentle way that the council should formulate its decision as far as possible in positive terms, so as to show the church to be, in his words, "the loving mother of all, benign, patient, full of mercy and goodness." He explicitly asked that the council as far as possible avoid issuing condemnations.

The bishops took the pope at his word and tried to do what he asked. They eventually began to see that this meant abandoning the traditional forms, especially the canon (Vatican II issued not a single one), and the adoption of form of discourse no council had ever before used or, perhaps better said, never used in such a consistent and altogether characteristic way.

Trent employed the canon because it was traditional but also because the bishops realized that exhortations, especially regarding the duty of residence, had proven insufficient. That solution had been tried for generations without success. The fact that the obligation of residence aroused such strong opposition in the council itself indicated that strong measures were needed if there was to be any hope of success. The bishops at Vatican II, on the contrary, were, except for a small minority, solidly behind the episcopal ideals presented in both *Lumen Gentium* and *Christus Dominus*. They believed they did not need to coerce support for them.

In essence Vatican II adopted and adapted a form of panegyric. Instead of prescribing or proscribing certain behaviors, it held up ideals to be striven for. A comparison between Trent's legislation on the behavior of bishops with Vatican II's Decree on the Pastoral Office of Bishops, *Christus Dominus*, illustrates the point perfectly. The former prescribes certain behaviors. The latter proposes an ideal. The former pursues its goal through threat of punishment, the latter through appeal to the bishop's conscience and goodwill.

Vatican II's style choice had profound and radical implications. It made Vatican II different not only from Trent but also from every council that preceded it. By that choice it implicitly, but powerfully and unmistakably, repudiated the Roman Senate model, and it set another in its place. The style choice made Vatican II so different that it in effect redefined what a council is and what it is expected to do. Such a redefinition, I think you will agree, is a difference of crucial importance. Failure to take account of the difference means a failure in basic hermeneutics for the council.

As I suggested earlier, even though the two councils very much differed from each other, they also had important similarities. We need, first of all, to note that on several occasions Vatican II maintained that what it was teaching was in continuity with the Council of Trent. True though that may be, it also shared certain communalities with Trent that at the time the prelates and theologians of the council did not clearly realize. I here call attention to five of them.

First, they both had to respond to a great crisis. That is obvious for the Council of Trent but generally denied for Vatican II, which is often singled out as being unusual for not having to face a crisis. In fact, however, Vatican II met in a period of profound crisis not only for the Catholic Church but for all Christian churches. It was a crisis all the more serious for being diffuse and not easy to analyze or define in a few words. Yet the crisis was real, pervasive, and far-reaching in its ramifications—perhaps the most serious and radical in the history of Christianity. We can call it, for lack of a better word, the crisis of modernity or the crisis of the modern world.

It is a crisis with roots deep in history. It was early propelled on its way by the Scientific and Industrial Revolutions but took on its sharpest characteristics in the wake of the French Revolution during the century and a half leading up to Vatican II, the period I have called "the long nineteenth century." In its official pronouncements, the church almost invariably assumed a negative stance toward every aspect of "the modern world." Yet by the time of Vatican II, it was no longer credible to maintain that stance, as the theologians and bishops at the council realized at least on some level.

"The modern world," or modernity or postmodernity, is a reality so complex as to be almost intractable! But let me name five aspects of it that are particularly pertinent to the council and that the council directly or indirectly tried to address. First is the newly urgent problem of multiculturalism. (What does this mean for a church so identified with the West as the Roman Catholic Church, especially in the postcolonial period?) Second is the newly urgent problem of religious pluralism. (Can the church credibly continue to disdain and belittle other churches and religions? Can the church take responsibility for the Holocaust?) Third is the crisis of authority produced by the most radical political and social shifts in world history. (What does this mean for a church that looks on itself and on the world as structured essentially hierarchically?) The fourth aspect is the closely related problem of the new social, economic, and cultural situations of most human beings today (urbanism, industrialism, mobility, women in the workforce, nuclear proliferation, bioethical dilemmas, and so forth). And the fifth is the emergence of a newly sharp historical consciousness, now applied in systematic fashion even to sacred subjects. (How can the church explain as apostolic truth a doctrine like the Immaculate Conception of Mary? How can the church deal with the discrediting of the classical worldview and issues like evolution?) I of course do not have space for even the most superficial discussion of these complex issues, but perhaps we can at least agree that, just as Trent faced a crisis, Vatican II did the same. Just as Trent tried to find solutions to the crisis, so did Vatican II.

The second trait the two councils have in common is a particular of the first—namely, being forced to deal with the problem of change. Trent had to deal with it because of Protestant attacks. According to the Protestant reformers, the church in its doctrine and practice was discontinuous with the apostolic past. Trent's response was, in blunt terms, to deny any discontinuity, to deny that change had occurred. That solution was no longer possible for Vatican II. To the council's credit, it addressed the question by accepting the fact of change in the church's teaching and practice. Unlike any previous council, Vatican II used the word "change" in a positive or neutral sense and went on to use words like "progress," "evolution," and especially "development."

It did not try to solve the paradoxical problem of change within continuity, but it deserves credit for facing it. In so doing, the council took an important step in qualifying the Catholic bias toward continuity to which

Trent had given impetus. Vatican II thereby provides us with a notable example of the recurring paradox of history: continuity and change are twins conjoined at birth. Under one aspect of the problem of change, Vatican II is like Trent, continuous with it, but, under another different from Trent, discontinuous with it.

The third trait the two councils share: they were both councils of reconciliation. Designating Trent a council of reconciliation requires considerable qualification and is certainly not immediately obvious. Nonetheless, it is a valid designation. Despite prejudices, skepticism, and serious missteps, the council did not give up the hope of some form of reconciliation with "the Lutherans" until almost the end—even though the reconciliation had to be on the council's terms.

For Vatican II reconciliation was more obvious and more effectively operative. When, on 25 January 1959, Pope John XXIII convoked the council, he announced as one of its aims the extension of "a renewed cordial invitation to the faithful of separated communities to participate with us in this quest for unity and grace, for which so many souls long in all parts of the world." Vatican II took up the challenge and produced two documents that are quintessentially reconciliatory: the Decree on Ecumenism, *Unitatis Redintegratio*, and the Declaration on the Relation of the Church to Non-Christian Religions, *Nostra Aetate*. But those two documents are symptomatic of the wider reconciliatory dynamic of Vatican II that extended to all five of those features I singled out as characteristic of the contemporary world. The final document of the council, *Gaudium et Spes*, is appropriately titled the "Pastoral Constitution on the Church in the Modern World." In it the council affirmed not only that the church helps the world and teaches it but also, most remarkably, that the world likewise helps and teaches the church. The document was addressed to "the whole of humanity" and sought to enlist all persons of goodwill in the mission of peace and harmony. Vatican II tried to make categorical repudiation of "the modern world" a thing of the past.

The fourth trait is much more concrete and more easily named and identified than the first three. Both councils dealt with the relationship between the papacy and the episcopate, especially when the bishops are acting together in collegial fashion in a council. Not only did they both deal with it, but in both councils it provoked major crises. Although at Trent the legates did all in their power to keep the problem from coming to the surface, they could not keep it from obliquely but unmistakably doing so. This issue underlay the problem of enforcing episcopal residency, and therefore it perforce had to raise its ugly head. During the third period it brought on the council its most dramatic crisis, which lasted for ten long months. Cardinal Giovanni Morone was finally able to broker a compromise, but a compromise that satisfied neither party. Although the compromise allowed the council to move forward and complete its agenda, it left the theoretical problem unaddressed and unsolved. The final documents of the council betray not the slightest suggestion that papal authority was a crucial, persistent, and divisive issue at the Council of Trent.

Vatican II tried to face the problem squarely with its teaching on episcopal collegiality in the third chapter of *Lumen Gentium.* Despite the fact that the teaching won overwhelming approval, a small minority continued to oppose it and in various ways eviscerate it of its effectiveness as an institution of church governance. As in Trent, this problem again and again provoked crises. At Vatican II the crises were resolved more swiftly than at Trent but just as unsatisfactorily.

The fifth trait is similarly concrete and easily identified: they both wanted to reform the Roman Curia. At the time of the Council of Trent, the reform of the curia was already a problem of long standing in the church that grew acute during the crisis of the Great Western Schism. It was high, therefore, on the agenda of both the Council of Constance and the Council of Basel. When Luther made it a major issue in his "Appeal to the German Nobility" in 1520, he cataloged in particularly provocative and exaggerated terms grievances that had become commonplaces.

No surprise, therefore, that reform of the curia was on the agenda at Trent. Like Constance and Basel, Trent wanted to simplify the lifestyle of the cardinals in the curia, eliminate their practice of amassing huge fortunes by holding multiple, incompatible benefices, abolish the practice of quid-pro-quo granting of dispensations and similar favors, curtail the naming of teenagers as cardinals, and, finally, force the cardinal bishops to reside in their dioceses just as other bishops were required to do. There was a deeper grievance, even though it never got officially articulated. It was the control over the council exercised by a group of curial cardinals the pope gathered to review the council's deliberations and decisions and thereby to control the council's freedom of action. The Council of Trent had only limited success in remedying these problems.

Nonetheless, by the time of Vatican II, no cardinals in the curia were holding multiple benefices or amassing huge personal fortunes. No teenagers were being nominated as cardinals—in fact, the very opposite had become a problem! But the control the curia tried to exercise over the bishops and, more specifically, over the council itself had not gone away. During the first period of Vatican II, the autumn of 1962, the resentment the bishops felt toward the curia almost reached a boiling point, and by the end of the period many bishops were determined to put its reform high on the agenda when the council reconvened the next year. Bishops began to speak openly about the complete abolition of the Supreme Congregation of the Holy Office of the Roman Inquisition.

Pope Paul VI defused the tension when, a few months after his election and just before the council reconvened, he addressed the curia. He told its members that reform was necessary and they should expect it. He reassured them by saying that he himself, with their cooperation, would undertake it. In so doing, he eliminated the possibility that the issue would come to the floor of the council. In effect, he removed it from the council's agenda.

Paul VI subsequently made changes but certainly not changes as radical as some members of the council thought were needed. For instance, the cry for the elimination of the Holy Office went unheeded. Paul renamed it the Congregation for the Doctrine of the Faith (CDF) and made other changes, but in time the CDF began to function more or less as it always had. It is not surprising, therefore, that in our own day we once again hear a great deal about the reform of the curia. *Curia semper reformanda.*

* * *

Two councils, two radically different eras, two very different sets of problems—yet the two councils unmistakably display the paradox of being both markedly discontinuous with each other and markedly continuous. They nicely illustrate the paradox of history, where *la longue durée* is constantly pitted against the obtrusive reality of change. We do not resolve the paradox by taking easy refuge in one or the other. *Plus ça change, plus c'est la même chose.* Vatican II was certainly not *la même chose*, the same thing, as the Council of Trent.

However, certain patterns recur in history. Our two councils clearly illustrate several such recurrences. Moreover, they teach us the important lesson that reform of any institution, especially one with such a long, rich, and complex history as the Catholic Church is not a task easily accomplished. Nor is it a task accomplished once and for all. In that regard it is like the reform of life to which Christians believe they are daily called. Reform, whether of an institution or of one's personal life, is an ongoing project.

Part III

The Church at Large

14

SOME BASICS ABOUT CELIBACY

The obligation of celibacy imposed on priests of the Roman Rite of the Catholic Church has from time to time been the object of great controversy, beginning with the Gregorian Reform of the eleventh century. The next serious outburst of controversy occurred in the sixteenth century with the Reformation. After a long period of relative quiescence, the issue reappeared when the sex-abuse scandals broke into the news, first in Boston in 2002. This time it was not so much an object of controversy as of curiosity and concern. Was there a relationship between priestly celibacy and sexual abuse? The editor of America magazine asked me to put the issue into historical perspective, and he published this article on 28 October 2002.

Before this year many American Catholics probably had never heard of, and surely had never used, the word "celibacy." But in the wake of the sex-abuse scandals, it has appeared so often in newspapers and journals and been heard so often on radio and television that it no longer can be classified as an unusual term. Yet, despite its current popularity, the word still seems a little mysterious. Even more mysterious is why and how the celibate state became a requirement for ordination to the diaconate, priesthood, and episcopacy in the Western Church. With sound-bite explanations and dips into church history, the media have tried to deal with it, but often with confusing results.

What I hope to do is provide the most basic information required to speak intelligently about celibacy. Much will be familiar to readers of this journal. I make no claim to originality or new insight, which in the present agitated context is probably a virtue, and I will use traditional categories of Catholic theology and asceticism. I divide what I have to say into two unequal parts. I will first provide six points of clarification. That way there will be less danger of confusion concerning what we are talking about. I will then review, all too briefly, the history of the issue in the Western Church, so that we have a better idea of how we got to where we are. That is the extent of my agenda; expect nothing more.

We need to begin by being clear about the meaning of the word. Celibate means unmarried. It signifies that state of life. In Romance languages the equivalent term, when applied to men (e.g., *celebe* in Italian), means bachelor. Sometimes in North America people use celibacy, however, as if it were a synonym for chastity or to indicate abstention from sexual activity—"I've been celibate for two months." That is incorrect and confusing usage.

Chastity is a virtue required of all men and women according to their state of life; it is opposed to the vice of lust. When we speak of priestly celibacy, the virtue of chastity is of course implied, but in this instance the virtue is assumed to give shape and spiritual meaning to that state in an especially enhancing way. Nonetheless, the virtue of chastity is distinct from the state of being unmarried. As will become clear below, celibacy must also be carefully distinguished from continence.

Second, the requirement of the celibate state for ordination is an ecclesiastical discipline, a ruling by the church for the church. To put it negatively, the requirement of celibacy is not a doctrine or dogma. It is not, as such, a "teaching." The media have in fact been fairly clear on this aspect of the issue, but it still needs to be mentioned. As a discipline, the requirement of celibacy is something that can change, has changed, and might in the future change. A few scholars argue, however, that while the discipline concerning celibacy may be subject to change, the tradition of continence for married deacons, priests, and bishops is of apostolic origin. If that is true, the church would feel less free to change. Nonetheless, the Second Vatican Council introduced the order of "permanent deacons," who might be married and, if so, are permitted to continue to have conjugal relations with their wives. It specifically determined, however, that these deacons could not go on to priestly ordination.

Third, while this is a discipline or law, the official approach today, as indicated in the new Code of Canon Law, promulgated in 1983, recognizes chaste celibacy as a charism, a special gift from God. The church ordains only those who have received this charism. It thus does not so much impose celibacy as invite to ordination those who have the gift.

Fourth, as a requirement for ordination, celibacy is peculiar to the Western Church (or Latin rite). Other churches in union with Rome (Ukrainian, Melkite, and others) have in this regard different disciplines whose origins reach far back into their traditions. They allow married clergy, but with certain restrictions, especially for ordination to the episcopate.

This means—and this is my fifth point—that even today there are priests from churches in full communion with Rome, hence fully Catholic, who are married. There are therefore legitimately married priests in the Catholic Church. The steady opposition of the American Latin-rite hierarchy to the presence of married Eastern Catholic priests in North America has generally prevented married clergy from those churches serving here. This policy was formalized in 1929 with the Vatican decree *Cum Data Fuerit.* In recent years some bishops in the Ukrainian and Ruthenian Catholic Churches in North America have not altogether followed this policy. Moreover, there are in the United States a small number of former Anglican priests, married, who have converted to Catholicism and are now legitimately functioning as Roman Catholic priests. They are not obliged to observe continence with their spouses.

Finally, we must clearly distinguish between the discipline of celibacy that is required of (almost) all priests of the Latin rite and the vow of chastity freely undertaken by priests (and others) who are members of religious orders. For the priests in religious orders, the vow fits into the triad of chastity, poverty, and obedience, which in principle commits them to a more total availability for ministry or, in the case of monk priests, for the worship of God. There is considerable confusion today about this distinction, with even some high ecclesiastics speaking as if the diocesan clergy had pronounced the traditional three vows, with all they imply. The members of religious orders also live together in community, which in practice has precluded wives and children. Even if the discipline of celibacy should be changed to allow diocesan priests to marry, priests who are members of religious orders, by definition and by their own choice, would not marry.

With those basics in place, we can turn to the history of celibacy in the Western Church. There are three crucial moments—the fourth, the eleventh, and the sixteenth centuries. But since the New Testament is the basis for Christian life and belief, a word must be said about it. Although the practice of celibacy was not common in ancient Judaism, it appears that some Essenes and the Therapeuticae, members of Jewish religious sects who lived a communal life analogous to that of later Christian monks, were celibate.

There is no suggestion in Jewish or Christian sources that either John the Baptist or Jesus was married. At least there is no mention of a wife or children for either man. Indeed, celibacy undertaken "for the sake of the kingdom of heaven" (Mt. 19:12) fits well with what we know to have been the focus of Jesus's life and preaching. Peter was certainly married, since Mark tells us he had a mother-in-law (1:29–31). And Paul claims in 1 Corinthians 9:5 that Cephas (usually interpreted as another name for Peter) was accompanied by his wife on his apostolic journeys. We know nothing about the marital status of the rest of "the Twelve."

In 1 Corinthians 7, Paul holds up virginity, continence, and celibacy as Christian ideals. For him, writing in an eschatological context while awaiting the Second Coming, these practices were aids toward a more fervent consecration to God. Paul even concludes that one "who refrains from marriage will do better" (7:38). He was careful, however, to insist that they were gifts from God and were not granted to everyone. When Paul wrote his letters, he was not married and affirms that he was celibate. But, on the basis of 1 Corinthians 7:8 ("To the unmarried and the widows I say that it is well for them to remain unmarried as I am"), some interpreters argue that Paul had been married and was now a widower. The First Letter to Timothy directs that "bishops" (3:2) and "deacons" (3:12) be "married only once." Whether this stipulation forbade polygamy or remarriage after a spouse's death has been debated among exegetes for many years.

Beginning with the third century, there is indisputable evidence that even in the West many priests and bishops in good standing were married. The following list of bishops is but a small sample that I have randomly selected: Passivus, bishop of Fermo; Cassius, bishop of Narni; Aetherius, bishop of Vienne; Aquilinus, bishop of Évreux; Faron, bishop of Meaux; Magnus, bishop of Avignon. Filibaud, bishop of Aire-sur-l'Adour, was the father of St. Philibert de Jumiäges, and Sigilaicus, bishop of Tours, was the father of St. Cyran of Brenne. The father of Pope Damasus I (366–384) was a bishop. Pope Felix III (483–492), whose father was almost certainly a priest, was the great-great-grandfather of Pope Gregory I the Great (590–604). Pope Hormisdas (514–523) was the father of Pope Silverius (536–537).

Being a married man with children was obviously no obstacle to the episcopacy or even to the papacy. We know for certain that one of the great fathers of the church, St. Hilary, bishop of Poitiers (315–368), who was declared a doctor of the church in 1851 by Pope Pius IX, was married and had a daughter named Apra. It is thus clear that during the patristic era and into the early Middle Ages, celibacy, as such, was not in force.

Celibacy is one thing; continence another. Until the fourth century no law was promulgated concerning clerical marriage or clerical continence after marriage for those in major orders who were already married when ordained. But we know that by that time clerical renunciation of marriage was not rare, nor was the practice of living apart from their wives by those who were married before ordination. There is no way of estimating how many conformed to this behavior, but it is clear that in some places it was considered normative and traditional.

We cannot underestimate, however, the dramatic change in status for all Christians that Constantine's recognition of Christianity early in that century brought with it. It gave fuel to a sometimes fierce asceticism, as Christians now withdrew into the desert from a world that had become too friendly. This period marks the beginning of Christian monasticism. With the age of the martyrs over, Christians had to have other means of following Christ to the limits and laying down their lives for him. With St. Jerome (345–420), as well as many others, virginity for those espoused to Christ began to be extolled with new fervor and consistency. But these ideas and ideals were by no means new for Christians.

In any case, many things changed for Christians as they "emerged from the catacombs" in the fourth century. Among these changes was the beginning of legislation concerning our subject. Around the year 305, nineteen bishops assembled from various parts of Spain for the Council of Elvira (near Granada). Also in attendance, but not voting, were twenty-four priests and a number of deacons and laypeople. The council promulgated eighty-one disciplinary decrees. Canon 33 is the one that concerns us, for it is chronologically the first of a long series of legislative measures extending down to the present dealing with the subject of marriage and the clergy. The text reads, "It has seemed good absolutely to forbid the bishops, the priests, and the deacons, i.e., all the clerics in the service of the ministry, to have relations with their wives and procreate children; should anyone do so, let him be excluded from the honor of the clergy."

The decree takes for granted that some clerics will be married. What is prohibited is for them to have conjugal relations with their wives. The decree thus concerns continence, not celibacy. It seems likely that the decree was meant to deal with infractions of what was considered normative rather than to initiate some new practice. If the contrary were the case in such a serious and potentially disruptive matter, we could certainly expect some reasons to be given for the change. But there are none. By the end of the century, the Council of Carthage (390) would justify its almost identical prohibition with the claim it was legislating only "what the Apostles taught and what antiquity itself observed." There is, however, one thing that is certainly new about canon 33 of the Council of Elvira: it made a practice or tradition into a law, violations of which would be punished.

In any case, from the early fourth century forward, councils, popes, and bishops issued a number of decrees enjoining continence on married men who had been ordained to the diaconate, priesthood, or episcopacy. That is the orientation of the church in the West through the patristic period into the Middle Ages. There was no prohibition against married men being ordained. There were, however, plenty of laws, letters, and exhortations enjoining continence. (It is interesting to note that the "Synod in Trullo" or "Quinisext" Council, 691–692, held in Constantinople, explicitly repudiated in canon 13 the "Roman" custom of requiring continence. The Western Church, however, never received [read: accepted] the canons of this council or considered it ecumenical.)

What lay behind this insistence on continence for married clergy? That is a question not easy to answer. In general, there were four motivations that seemed to be operative all at once, singly, or in some combination. The first was the conviction that continence for those ministering at the altar was traditional, with at least some commentators believing the tradition was of apostolic origin. That conviction was itself sufficient for insisting without question on its observance. Second, the practice was often explained by arguing for the total dedication required in the minister of the sacraments and by arguing that an incontinent cleric could not urge virgins and widows to continence. The argument from ritual purity, with allusions to Old Testament precedents, also appears frequently in the sources. Finally, as is clear from a curious decree of Emperor Justinian in 528, some Christians were concerned that bishops would squander on their wives and children resources given the church for worship and for the aid of the poor. This last, however, is in these centuries a relatively infrequent and subdued theme.

Although the context would be radically different, these four arguments are fundamentally the ones that the Gregorian reformers of the eleventh century would borrow and develop. The second decisive moment comes with those reformers. The Gregorian Reform, also known as the Investiture Controversy, was one of the greatest turning points in the history of the church in the West. From the fourth century onward, the gradual incursion of the "barbarian" tribes into the West had transformed the structures of the Roman Empire and gradually weakened them. Bishops began to take over more and more civic duties, including the military defense of cities. The situation deteriorated badly, as Europe entered "the Dark Ages." Although Charlemagne was able in the ninth century to establish some semblance of centralized order, his accomplishments were soon dissipated by internal dissensions and attacks from the outside by Vikings, Magyars, and Moors. Despite all, society began to recover in the late tenth and early eleventh centuries, and with recovery came a yearning to reestablish proper order.

Two interlocking abuses among the clergy shocked reformers in the eleventh century: simony and incontinence—that is, clergy living openly with their wives or in concubinage. These abuses were related because clerical offices, like bishoprics, were sometimes being sold to the highest bidder, no matter what his morals, or being passed on, with their considerable revenues, from father to son.

With the gradual recovery of society in the eleventh century came recovery of substantial collections of canon law from the patristic period. For thirty-five years beginning in 1049, a series of energetic popes emerged who were determined to set things right. Their principal weapon was the canonical collections that provided them with their blueprint for how society and church were to be ordered. These collections included many documents from the patristic period related to our subject. The popes launched a program of reform that, in the name of restoring the authentic past, created something entirely new, especially a papacy with claims of authority far exceeding in theory and practice anything that had preceded it. The reform reached its culmination with Pope Gregory VII (1073–1085), one of the most important popes in the history of the papacy. The reform movement is named after him.

The movement began, however, with the more modest, though still formidable, goal of bringing the behavior of the clergy into line with the reformers' interpretation of the ancient canons. To that extent, it was a holiness movement. In the wake of the Gregorians' efforts, the law of celibacy began to emerge in much the form we know it today—that is, as a prohibition against ordaining married men and entering the married state after ordination. The very first of "the Gregorians," Pope Leo IX (1049–1054), for instance, presided along with the German emperor at a synod in Mainz in 1049 that condemned "the evil of clerical marriage"— *nefanda sacerdotum coniugia*. If this prohibition is to be understood as somehow qualified for those already married before ordination, the limitation is not clear from the text itself.

The focus of the reformers was, however, more in accord with the older tradition in that they insisted on continence—absolutely. Along with other sanctions for incontinent priests, they forbade the laity to assist at the Masses of priests they knew were not conforming to the requirement. They found a good argument for their ideals in canon 3 of the Council of Nicaea (325), which forbade clerics in major orders to have any women in their households except their mothers, sisters, or aunts. They interpreted the canon, incorrectly, as a prohibition of marriage.

With the passage of time, the absolute prohibition of marriage assumed ever greater prominence and gradually became accepted by a seeming majority of lay magnates and the upper clergy as the tradition of the church. In 1059 St. Peter Damian, a cardinal and one of the most effective spokesmen for the Gregorian program, wrote his book *On the Celibacy of Priests* (*De Coelibatu Sacerdotum*), which by its very title helped promote this trend and give prominence to the word itself.

But no aspect of the Gregorians' program went uncontested, including this one. Otto, the bishop of Constance, refused to enforce with his own clergy Gregory VII's directives regarding clerics and women. When Bishop Altmann of Passau tried, on the contrary, to implement the reforms, the clergy attacked him and, with the help of imperial troops, drove him out of his diocese. A cleric, probably Ulrich, the bishop of Imola, took up his pen about 1060 in a defense of clerical marriage that assumed conjugal relations after the ordination of the spouse. Ulrich's

"Rescript" influenced other writings in the same vein that continued to appear into the twelfth century. But by the time of the Second Lateran Council (1139), the Gregorians had substantially achieved their aims in this regard and won widespread support for them from lay and ecclesiastical leaders.

Some five hundred bishops gathered for Lateran II. Canons 6 and 7 of that council forbade all those in major orders (now including subdeacons) from taking wives and forbade the faithful from assisting at the Masses of priests they knew to have wives or concubines. These two decrees represent a culmination of the reform movement, and, although they might still be interpreted in the older sense of prohibiting marriage after ordination, they came to be understood as absolute prohibitions. From this time until the Reformation, the prohibition of marriage for all clerics in major orders began to be taken simply for granted. That does not mean the prohibition was necessarily observed.

The third decisive moment came in the sixteenth century with the Reformation. Since Luther and the other reformers found no justification for celibacy in the New Testament, they denounced it as just one more restriction on Christian liberty imposed by the tyrant in Rome. Luther also argued that celibacy was responsible for the debauchery of the clergy that he found prevalent. He and the other reformers all married. Although the question of married clergy was not at the center of the Reformation agenda, it in fact gave that agenda an institutional grounding that would serve it well. These ministers would be a powerful force resisting reconciliation with the traditional church until they could be assured it meant they could bring their wives and children with them as they continued to exercise their ministry.

The Reformation was certainly the most massive frontal attack that the traditions of clerical celibacy and continence had ever received. It had to be answered. The Council of Trent (1545–1563) finally took up the matter in the final period (1562–1563) of its eighteen-year history. The theologians deputed to deal with it were divided in their opinions, with a few of them maintaining that celibacy for the clergy was of divine law and could not be abrogated, but most of them held more moderate opinions. The matter was further complicated by political pressure from German Emperor Ferdinand and Albrecht V, duke of Bavaria, both devout Catholics who wanted celibacy abrogated. If that were not possible, they wanted a dispensation from it for their own territories. On 24 July 1562, for instance, Sigismund Baumgartner, a layman and the ambassador of the duke to the council, spoke at length before the bishops arguing precisely along those lines.

The decrees and canons of the Council of Trent run to almost three hundred pages in a standard English translation. The council in several places touched on issues related to our subject, as when canon 10 of session 24 condemned the opinion that marriage was better than virginity or celibacy. It issued, however, only one brief canon, a paragraph, that addressed this burning matter directly (canon 9, session 24). That canon is notably cautious. It makes no assertions about the origins of the tradition, about its importance, or about its necessity. It simply condemns three opinions concerning celibacy: first, that clerics in major orders and religious priests who have made a solemn vow of chastity can validly contract marriage; second, that the regulation of celibacy is a disparagement of marriage; and third, that those who, after making a solemn vow of celibacy, cannot observe it are free to contract marriage.

The canon obliquely reaffirms the discipline of celibacy, but it does not do so explicitly and directly. It left open the possibility of exceptions and dispensations. German leaders continued, in fact, to press their case with Pope Pius IV after the conclusion of the council. The pope, under pressure from King Philip II of Spain to stand firm, submitted the matter to a consistory of cardinals. His successor, Pope Pius V (1566–1572), left no doubt that the matter was definitively closed.

In the centuries between then and now the issue occasionally surfaced again, especially during the French Revolution, but by and large it has been quiescent within Catholicism until quite recently. Canon 132 of the Code of Canon Law of 1918 stated, "Clerics in major orders may not marry and they are bound by the obligation of chastity to the extent that sinning against it constitutes a sacrilege." Although a few bishops at Vatican II (1962–1965) advocated abrogating or modifying the law, Pope Paul VI in 1965 prevented it from being formally discussed at the council. In the code of 1983, the one currently in effect, the law of celibacy was reformulated in canon 277, which echoes themes that have recurred in the history of the issue: "Clerics are obliged to observe perfect and perpetual continence for the sake of the kingdom of heaven and therefore are obliged to observe celibacy, which is a special gift of God, by which sacred ministers can adhere more easily to Christ with an undivided heart and can more freely dedicate themselves to the service of God and humankind."

15

WERE MEDIEVAL
UNIVERSITIES CATHOLIC?

In the United States, presidents of universities that call themselves Catholic often have to defend their institution from the accusation that they have gone secular and no longer deserve the name. Bishops have raised this question, sometimes in threatening ways, and the Holy See itself has from time to time set down norms for universities to follow to ensure their Catholic character. Sometimes behind these efforts lurks a mistaken myth about the origins of universities in the thirteenth century and the nature of their Catholic character. In this article published in America *magazine, 27 September 2012, I deal with that myth and try to dispel misapprehensions about the universities of the Middle Ages. The issue deserves much more detailed treatment than it receives here, but I believe I have been able to show how medieval universities, including the University of Paris, differ from the pious image often projected on them today.*

Perhaps the greatest and most enduring achievement of the Middle Ages was the creation of the university, an institution for which there was no precedent in the history of the West. It sprang into existence seemingly out of nowhere in the late twelfth century primarily in two cities, Paris and Bologna. Both claim to be Europe's first. By the early decades of the thirteenth century, others had emerged modeled on them—Oxford on the Paris model and Padua on Bologna. From that point forward, universities proliferated across the face of Europe and became a standard, important, and self-governing institution in larger cities.

Medieval universities, although they differed among themselves in significant ways, all quickly developed highly sophisticated procedures and organizational strategies that we recognize as our own today. The list is long: set curricula, examinations, professorial privileges and duties, a full array of officers of various kinds, division into different "faculties" (we call them schools), and the public certification of professional competence through the awarding of degrees.

The invention of degrees was particularly important. A man could practice medicine without a university degree (and the vast majority of doctors did so), but with a degree he enjoyed greater prestige and could exact higher fees. He was a professional with documentation to prove he had passed the scrutiny of his peers. A university degree spelled upward socioeconomic mobility, whether in the church or in society at large.

In the Middle Ages there were four university faculties—law, medicine, theology, and arts. The first three trained young men aspiring to distinction in a profession. Theology, we must remember, was a professional subject like law and medicine. Not a single course in it, therefore, was taught in the other three faculties. (For that matter, neither was a course in catechism.) Theology was not, therefore, considered one of the liberal arts. A degree in theology qualified an individual for a university chair (or its equivalent in religious orders), which would enable the holder to teach others pursuing such a career. It might also commend him as a candidate for a bishop's miter, although a degree in canon law might better commend him.

The arts faculty was the entry faculty where one learned the basic skills of the trivium and quadrivium. As Aristotle's works on physics, metaphysics, the heavens, animals, and other subjects were translated into Latin, they began to dominate the arts curriculum. This faculty thus evolved, especially in Italy, into a professional school where the cultivation of natural philosophy gradually took precedence over the other branches and became the seedbed for modern science. The professors of natural philosophy drew better salaries, attracted more students, and enjoyed greater prestige than professors of metaphysics.

Not all universities had all four faculties. Even when they did, the faculties were not equal in strength and prestige. Bologna was renowned for law. It had been founded by wealthy students intent on a career in law who banded together to form a university to hire experts to teach them. Bologna did not have a theological faculty until 1364, nearly two centuries after its founding. Even then the faculty consisted essentially in a kind of consortium of the "houses of study" of the religious orders in the city. Most large Italian universities had only one or two professors of theology and one or two of metaphysics in a professorate of fifty to one hundred. Instead, they were renowned for law, medicine, and, in time, natural philosophy.

The pattern was different in universities in northern Europe, where theology was strong and law and medicine weak or nonexistent. What is important to recognize for both northern and southern universities, however, is that the faculties operated independently of one another and communicated with one another only on the most formal level.

They all, however, had the same scope: intellectual problem solving through the acquisition of professional skills. Intellectual problem solving was perhaps nowhere more evident than in the arts and theology faculties because of their appropriation of dialectics (disputation or debate) as central to their method. Logical, left-brain, agonistic, analytic, restless, and relentless questioning was the method's hallmark, in which the resolution of every question led only to further questions. It is no wonder that virtually all the heretics from the thirteenth until the sixteenth century were Scholastic theologians; their very method led them into asking questions that challenged received wisdom.

When today Catholic educators and prelates speak of the origin of Catholic universities, they locate them in the Middle Ages. Although such talk is rarely free of an idealized vision of the "ages of faith," it is, in this instance, not unreasonable. Catholicism permeated medieval culture. It therefore permeated the culture of the universities. Faculty and students were all Catholics. Many universities held papal charters. Theology enjoyed an uncontested place among the disciplines in some universities.

But would medieval universities satisfy the norms held up today to qualify as "authentically Catholic"? A composite profile of such norms drawn from such documents as *Ex Corde Ecclesiae* would look something like this: the university explicitly professes the Catholic faith, is unquestioning of the magisterium, installs theology as a core subject, contributes to "the common good" of the church and of society at large, and professedly fosters the students' moral and religious formation as well as their commitment to the church. A Catholic university is a religious university.

One difficulty in answering the question is that medieval universities, unlike many universities in the United States today, did not issue mission statements. Unlike the humanist schools that developed later, they did not profess to operate out of a clearly articulated philosophy of education. They just did what they did. And what they did was engage in intellectual problem solving, which entailed the development of professional skills that led to career advancement. Intellectual problem solving and career advancement were the core values of the medieval university. They are secular values, identical to the values operative in today's secular universities.

Without a mission statement, there was no way for the medieval university to profess that it was concerned, for instance, with the common good or with the students' religious and moral development. In fact, the medieval university, as such, took no systemic measures to deal with such concerns. That does not mean that in the university milieu these concerns did not find expression. Although the medieval university made no provision for the morals of its students, residences of various kinds officially or unofficially affiliated with it took on this task in some cases. The Collège de Montaigu at the University of Paris, where in succession Erasmus, Calvin, and St. Ignatius of Loyola lived as students, was famous (or notorious) for the discipline it imposed.

Even though the university as such did not concern itself with "the common good," the theological faculties in northern Europe took on at least one such task. They became the self-appointed guardians of orthodoxy, not in the least shy about condemning those who deviated from the orthodox standards of the day. These faculties, rather than obeying the magisterium (a thoroughly modern concept), *were* the magisterium. The faculties of Cologne and Louvain, for instance, condemned Luther before the papacy did.

Were medieval universities Catholic universities? It is a question easier to ask than to answer. One thing, however, is certain: the contemporary grid for an "authentically Catholic" university does not neatly fit the medieval reality. There are even grounds for asserting that in their core values, medieval universities more closely resemble the contemporary secular university than they do today's Catholic model. If we are looking

for historical precedents for that model, we do not find them clearly in the
Middle Ages.

16

EXCOMMUNICATING POLITICIANS

American bishops were much in the news after 2002 as the sex-abuse scandal broke, but they were at about the same time also in the news because of the uncompromising stand some of them took on legislation or potential legislation, especially regarding abortion. They threatened various sanctions against politicians who supported such legislation. I was once again asked by the editor of America *magazine to provide a historical perspective. The article appeared on 27 September 2004. Although the issue seems somewhat to have lost its urgency, it still occasionally rears its head.*

Denying Communion to politicians because of their voting records or policy decisions, as has been done recently by a few American bishops, has caught the attention of the nation. Withholding Communion is not the same thing as excommunication in the strict sense. Church practice has allowed even an ordinary parish pastor to deny Communion to "notorious public sinners." The classic example of such a sinner is a madam who runs a bordello in a small town, where her profession is known to everybody. Whether or not the political figures being denied Communion today fit into this category I leave to others to judge. The bishops' actions do raise the question, however, of how the church has traditionally dealt with political figures who in one way or another have run afoul of the church, or at least of churchmen.

The best-known instances of formal action against such figures are excommunications, of which church history provides some spectacular examples. At least up until the nineteenth and most especially the twentieth century, the culprits have been monarchs or their officials—not, as is the case today, elected officeholders. But despite that major discrepancy between past and present, it might be instructive to review some major excommunications. They can help us frame our situation today. They may perhaps also serve as cautionary tales.

Despite the excommunications that grab our attention in history books, we need to realize that, given the potential for conflict in how the church and the state relate to each other, political excommunications have been relatively rare. The first clear instance that I know of did not occur until the latter part of the eleventh century: the excommunication (and deposition) of Emperor Henry IV by Pope Gregory VII. The reasons for the relative rarity of this form of punishment are many. The self-interest of both parties is certainly one of them. The punishment disrupts the smooth functioning of society, which is obviously a desideratum for both church and state. It also often puts the faithful in quandaries that the church has wanted to avoid whenever possible. Until recent centuries, moreover, high churchmen and magnates were drawn for the most part from the same social class and had the same or a similar education in the "classics," especially of Latin literature, where moderation, forbearance, and the settling of disputes through negotiation were consistently held up as ideals. Most important, excommunication was the ultimate sanction, to be used only in the most extreme cases.

The best-known instances from the patristic era of episcopal confrontation with a political figure involved St. Ambrose, archbishop of Milan, and Emperor Theodosius I, known as the Great. We sometimes read that Ambrose excommunicated Theodosius, but that is not precisely the case, at least not as we understand excommunication today. In 388 the Christians at Callinicum on the Euphrates sacked and burned the Jewish synagogue there. They did this with the encouragement of their bishop. Theodosius ordered the bishop to restore the synagogue at his own expense. Ambrose vehemently opposed this order on the grounds that, in rebuilding the synagogue, Christians would be committing an act of apostasy. When Theodosius appeared for Mass in the cathedral in Milan, Ambrose denounced him publicly and refused to continue celebrating the

Eucharist until the emperor on the spot retracted the order. Theodosius acquiesced.

When two years later a rioting mob in Thessalonika murdered a high-ranking general, the enraged emperor gave orders that citizens of the town up to a fixed number were to be killed. A great many people, perhaps as many as seven thousand, were slaughtered in a blood orgy that lasted for three hours. Almost immediately Theodosius seems to have regretted what he did. In any case, for this serious crime Ambrose wrote a strong letter to the emperor and later claimed that the emperor had done public penance for the atrocity he committed. Different versions of the story began to circulate about precisely what happened in this affair, but that much is certain.

The stories about Ambrose's confrontations with Theodosius later gave ample warrant to bishops and popes who decided drastic action against rulers was needed. Gregory VII explicitly adduced that "excommunication" as a precedent for his real excommunication of Emperor Henry IV in 1076 and for his second excommunication of him in 1081. Henry, it has to be said, was not a nice man. He defied Gregory's insistence that bishops be canonically elected, not appointed by Henry, and he flaunted his actions in ways Gregory could hardly ignore. Such elections were the primary plank in the so-called Gregorian Reform that Gregory was spearheading. It was a plank that no ruler in the Middle Ages, surely not the headstrong Henry, was prepared to accept without considerable qualification.

Gregory had to defend his actions because his critics, including some of the bishops who supported his program, protested that Gregory's actions were a novelty in ecclesiastical procedures. In any case, those actions led to a bloody civil war in Germany and, once Henry triumphed there, to his descending on Italy with his troops and laying siege to Rome. This resulted in one of the worst sacks in the history of the city and drove Gregory into exile, where he died shortly thereafter. The successors of both Gregory and Henry later worked out a compromise, which in different ways more or less prevailed in Catholic Christendom into the nineteenth century. In essence, the compromise gave both church and state a voice in the selection of prelates, with both the church and the state having the equivalent of a veto over the other's choice.

Whether or not there was earlier precedent for what Gregory did, his actions provided clear precedent for subsequent popes. Both Gregory IX

and Innocent IV excommunicated Emperor Frederick II. They laid numerous charges against the emperor, many of which were justified, but
they especially feared his military and political might in central Italy,
where he encroached on the territory of the Papal States. Frederick, perhaps the most formidable enemy the medieval popes ever faced, holds the
dubious distinction of being the subject of a long decree of an ecumenical
council, Lyons I (1245). The decree lays out his crimes in great detail.
Frederick conveniently died shortly afterward, before he could do even
more harm.

Boniface VIII's conflict with King Philip IV of France in the late
fourteenth century is as well known to medievalists as earlier popes'
conflicts with Henry and with Frederick. Boniface was impetuous and
imperious; Philip calculating and devious. The conflict began with Boniface's objection to the secular power's imposing taxes on the clergy in
violation of canon law, but it soon devolved into a test of wills, especially
after the king ordered the arrest of a French bishop on charges of blasphe-
my, heresy, and treason. In the face of Boniface's vehement objections to
the king's violation of canon law and his manipulation of the French
episcopacy, Philip rightly began to suspect the pope was preparing to
excommunicate him. He retaliated by calling for the deposition of the
pope, accusing him of atheism, of sodomy, of demon worship, and,
among still other things, of declaring he would "rather be a dog or an ass
than a Frenchman." Meanwhile, two high-placed henchmen of the king
broke into the papal palace at Anagni south of Rome and threatened the
pope with physical harm. By a stroke of luck, they could not carry out
their plan, but the pope, old and infirm, died shortly afterward, surely in
part because of the shock. The two royal ministers who attacked the pope
were almost immediately excommunicated, but the king never was.

The affair thus ended badly for Boniface—indeed, for the church.
Confusion and dissension ensued in the papal curia and during the next
two conclaves. This situation prepared the way for the seventy-year residence of the popes in Avignon, the papal enclave in southern France. For
as long as Philip lived he continued to demand that Boniface be posthu-
mously put on trial for heresy and other crimes. Despite the king's insistence, the trial never took place. The Avignon residency set the stage,
nonetheless, for the Great Western Schism later in the fourteenth and
early fifteenth centuries, when two, and then three, men claimed to be the
legitimate pope.

The excommunications of King Henry VIII of England by Pope Clement VII in 1533 and of Queen Elizabeth I by Pius V in 1570 are perhaps the best-known cases. The pope had for several years threatened Henry with excommunication if he did not take back his first wife, Catherine, but by the time of the actual pronouncement against the king, there were, of course, other reasons for the action. The excommunication of Elizabeth and the explicit releasing of her subjects from their oath of loyalty to their sovereign were largely motivated by the hope that these actions would lead to the deposition of the queen. It had, of course, just the opposite effect. It created an upswing of support for Elizabeth against the interference of a foreign power and made the situation of Catholics in England almost impossible, as they had to choose between their country and their religion.

A somewhat similar dilemma faced Italians in the nineteenth century, when efforts to unify the country led to the seizure of the Papal States, beginning in 1860, and of Rome itself in 1870. Pope Pius IX and his advisers were not only adamantly opposed to these measures but also believed, quite correctly, that some leaders of the movement, especially Camillo Cavour, had further plans for lessening the role of the church in Italian life. In 1855, for instance, Cavour, as prime minister of the Kingdom of Sardinia (House of Savoy) under King Victor Emmanuel II, promoted a bill to suppress all religious orders except those dedicated to preaching, teaching, or nursing. Pius IX denounced the bill, as was to be expected, and let it be known that there could be no compromise with such enemies of religion. Five years later, in March 1860, when under the aegis of the House of Savoy the seizure of the Papal States had begun, Pius excommunicated "all usurpers of the Papal States, all those who carry out their orders, all those who advise them or support them." This huge net caught a lot of fish, but, except for the king himself, none more important or prominent than Cavour.

A year later Cavour took suddenly ill, and it soon became clear he was dying. He called to his bedside his old Franciscan friend, Giacomo da Poirino, who administered to him the last rites but did not extract from him a formal retraction. The friar was called to Rome to answer for his actions, where he had two stormy audiences with the pope. As part of the aftermath he was forbidden henceforth to hear confessions and was removed as pastor of his church in Turin. When in 1870 Rome fell and was declared the capital of Italy, Pius retreated to become the self-styled "prisoner of the Vatican."

Victor Emmanuel II, a devout believer, was, of course, also caught in the excommunication. In the hope of working out a reconciliation between the state and the church, he secretly carried on a correspondence with Pius IX. Despite the relationship he thus developed with the pope, his efforts to heal the breach came to nothing. In 1878, however, when the king was dying in Rome at the Quirinal Palace, which just a decade earlier had been the summer residence of the popes, Pius IX released him from all canonical penalties, permitted him to receive the sacraments, and even sent him his blessing.

The papal stance against the new Kingdom of Italy and those who supported it was bitterly hostile, culminating with the non expedit that absolutely forbade Catholics to vote or to hold office. The decree handed the political order of the nation over to "the enemy." Many Catholics simply ignored the decree by casting ballots, and with each election that number increased until the decree was rescinded in the early twentieth century. The matter was not fully settled, of course, until 1929, when Pope Pius XI negotiated with Benito Mussolini for the creation of the sovereign state of Vatican City.

In the United States the best-known excommunication of a political figure was the action taken on 16 April 1962 by the archbishop of New Orleans, Joseph F. Rummel, against three Catholics who opposed the archbishop's plan to desegregate the Catholic schools in the archdiocese. The three included Leander Perez, the political boss of both Plaquemines and St. Bernard parishes (counties). In 1953, a year before the Supreme Court's ruling in *Brown v. Board of Education* that racial segregation was unconstitutional, Archbishop Rummel issued a pastoral letter that declared "the unacceptability of racial discrimination" in the churches of the archdiocese. The letter set off a decade of turmoil as prominent Catholic politicians began an organized fight against Rummel's policy. In 1956 Rummel issued another letter to prepare for the eventual desegregation of Catholic schools, which caused even further turmoil, and finally, in March 1962, he announced that at the opening of the new term all Catholic schools would accept all qualified students.

During these years opposition to Rummel had grown ever stronger among Catholic segregationists. Perez, whose reputation for shady deals was almost as strong as his political clout in the two parishes, was among the most notorious. He helped write hundreds of Louisiana's segregation laws and denounced racial mixing as a Communist plot. After Rummel's announcement about the schools, Perez called for the withholding of financial support from the church. Rummel sent letters to the most vocal of the segregationists warning them, as canon law required, that they would be excommunicated if they persisted. Most of those who received the warning ceased their activities, but Perez and the two others did not. With that the archbishop excommunicated them and went ahead with his plan. Perez, undaunted, continued to agitate against desegregation and in 1968 was George Wallace's campaign manager in Louisiana. Shortly before his death on 19 March 1969, he was reconciled to the church and received a Catholic burial.

As we look back on these cases, what are we to think about them? I am sure different people will draw different conclusions. I would make just three observations. First, I would again underscore the relative rarity of these public condemnations and humiliations of political figures. The reasons for this reticence are many, as I have tried to suggest, but surely cutting persons off from access to the sacraments would seem to be a measure to use only in extreme cases when all else has failed and the good to be gained from it seems commensurable. I also would underscore that, with some exceptions, the actions of the excommunicated in the cases cited were direct, programmatic, and often deliberately provocative. In that regard, it would be possible to assemble a long list of rulers and politicians who, despite defiant actions, were never excommunicated, because it was deemed this would do more harm than good. The list might begin with King Philip IV of France but would certainly include Francis I of France, who did everything in his power to derail the Council of Trent. Finally, what strikes me forcefully about most of these excommunications is how spectacularly they fulfill the well-known law of unintended consequences.

Almost every action we take in our lives sets that law into motion, of course, and the more dramatic the action we take, the more dramatic we can expect the unintended consequences to be, for better or for worse. Whatever else is to be said about formal excommunications of public figures or even of publicized refusals of Communion to them, they are dramatic actions that can be expected to have serious and long-range repercussions beyond what the authors of those actions intend.

17

ONE PRIESTHOOD, TWO TRADITIONS

One of the happy peculiarities of the Catholic Church is that it has two corps of priest ministers: clergy who are members of a diocese and clergy who are members of a religious order. What's the difference between them? In the first place, the religious clergy take the three vows of poverty, chastity, and obedience and generally live in a community, whereas the diocesan clergy do not take those vows and do not live in a community. These distinctions are important, of course, but we must remember that diocesan clergy make a solemn promise of chastity, live under the authority of the local bishop, and have been repeatedly urged by Pope Francis to pursue a modest lifestyle. Although (especially these days) they often live alone, in the United States a fair number live in a rectory with one or more other priests. But from a historical perspective there is another important difference of which insufficient account is taken. The two sets of clergy have operated with a pastorally significant, though generally unexpressed, division of labor. The diocesan clergy minister most generally in parish churches, where they feed their flock with word and sacraments. The religious clergy, of course, also engage in parish ministry, but most characteristically they engage in other ministries and to other flocks. I elaborate on that division of labor in this article.

"Happy to meet you, Father! What's your parish?" This question is the almost inevitable initiation of a conversation about being a priest, yet not being in a parish, about being a priest and at the same time being a member of a religious order. For many Catholics being a priest means, by definition, doing parish ministry under the diocesan bishop, and even for many priests in religious orders, "real" priestly ministry means celebrating the Eucharist in a parish on Sunday morning. This identification of priesthood with parish and diocese is the result of a long tradition of thinking in the church that gained great impetus with the Council of Trent and reached a kind of climax with the Second Vatican Council and its aftermath. Books and articles about the history of priesthood deal almost exclusively with this tradition, reinforcing the impression that there is no alternative.

But there is, of course, an alternative—the tradition of priesthood within the religious orders, the tradition of priesthood within the context of the consecrated life. In this essay I will deal precisely with the relationship between them—an issue that obviously cannot be dealt with without touching on many other issues. Nonetheless, our focus here is that relationship, multifarious and distressingly complicated though it is.

The issue is not new in the church. During the first millennium it often took the form of ascetics propounding the thesis that the consecrated life was utterly incompatible with priestly orders and hierarchy. "A monk ought by all means to fly from women and bishops," said John Cassian in the fifth century, repeating what he took to be already an "old maxim of the Fathers." The tone of the discussion was sometimes angry and reproachful, almost always firm and eager to establish clear boundaries between the two ways of life.

Bishops, of course, had their own reservations and even antagonisms toward monks. By the early years of the second millennium in the West, in the wake of the Gregorian Reform, the antagonism took more public and aggressive form. At the First Lateran Council in 1123, for instance, the bishops turned the tables. They fired the first salvo in what would be the classic battleground from that time forward—where, by whom, and under whose authority Christian ministry is rightly performed. Canon 16 of the council reads in part, "Following in the footsteps of the holy fathers, we order by general decree that monks . . . may not celebrate masses in public anywhere. Moreover, let them completely abstain from public visitation of the sick, from anointings and also from administering penances, for these things in no way pertain to their calling."

In 1123 the bishops directed their salvo against monks because the mendicants such as the Franciscans and Dominicans, the principal target for later centuries, had not yet come into existence. Once the mendicants appeared in the thirteenth century, the conflict burst even more contentiously into the public arena with the bitter conflicts between "the regulars and the seculars" in the universities and in the bishops' great attacks on the pastoral privileges the popes had granted the mendicant orders.

The attack raged so severely and relentlessly at the Fifth Lateran Council in 1516–1517 that Giles of Viterbo, the superior general of the Augustinians, was convinced that the bishops wanted to destroy the mendicants utterly and delete from memory their very name. In his correspondence Giles relates his desperate and prolonged efforts to save what he could, running from the bishops to the cardinal protector, to the pope, and to the representatives of the civil powers. On that occasion the orders were saved through the intervention of Pope Leo X, who, like his predecessors and successors, saw them as allies in the papacy's ongoing power struggle with the bishops.

The decrees of the Council of Trent, 1545–1563, do not reflect how persistently the bishops recurred to their now standard grievances against the orders or how much they wanted to bring the orders' ministries under episcopal control. After Trent some bishops welcomed the orders, which now included newer ones like the Jesuits, into their dioceses as partners in a common task, whereas others tried to limit severely their activity and would have dispensed with their ministrations altogether if they could. The powerful and widely emulated archbishops of Milan—St. Carlo Borromeo (1560–1584) and his cousin Federico Borromeo (1595–1631)—worked toward an ideal of having practically all preaching in their archdiocese performed by diocesan clergy, but even their resources were too limited to allow them to attain it.

In subsequent centuries the relationship between the two traditions of clergy continued to be marked by ambivalence and even raw antagonism. Nonetheless, along with rivalry, conflict, jealousies, and petty and major struggles for power, there was often cordial cooperation, as well as a division of labor that served the church well. The diocesan clergy ministered for the most part to the faithful, especially through sacrament and ritual in the parishes or their equivalents. It was for this task that they were trained. The regular clergy also ministered to the faithful, especially through other instruments like schools, shrines, and retreat houses. Many went beyond the faithful in the pews to seek out the sick and the homeless and to work for the conversion of the pagan and the infidel. The missionary clergy were almost exclusively the religious clergy.

This division of labor was distinctive of Roman Catholicism, because the Protestant churches had abolished the religious orders and congregations. This meant, as well, that they had no equivalent to the many active congregations of women that sprang up, especially beginning in the seventeenth century, and that were, perhaps, even more distinctive of Catholicism.

VATICAN II

With the Second Vatican Council, the relationship between the two traditions of clergy reached, quietly and almost unobserved, a new crisis. As part of its sweeping and all-inclusive agenda, the council at a certain point realized that it needed to make a statement about priests, as well as about bishops, and especially to indicate for them the ideal in ministry for which they were to strive. The result was three decrees: *Christus Dominus* (Decree Concerning the Pastoral Office of Bishops in the Church); *Presbyterorum Ordinis* (Decree on the Ministry and Life of Priests); and *Optatam Totius* (Decree on the Priestly Training).

Although not among the documents that received the closest scrutiny and consideration during Vatican Council II, they were rightly greeted with enthusiasm on their publication for being major improvements on any official statements on the subject up to that time. *Presbyterorum Ordinis* was in several regards outstanding. In the first place, it sedulously tried to avoid identifying priesthood exclusively with the power to consecrate the Eucharist by giving equal importance and force to each aspect of the threefold ministry of word, sacrament, and governance—prophet, priest, and king. This was a radical departure from the extremely brief decree on holy orders at Trent, where priesthood was in fact narrowly described as "the power to consecrate, offer, and administer his body and blood, as also to remit or retain sins." Partly to forestall such a description, *Presbyterorum Ordinis* for the most part used, as in its very title, *presbyter* rather than *sacerdos* to indicate what it was talking about—an important distinction consistently ignored in English translations, where *priest*, with its denotation of somebody who offers sacrifice, carries the day.

Most important of all, the document defined the presbyterate as instituted for *ministry*. It is almost impossible for us to recover what a dramatic shift in perspective such a definition betrays. The definition means that ordination is not for the celebration of the Eucharist or for the hearing of confessions per se; it is not for the enhancement of the person of the minister by conferring on him special "powers," but rather ordination is for the service of the people of God. We perhaps catch some glimpse of how radically the document departs from an earlier theology by noting that the word "ministry" plays an utterly insignificant role in the correlative document from the Council of Trent.

Optatam Totius was basically a practical decree, but *Christus Dominus* and *Presbyterorum Ordinis* incorporated the best research and thinking then available on their respective subjects, although admittedly these were not subjects where research was particularly plentiful or profound. Diocesan clergy found the documents uplifting and encouraging, not least for their seeming promise of a more collegial relationship between priests and bishops. Priests in many religious orders found them confirmatory of the primacy they had given to various forms of ministry of the word from their founding years.

Not until some years after the council did members of the religious orders begin to detect perturbing implications for themselves in these documents and in some of the ways the documents were interpreted and implemented, especially as they impinged on the training of candidates for the priesthood. Was, for instance, a single "Program for Priestly Formation" appropriate for candidates from both the dioceses and the orders, with its implication that both would engage in identical forms of ministry? An altogether crucial question began to emerge—an old question, perhaps, but in new form and with new urgency: How do priests in religious orders and congregations fit in the ministry of the church?

The three most directly pertinent documents of the Second Vatican Council are subtle and in many respects pliable in their rhetoric; yet they suggest that the specific difference between religious and diocesan priests lies in the fact that the former take vows of poverty, chastity, and obedience, whereas the latter do not. The ideals that these vows entail, however, are so vigorously enjoined on diocesan priests in *Presbyterorum Ordinis* that, in the long run, the difference seems to be at most one of emphasis or to consist simply in the juridical fact of public vows, or perhaps life in community. The difference seems thus reducible to some rather vague particularities of spirituality that are difficult to define.

The conclusion seems to follow that there is one priesthood, as the document firmly states, but that priests can be animated by different spiritualties. There are no further differences. Although *Presbyterorum Ordinis* concedes in its opening paragraph that its provisions are to be applied to "regular clergy" only insofar as they "suit their circumstances," the document seems to assume that they in fact suit their circumstances quite well. The topic sentence in that paragraph sets the tone for everything that follows: "What is said here applies to all priests."

Some things surely do apply to all, especially things that the documents state forthrightly and directly. First and foremost among them is the firm location of a priestly identity in *ministry*, a location crucial for both diocesan and religious clergy. Yet it is in this very issue of ministry that perhaps the major problem lies. The difficulty with the documents in this regard is not so much what they explicitly say about ministry as how they frame it—and perhaps for that reason their radical implications for priests in religious orders were not at first grasped.

In other words, underlying the documents are certain assumptions that are not immediately obvious but that provide the basic design for priestly ministry as the council conceived it. That design consists essentially of four components:

1. Priestly ministry is a ministry by and large *to the faithful.*
2. It is a ministry that takes place in a stable community of faith—that is, *in a parish.*
3. It is a ministry done by clergy *"in hierarchical union with the order of bishops."*
4. The *warrant for ministry*, including preaching, is *ordination* to the diaconate or presbyterate.

This design clearly corresponds to the ministerial traditions and situations of the diocesan clergy—in theory since the early centuries of Christianity and ever more in practice since the Council of Trent. But does it correspond to the traditions and situations of the regular clergy? Not so clearly. In many instances, in fact, it runs counter to them.

As for the first component of the council's design for priestly ministry, the Dominicans, to take an obvious example, came into being in the thirteenth century not to care for the faithful but to preach conversion to the Albigensian heretics. As for the second, many orders carried out their ministries principally in schools, third orders and sodalities, hospitals, soup kitchens, and printing presses, and they were the great missionaries. They were, moreover, often forbidden to undertake parishes. As for the third, while they had to respect episcopal rights to regulate public worship and other matters in their dioceses, members of religious orders relied on their own superiors or chapters to decide when, where, by what means, and to whom they would minister. As for the fourth, at least in the Society of Jesus, the primary warrant for ministry was entrance into the order, for even the novices were expected to engage in all the "usual ministries" of the Society, except, of course, the hearing of confessions. The novices and other unordained members preached, for instance, during Mass and on other liturgical occasions.

In the active orders, their constitutions, rules, officers, and superiors, yes, even their so-called privileges, were not operative only for the internal discipline of their communities, as *Christus Dominus* by some historical sleight of hand seems to indicate. They looked just as much, if not more, to effective ministry. The commitment to ministry affected the scope even of the vows traditional to religious life. For the Dominicans, poverty was not simply an ascetical principle helpful to the spiritual development of the individual friar but also a condition of effective ministry for dealing with the Albigenses' criticism of clerical wealth and corruption.

I have in several publications elaborated on the relationship of ministry to religious life. Moreover, I consider my book *The First Jesuits* an extended case study of the question as exemplified in the foundational years of one major order. I will not, therefore, pursue these aspects of the question any further here. I would, however, underscore that I think them of fundamental importance—the basic points of reference to which the discussion must always return.

I here propose that we need to approach the question of ministry in religious life with a new method. We need to approach it as part of the history of ministry rather than exclusively as an aspect of the history of asceticism beginning more or less with Pachomius and "The Fathers of the Desert." The latter approach suggests that ministry is a kind of add-on to religious life. The former indicates that, at least beginning with the mendicants in the thirteenth century, ministry is constitutive of the identity of many of the new orders. Why not, in other words, do the history as from Paul to Ignatius rather than the traditional from Pachomius to Ignatius? Method, here as always, determines the outcome of the research.

What is crucial, in any case, is to move the discussion beyond the vagueness of spirituality and charism, where religious have often tried to argue their position. It must be moved to the more concrete ground of ministry—it must be moved to practice. Such a move will impart substance and energy to words like spirituality and charism. Such a move will allow us to speak with clarity and will dispel the vagueness of the abstract theological categories that so far have been devised to explain the difference between the two traditions.

TRENT AND "PAROCHIAL CONFORMITY"

Perhaps I can at this point further illustrate the contrast between the two traditions through a few observations about the Council of Trent and its significance for the future development of ministry. Some critics of Vatican II have barely managed to conceal their sneer when they describe it as a "pastoral council," implicitly contrasting it with the presumably more robust "doctrinal councils" like Trent. While it is undeniably true that Trent issued a number of important doctrinal decrees, it issued a perhaps even larger number "about reform." For Trent reform meant, for the most part, reform of the ministry of bishops and priests or reform of their lifestyle in order to bring it more in conformity with the ministry they were to perform.

Trent was, therefore, very much a pastoral council. Indeed, the degree to which it descended to nuts-and-bolts provisions about ministry made it much more practical than Vatican II ever pretended to be. Few councils have been more concerned with the great central Christian mysteries than Vatican II, few more convinced of the power of ideas to effect change when appealingly presented. Few, therefore, have been more doctrinal. Ironically, given Vatican II's reputation for being a pastoral council, few councils have been, in proportion to the quantity of its decrees, less prescriptive about specifics concerning ministry.

If Vatican II was, therefore, just as doctrinal as Trent, Trent was in its reform decrees just as pastoral as Vatican II. We have been misled about this aspect of Trent because, besides a few recent social historians, scholars have concentrated their researches almost exclusively on Tridentine doctrine. But the impact and implications of Trent's pastoral decrees have been immense—still affecting us today and still pertinent for the relationship between the two traditions of priesthood we are discussing.

In that regard, I will look at Trent from only two of several possible perspectives. The first is Trent's focus on the parish, and the second is the significance of the norms and means Trent proposed for reforming or improving ministry. These perspectives allow us to rise above the confusing mass of detail and legalistic jargon in Trent's decrees *de reformatione* to see the ecclesiological and pastoral vision from which they flow.

Trent wanted principally to reform three institutions: (1) the papacy and the papal curia, (2) the episcopacy, and (3) the parishes under their pastors—through whom the laity would be reformed. The council was consistently frustrated in dealing with the reform of the first institution and finally had to abandon the project for the most part, but it was successful in dealing with the other two—bishops and pastors—which in any case are closely related to one another. The council made use of traditional legislation concerning bishops and pastors but created something new by marshaling it in such a thorough and coherent way.

The ultimate purpose behind the Tridentine legislation on these subjects was to transform bishops and pastors of parishes from collectors of benefices into shepherds of souls. In its doctrinal decree on the sacrament of orders, the council had practically nothing to say about ministry. But ministry was to a large extent the scope of Trent's reform decrees. Those decrees looked, in the last analysis, to a more effective ministry by bishops and pastors, a ministry located in the *parish*. As a fundamental step in the direction of such a ministry, bishops would have to reside in their dioceses and pastors in their parishes. The battle to put teeth in the legislation requiring residency was waged sometimes on the sidelines, sometimes at the center of the council during much of the eighteen years that it lasted. Further provisions followed, with this one as their indispensible premise.

Two features of these provisions need to be noted. First, in the course of the centuries, they were a slowly moving but massive force in transferring religious practice ever increasingly into the parish—almost as into its only legitimate place of exercise. Parishes existed well before Trent, and, as essentially urban institutions, they took on more importance as European cities revived from the eleventh century forward. Even by the sixteenth century, however, and well beyond, they were only one institution in a vast array of others where Christians might find their devotion and engage in the practices of their faith.

Among these institutions were shrines, monastery and manor chapels, the collegiate churches of the mendicants, and, as research in the past decade has shown in such stunning fashion, the various confraternities or sororities or religious "guilds" that flourished in the cities and towns of Europe. That research has revolutionized our understanding of how Christianity was practiced from the late Middle Ages well into the modern era. Not only has it demonstrated how lively religious practice was and how well informed people were about basic Christian belief, but it also has shown how often parish churches played a secondary role. Of course, the situation differed greatly from place to place, from city to countryside. The parish church was where baptisms, marriages, and the "Easter duties" of annual confession and reception of Communion were performed and registered, but often little more. Religious devotion was more often sought and lived elsewhere—in institutions like the confraternities that to a great extent were managed by laymen and laywomen or like the third orders and sodalities under priests from the orders. It would be difficult to exaggerate the importance of these institutions or how they defined the practice of Christianity for serious adults in urban settings.

Although the bishops at Trent wanted to regulate such institutions better, they did not want to squash them. Their focus, however, was on the parish, so as to leave the impression that no other locus of ministry existed or was important. Moreover, after the council, zealous and ambitious bishops took the Tridentine legislation as a mandate to strengthen the role of the pastor and increase the level of practice in the parish. This led the British historian John Bossy to write about the "parochial conformity" of the modern era. That conformity constituted a break with the earlier tradition of a much greater variety of institutions in which the faithful could practice their religion, a break with the more spontaneous and self-determining character of most of those institutions. This conformity, so the argument goes, led to lassitude and loss of engagement on the part of the laity.

The reform legislation of Trent paved the road toward Vatican II, which would, in its turn, frame priestly ministry as (1) for the faithful, (2) in a parish, (3) under a bishop. The kind of thinking inherent in the question "Father, what's your parish?" was in fact also promoted by the

Reformation, so that it received in the Catholic Church an indirect but powerful impetus from that seemingly unlikely source. With the destruction of shrines, the abolition of religious orders, and the dispersal of confraternities, the Reformation created an exclusively parish-based clergy and public practice, no matter what nomenclature for the phenomenon different Protestant churches adopted.

In Catholicism a much richer and more varied reality continued to hold sway. After the Council of Trent, the mendicant orders experienced a tremendous growth in numbers and influence, and they were joined by new groups like the Capuchins and the Jesuits. Perhaps in no other field of ministry was their contribution more significant than evangelization of the "Indies" in America and Asia. Nowhere is the narrowness of Trent's focus more apparent than in the fact that, despite being held just when the evangelization of the newly discovered territories was at its peak in the mid-sixteenth century, the council bypasses it without a word. It was members of the mendicant orders, eventually joined by the Jesuits, who were the evangelizers. From Trent's decrees on ministry we derive a legitimate but narrow perspective on where, by whom, and unto whom priestly ministry in the Catholic Church was in fact being performed.

TRENT AND SOCIAL DISCIPLINE

Besides this almost exclusive focus on the parish, there is a second feature of Trent's provisions on ministry that is pertinent to our topic. Trent would reform ministry by reaffirming some ancient canons, especially those requiring or assuming bishops be resident in their dioceses, and by drawing up some new ones, which were generally just further specifications of long-accepted principles. Trent would thus accomplish its goal by reaffirming certain prescriptions for behavior and instituting means to assure their observance through closer surveillance and, when necessary, through punishment for delinquency. Trent reformed by passing tough laws.

The Tridentine decrees might well have remained a dead letter, as they in fact did in certain countries for a long while, if they had not been taken up by persons like Carlo Borromeo, who made them a rallying cry for his activity as the first bishop to reside in the archdiocese of Milan in fifty years. He made them a rallying cry, yes, but he also expanded on them in relentless detail in his many diocesan and provincial synods, the proceedings of which were published as the *Acta Ecclesiae Mediolanensis*. Throughout Europe the *Acta* became the blueprint for what a "reformed" diocese should look like, more influential probably than the original Tridentine decrees themselves.

Catholic historians have tended, until recently, to make almost unqualifiedly positive assessments of this development. In the past two decades, however, such a benign assessment has been challenged even by historians rooted in the Catholic tradition, such as Jean Delumeau in France and John Bossy in England. Bossy objects to the use of the term "reform" in such regards because it is a term derived "from the vocabulary of ecclesiastical discipline" meaning the restoration of some ideal form by the action of superiors. What surely happened, according to Bossy, was a movement from more natural, spontaneous, and fraternal realities to things more rationalized, impersonal, bureaucratic, and punitive.

The term and concept of *social discipline* is increasingly being applied to what we used to call reform. The term was originally used by the German scholar Gerhard Oestreich to indicate the processes whereby, in the drastically rearranged landscape of post-Reformation Europe, the growth of centralized and hierarchical institutions of state and church— both Protestant and Catholic—transformed the social order. Although criticized for assuming a simple top-down transmission of social norms and for taking insufficient account of the interactive nature of social change, it nonetheless captures a crucial element of what was happening. Social discipline is a modern concept, but it finds justification in the sources themselves, where *discipline*, not *conversion*, is the key term. It highlights the fact that reform meant the attempt to impose discipline on bishops, pastors, and the faithful. With Trent and the post-Tridentine bishops, the starting point for ministry was abstract norms, and the goal at which ministry aimed was to make conduct conform to them. The result would be a disciplined clergy and people.

What was entailed can be clarified by a concrete example. Trent, in its thirteenth session, merely reiterated the requirement first laid down in 1215 at the Fourth Lateran Council that all adult Christians must receive Communion at least once every year at Easter. In the Archdiocese of Milan, Carlo Borromeo implemented in 1574 a rigorous process to ensure observance of the decree, including a little slip of paper (*bolletino*), standardized and in printed form, that the confessor gave to the penitent when the confession was completed. The confessor had to fill out this form for all persons whose confessions he heard, and then the penitents had to show it to the pastor before being allowed to receive Communion. The pastor checked their names against the parish register so that eventually he had a list of all those who had failed to observe this law. In another measure, pastors were ordered to submit any *bolletini* of obstinate public sinners for episcopal inspection before approving them. The known behavior of such penitents suggested that absolution had been granted all too easily, and the *bolletini* made it possible to identify the lax or negligent confessors.

Measures like these may or may not have been indicated by sixteenth-century circumstances, but they powerfully manifest, almost to caricature, a tradition of ministry that begins with office and canonical discipline. This is the tradition that Trent and post-Tridentine bishops mobilized for the diocesan clergy and that has continued, much modified and enriched by other considerations, down to the present.

There is, however, another tradition of ministry represented by the regular clergy, where the starting point has been not canonical norms but experience. Religious orders differ so much among themselves regarding ministry and priesthood that it seems almost ridiculous to try to cover them all under the rubric of a single tradition. I nonetheless indicated above how many of them were similar in that, by and large, they did not fit the four criteria of the documents of Vatican II to the same degree as the diocesan clergy. Indeed, they often almost contradicted them. The religious orders are thus conjoined by a kind of *via negativa*—by what they are *not*.

Is there, as well, some positive factor that binds them together to the extent that we might even more coherently speak of a tradition in ministry among them? Although it seems foolhardy to try to generalize about the consecrated life as related to ministry and priesthood, perhaps we can attain some clarity by looking at three classic models—Benedictines, Dominicans, and Franciscans (and later Jesuits).

The Benedictines began their history with no further purpose than to lead the consecrated life in its purity, withdrawn from the world; whatever services they undertake for persons outside the monastery are, at least in theory, conditioned by that purpose. Only much later were large numbers of monks ordained, and ordained with a sometimes tenuous relationship to ministry. For the Benedictines, moreover, the vow of stability gives form to the ministries because, even in conjunction with their great missionary tradition, their ideal remains that whatever ministry is performed it be performed within the monastery or its environs.

Dominic was a priest who gathered other priests to engage in a specific ministry to heretics in southern France, in which a poor lifestyle was integral to the ministry. In this experience, preaching emerged as the primary ministry of the group. Francis, a layman, had a series of deep religious experiences that led him to a ministry of preaching and conversation, which at one point took him far outside Europe to preach to the infidel.

Ignatius experienced a deep religious conversion that led him to Jerusalem and then in Europe to a ministry of preaching, catechizing, conversation, and retreat directing; after engaging in these ministries for some years, he sought ordination to the priesthood. The order he and his companions founded was for ministry "among the Turks or any other infidels, even those who live in the region called the Indies, or among any heretics whatever, or schismatics, or any of the faithful." With such ministry in view, they created for themselves a special vow "concerning missions" that imbued the new order with a radically missionary character so that they would be ready at a moment's notice to travel to any part of the world for "the help of souls."

As different as these models are among themselves, they have one thing in common regarding ministry—they originated in some kind of *experience*. The experience was either a recognition of a pastoral *need* or some kind of personal *conversion* or *vision*, or a combination of both. The movement, thus, was from below, not top-downward. Its goal was not discipline but meeting some actuality. These factors lend a certain design to ministry that is different from that represented by the Tridentine tradition.

The design leads to consequences. With the early Jesuits, for instance, the most telling word in their pastoral vocabulary was not *discipline* but *accommodation*. This does not mean that they disdained ecclesiastical norms, for they often showed themselves overzealous in this regard. Nor does it mean that accommodation was their monopoly. Accommodation in fact had found objective expression in medieval casuistry through recognition that concrete circumstances determined the morality of any given act—all priests had access to confessors' manuals in which such accommodation was explained.

But what is interesting about the Jesuits in this regard is how accommodation was elevated to a general mode of procedure in ministry, which led to some amazing implementations of it. In Brazil in the sixteenth century, for instance, they used native women as interpreters in the sacrament of penance. That is an example of how a law—namely, the confidentiality of confession—was modified for the good of the penitent, in accommodation to the experience of a special situation.

A more stunning example, fraught with immense consequences for the ministry of the church in the modern era, was the Jesuits' decision to begin operating schools as a formal ministry. They created this ministry for the church in response to a need and an opportunity that they saw, even though it ran contrary to some fundamental guidelines they had initially set for their ministries. This ministry differed in obvious and significant ways from the pattern of sacraments, rites, and preaching in a parish that Trent envisaged for the diocesan priest. It was, moreover, created, not received of old. It took place in a classroom, not a church. It was to a specific group, young boys—sometimes including Protestants and nonbelievers. It operated with a curriculum dominated by the pagan classics, which were treated as instruments of moral instruction for the Christian.

So much for the sixteenth century! The tradition of accommodation persists in the scope of religious orders, as indicated by the homily of His Holiness John Paul II delivered to the Jesuits' thirty-third general congregation in 1983. The pope's message was an updating of ministries for the Jesuits. He urged them, among other things, toward "the education of young people, the formation of the clergy, deepening of research in the sacred sciences and in general even of secular culture, especially in the literary and scientific fields, in missionary evangelization . . . ecumenism, the deeper study of relations with non-Christians, the dialogue of the Church with cultures . . . [and] the evangelizing action of the Church to promote the justice, connected with world peace, which is an aspiration of all peoples." The list was not meant to be exhaustive.

These ministries, or formalities of ministry, do not quite coincide with the framework for priests provided by the three key documents of Vatican II. Although this homily was addressed to members of only one order, it suggests the broader division of labor that has marked priestly ministry in the Catholic Church for long centuries indeed. Each order or congregation could certainly add to the list from its own perspective on how its traditional ministries are being accommodated to the present situation.

CONCLUSION

In these pages I have drawn a sharp distinction between the two traditions of priesthood. I have pressed this distinction to its extreme by creating models or pure types—that is, mental constructs rarely, if ever, verified to the full in historical reality. In describing Carlo Borromeo's legislation on confession, for instance, I have drawn a picture of a hollow shell without spiritual content. This is how most historians today tend to view it, for Borromeo has become in this regard a favorite whipping boy. His massive influence, coupled with his well-documented obsession with rules and regulations for every aspect of religious practice, almost invites this assessment. Yet we know that San Carlo was a deeply spiritual person who at the time of his religious conversion as a young cardinal made the full thirty days of the *Spiritual Exercises* of St. Ignatius. For the other side, I have chosen to ignore the "observatism" that often dominated thinking and acting in institutions of the consecrated life, so that exactitude in following rules and rubrics became the very definition of "religious perfection." In other words, the two traditions are children of the same parent and bear strong family resemblances to each other.

Nonetheless, I think that the differentiation between them that I have tried to draw corresponds to some utterly fundamental realities of the Roman Catholic tradition in ministry—especially since the thirteenth century, but even earlier. These two traditions have interacted over the course of the centuries and have been mutually influential in numerous ways—both positive and negative. Both of them have given shape to the reality of priesthood in its actual practice, and both can claim legitimacy in the New Testament and in the long history of the church. Both have served people's spiritual (and sometimes material) needs.

Although there has been considerable and healthy overlap, a practical division of labor has in fact prevailed between diocesan and regular clergy through the ages. The "local," or diocesan, clergy have ministered primarily to the faithful according to time-honored rhythms of word and sacrament in parishes. They are the backbone of the church's ministry to its own. Religious, when they ministered to the faithful, did so in similar ways but particularly in other ways that new circumstances seemed to require. This division of labor has taken the religious even further afield, away from the faithful, in order to minister in some fashion or other to heretics, infidels, pagans, and public sinners.

No other Christian church has two such corps of ministers. Taken together they constitute a special richness in Catholicism. While tensions have always existed between them and sometimes erupted into ugly and scandalous battles, the genius of the Catholic Church up to the present has been its ability to contain them both within itself and not settle for neat resolutions that would reduce one to the other.

CONCLUSION

My Life of Learning

While I was writing my dissertation many decades ago, I heard a senior scholar remark that any academics she knew who had published memoirs about their careers were pompous asses. I never forgot that remark, and I often found her assessment verified. When in 2006 I was invited to deliver an address to the Sixteenth Century Studies Conference on my own "life of learning," I fully realized that I myself was about to fall into the category of pompous ass, but the invitation was too tempting for me to resist it. The lecture was later published in the Catholic Historical Review. *I include it here because, as I said in the introduction to this volume, I think it might give readers a further insight into what they have read because they will have a slightly better understanding of the person who wrote it.*

Aunt Annie, Uncle, and their grown son Paul lived next door to us. They were Easthoms, my mother's family on her mother's side. The Easthoms were supposedly Methodists, but they smoked, drank, carried on, and never were known to darken a church door. I liked them a lot. They got along marvelously well with the Gallaghers, my mother's family on her father's side. The Gallaghers were Catholics, but the difference in religion was taken in stride through several intermarriages of the two families.

Aunt lived with Mother, Dad, and me. She, too, was an Easthom, Uncle's sister. We had Easthom relatives all over that little easternmost plot of Ohio right on the Ohio River. One of my favorites was my Great-Uncle Noble Easthom, brother to Aunt and Uncle. I liked him as much for his neat name as for anything else. Although the Easthom women had not the slightest inkling of it, they were DARs, but of the underachieving variety. The whole clan lacked ambition and was intent simply on enjoying life as much as possible, as long as not too much exertion was required in doing so.

In that regard the Gallaghers could hardly have been more different. They were energetic, ambitious, and intellectually curious. They were also social climbers. Michael Gallagher, my mother's uncle and her legal guardian after her parents died, made a comfortable fortune for himself in mining and railroads, and he rose to prominence in the inner circle of his fellow Ohioan, that great American president, Warren G. Harding. To the relief (and somewhat to the surprise) of the family, Uncle Mike escaped unscathed in the Teapot Dome Scandal. Yes, except for the Easthoms, all my relatives, including my father's family, were staunch Republicans. The Easthoms were as unpolitical as they were unchurched, except that they, for good reason, kept an eye on local elections to see who might be elected sheriff.

I assume it was my grandfather's ambition for my mother, his only child, that motivated his sending her off at age ten to Mount de Chantal Academy, a relatively near, highly esteemed convent boarding school, whose curriculum I described in my *Four Cultures of the West*—six years of French, four years of Latin, several sciences, and so on, and, of course, a strong program in vocal and instrumental music. Besides my mother, five of my female cousins went to the Mount, loved it, and never got together without talking about it, which meant that the ethos of the school had a profound influence on my life.

The six years of French, for instance, stuck with my mother, and we were therefore Francophiles. Even before I could read, Mother taught me snatches of French verse, which in subtle ways opened vistas for me of life more exotic than in Tiltonsville, Ohio, population three thousand.

I was about ten when I discovered in the library of my grammar school a little book called something like *The Kings of France*. I devoured it, could not get enough of it, went back to it again and again. Not only was it about France, but it was also about *kings*—about the good old days. I now see that my passion for *The Kings of France* was an early sign that I was headed for no good.

Despite my father's surname, his family was in language and spirit German. His parents died in an influenza epidemic before he was a year old, and he and his two sisters were raised by their maternal grandparents, German immigrants. Hard to believe, but the O'Malleys spoke German at home! My dad's two sisters married men of 100 percent German background, which meant that that side of my family had decidedly Teutonic sympathies, only slightly tempered by the Great War and the rise of Hitler. They all lived in the big city of Wheeling, West Virginia, ten miles away, which is where my father also had his business. This side was as Catholic as Catholic could be, much stricter in their outlook and practice than either of my parents. I suspect that it was from my father's family that I somehow picked up my early interest in the Reformation.

That interest was also sparked, I am sure, by having so many Protestant relatives and by going to a public school where my classmates were about 50 percent Methodist and 50 percent Catholic. The two churches were the focal points for the social life of the town. In that regard the Catholics had a decided advantage in that their church sponsored bingo and card parties and at church picnics sold beer and wine.

Long before anybody in our milieu had heard the word "ecumenical," we kids were altogether ecumenical in our social relationships. Of my two best friends, one was a Methodist and the other, as best I could tell, casually agnostic. I cannot recall that we ever once had a conversation about religion.

In any case, I was, from a tender age, a confirmed and irredeemable history addict. My mother was as responsible for my addiction as anybody. When I was about eight I began piano lessons, and Mother insisted with two successive teachers that I was to learn the history of music as well as keyboard skills. She herself picked the texts the teachers were to use. In high school, even though history courses were miserably taught by coaches and intended as easy-pass options for the football team, I took every one of them. I lapped them up, and therefore I'm sure that, totally unawares, I was roundly hated by the jocks for whom the courses were designed.

In my first year in high school I had two remarkable teachers. Miss Funari taught Latin. Her course was certainly one of the most important intellectual experiences of my life. Under her tutelage I for the first time came to understand language and how it works. Mr. Kerr taught English. Every Friday he made us produce a different kind of paper—an essay, a poem, a story. He took me aside several times for encouragement about my writing, which meant a lot to an impressionable fourteen-year-old.

By the end of high school I was fairly sure I wanted to be a priest, and I think I wanted to be so for the right reasons—but that is a story for another occasion. In my voracious but undisciplined reading, I'd often come across the Jesuits and knew that they were teachers, a vocation to which I was also attracted. Although I'd never laid eyes on a Jesuit in my life, I wrote away (as they say) toward the end of my senior year.

If I were serious about joining, I was told in reply, I should go to Cleveland, about a hundred miles away, to be interviewed. That's what I did. In retrospect I marvel that my parents, otherwise levelheaded, went along with this madcap venture of their only child—once I took the trouble to tell them what I had perpetrated in my correspondence.

The Jesuits put me off for six months, ostensibly to give me time to do a crash course in Latin, but I'm sure it was also to give them a chance to look over this naïve eighteen-year-old who appeared out of nowhere and knocked at their door. After I was admitted, the person who supervised my first two years in the order, the master of novices, was a remarkable man, William Young. He had studied theology in Spain, read classics at Oxford, and went on to translate into English selections from the correspondence of Ignatius of Loyola and other important works related to Jesuit history. In that last regard he was a pioneer. Learned himself, he insisted with us novices that learning was an ideal of the Society of Jesus toward which every member should strive. I was not yet twenty, happily susceptible to this indoctrination.

I moved through the Jesuit training, which included three years of teaching history at a Jesuit high school in Chicago, an invaluable experience for me in making complex issues comprehensible. The final phase of the training was four years of theology, which included ordination to the priesthood. During that phase I had several wonderful teachers. In fact, the general outlook of the faculty was, for Catholics in the United States in the late 1950s, remarkably "progressive" and au courant with what was happening theologically in France and Germany on the eve of the Second Vatican Council.

By this time there was no doubt in my mind or in the mind of my superiors that I would do a doctorate in history in a university of my choice. Although I knew precious little about the sixteenth century and the Reformation, I was attracted to it for reasons I suggested earlier, but now also because of the growing interest of Catholics in the ecumenical movement.

For my final year of training as a Jesuit, I set off for Austria, where I would perfect my German. Before I left the States, however, I visited three universities to which I would apply for my doctoral program—Ohio State, Princeton, and Harvard. My fourth and perhaps best option was to study at the University of Bonn with Hubert Jedin, the great historian of the Council of Trent. Once arrived in Europe, I went to see Jedin, who received me graciously. I therefore also applied there.

The year in Austria proved extremely difficult for me emotionally. It was a total-immersion experience and culture shock in capital letters. I was, moreover, often bored to utter distraction in this small village in Carinthia, where the ten months would never end. Nonetheless, this was one of the great transforming experiences of my life, as I realized in a depth no book could ever teach me how difficult it is to empathize with and understand a culture not one's own, whether those were cultures of the sixteenth or of the twentieth century.

I was accepted at the schools to which I applied. Since I was interested in church history, the logical place for me was Bonn, the most illogical Harvard, which is, of course, where I decided to go. As ungrounded a choice as my decision to enter the Jesuits, it turned out to be, like the Jesuit one, inspired.

Even at this early stage I had a half-formulated goal of integrating my church history into secular history, and I am sure that at some level that goal influenced my choice of Harvard. As the years have rolled on, the integration of religious history with cultural history has become ever more important to me and guided my scholarship at the deepest level.

But first I had to get from Austria to Cambridge, Massachusetts. The only other American whom I knew in Austria went to work persuading me to travel with him for a week in Italy on the way home—Venice, Verona, Florence, and Rome. I resisted. I did not want to go. I had no interest whatsoever in Italy, and the only word of Italian I knew was "pizza." Finally, desperate to get my friend off my back, I agreed to make the trip.

We arrived in Venice on a glorious day in July. I could not believe my eyes—the sheer physical beauty of the architecture and the people. Then the food! Venice was thrilling in a way no other city I had visited was thrilling. Then Verona, and then Florence, where we arrived at midday. That afternoon I ventured out alone and strolled toward the cathedral. I'll never forget the moment my eye caught Giotto's Campanile. It took my breath away.

Something was happening to me, and I liked it. Meanwhile, that afternoon I kept walking past *gelaterie*, where the ice cream offerings were cleverly displayed so as to tempt the weak. Desire welled up within me. But I knew no Italian. Then I remembered: fortune favors the brave. I walked into one, pointed, got two dips, managed to pay for them, and walked out into the sunshine.

As I licked away at my ice cream cone, I said to myself, "This is a good country." Then, like a bolt of lightning out of the heavens, the fateful question struck me: Why don't you go into Italian history? *Yeah, why not?* was the fateful answer to the fateful question. And thus it came to pass. I put it this way: Luther had his Tower Experience; I had my *gelateria* experience.

At Harvard I met Myron Gilmore, my academic adviser, who also happened to be an Italophile. I also met Heiko Oberman, and my first semester I enrolled in his seminar on late-medieval nominalism. Oberman, young, feisty, determined to prove himself and to test every student in the fiery furnace of his blunt Dutch criticism, shaped me like no other teacher up to that point. I learned in a new (sometimes painful) way what evidence was, how not to move beyond it, how important it was to examine one's presuppositions and to discard them when the evidence proved them unfounded. Suffering bonded us students in the seminar together, and I formed friendships that have endured through the years. I fortunately had a good background in medieval Scholasticism, and my Latin was fluent, so I was able to hold my own.

Second semester was challenging in a different way in Gilmore's seminar on Machiavelli, which I had no choice but to take. Just four students, no place to hide, and I knew nothing about the Renaissance or humanism, and, of course, nothing about Machiavelli, except that he was a bad guy. For three and a half months every Monday evening I pasted a knowing smile on my face to try to conceal that I had absolutely no idea what anybody was talking about.

Somehow I got through it, finished the year, and then sailed into preparation for the general examination to be taken at the end of the next year. In this preparation, Giles Constable, the distinguished medievalist, played an important role as one of my mentors, and I still marvel at how generous he was with his time for me.

Meanwhile, my thoughts turned to a dissertation topic. Myron suggested Giles of Viterbo, of whom, of course, I'd never heard before. I pasted that faithful old knowing smile on my face and said it sounded like a good idea. One day I noticed a poster in the office of the history department announcing a new predoctoral fellowship for research at the American Academy in Rome. That sounded like something worth trying for, because I had found out that most of Giles's manuscripts were in Rome. So once again I wrote away, giving Myron Gilmore as a reference. A few weeks later Myron accosted me. "John, did you apply for a fellowship to the American Academy in Rome?"

"Yes."

"Do you have any idea what the American Academy in Rome is?"

"No."

"You'd better make an appointment to see me."

I got the fellowship, which led to two of the happiest and most formative years of my life. Distinguished scholars, guests of the academy, regularly joined us fellows at table. It was stimulating and fun. It was as transforming an experience on a happy note as my year in Austria had been transforming on a painful one. An added bonus was that Myron and Sheila Gilmore, of whom I had grown very fond, were in Rome during my first year.

The academy had a strong art history component. I had never taken an art history course in my life, but in conversation at the table I began to get a first-rate art history education. My appetite was whetted and made keener by having so many masterpieces just a few hundred yards away. I was hooked, but of course I never expected to have any professional relationship to the field.

O happy days! O delicious months! O sweet years! Yet there *was* a little cloud on the horizon—the dissertation. Practically nothing of Giles's large corpus had been printed. So, without any training in paleography, I was stuck with trying to decipher his manuscripts. My heart sank when I saw the first one, some 650 pages. That day I got through about half a page. I became more proficient with practice, but then I realized I could not make much sense of what I'd deciphered. This went on day after bleak day, month after increasingly desperate month.

One day I bumped into Myron at the academy. After a few pleasant-ries he asked the question I dreaded: "How's the dissertation going?" I could not bear to tell him the depths of my despair.

"All right," I lied.

"Oh, I'm so relieved to hear it," he replied. "I was a little worried. A student of Sir Isaiah Berlin tried to write a dissertation on Giles. He had a terrible nervous breakdown."

Well, the good news was that I knew where I was headed. But bit by bit things got better, and by March of my second year I was able to deliver a draft to Gilmore, who meanwhile had become director of Villa I Tatti, the Harvard Center for Italian Renaissance Studies in the former home of Bernard Berenson outside Florence. Myron liked the disserta-tion, and that was that. Things were simple at Harvard in those days, and I did not have to face a committee.

I need to mention that while I was at the academy, the Second Vatican Council was in session not more than a mile or so away. Through the academy I had tickets to two of the great public sessions, and through some clerical contacts I managed to slip into a number of the press brief-ings that occurred every afternoon. I was, of course, keenly interested in the council because I was a priest and knew that the decisions of the council would probably affect that side of my life.

I also had a more specific, professional interest in it. My work on Giles focused on his activities as a reformer of the Augustinian order when he was prior general, 1506–1518. The council had taken *aggiorna-mento* (updating) as one of its leitmotifs, and I understood *aggiornamento* as a soft word for reform. The council provided me with a good foil for understanding aspects of the sixteenth century, and the sixteenth century provided me with a foil for understanding things happening in the coun-cil. What I was learning was that everything is grist for the historians' mill, including their personal experiences and the events they are living through.

This was exciting and stimulating, but I did not dream at the time that within a few years I would begin writing about the council on a profes-sional basis or that I would continue to do so through the next thirty-five years. Truth be told, I am right now trying to write a book on the council. I had from the beginning of my doctorate, of course, wanted to contribute to scholarship, but I also hoped that I would be able to bring that scholar-ship to bear on contemporary issues.

Somehow or other I've never been able to shake a preoccupation with the "so what?" question, a trait I inherited from my father. My interest in the council provided me with my first opportunity to publish along that line, which in a modest way I have been able to do ever since, on various topics in both professional and more popular media.

When my time at the academy drew to a close, my superior in the Jesuits assigned me to the University of Detroit. I had never been there before and soon came to, well, detest the place. I was rescued. Heiko Oberman had asked to read my dissertation. He invited me to publish it in a new series he was editing with Brill. I was delighted and honored. I felt, however, that the dissertation had been done in great haste and that I needed time to double-check and revise it. My dean, not so impressed with the invitation from Oberman as I was, said that the university had no provisions for a leave and, besides, had no money for one . . . but maybe in three or four years things might change. That pronouncement did nothing to warm my feelings toward him or toward the institution for which he spoke.

I wrote to Myron telling him what had transpired and asked him if, possibly three or four years from now, he thought my project might be suitable for I Tatti. I tried to be clear that I was speaking of the hypothetical future. Gilmore—bless him!—thought I was asking for the next year and replied that, yes, he had a fellowship for me. (As I mentioned, things were simpler in those days!) The very morning I got the letter, I announced it to the dean and told him in no uncertain terms that I was accepting it. Miraculously, he was able immediately to come up with a leave from the university. I was on my way.

The two years I spent at I Tatti were the icing on the cake. More wonderful conversations with top-notch scholars, many of whom, of course, were art historians, surrounded as we were every day with Berenson's marvelous art collection. Most important, the years came at just the right time in my career—dissertation finished, a year away from it that provided distance and a change of pace, then back to it before it got stale, and finally time to get a head start on other projects. Back to the University of Detroit. Shortly after I returned there, my book on Giles was published. During my absence the race riots had occurred, and much of the city was in shambles—a tragedy from which Detroit has never recovered.

Something else had happened while I was away. Despite tragedy in the city, the atmosphere in the university and the Jesuit community had changed for the better with a new president. Moreover, a number of my Jesuit contemporaries, fresh from first-rate PhDs, had arrived on the scene. It was a much happier, more stimulating place, and I a much happier person.

By some process I do not recall, I got to know Tom Tentler, the author of *Sin and Confession on the Eve of the Reformation*, and Charles Trinkaus, the author of *In Our Image and Likeness*, both of whom were teaching at Ann Arbor. Charles invited me to give a paper at a conference he was organizing on religion in the Renaissance and late Middle Ages. I readily accepted and only later realized I did not have the slightest idea for a topic, since I could not simply rehash Giles. I spent the summer before the conference in Rome, working desperately in the Vatican Library trying to find material on some new topic that would move me beyond Giles.

I passed three or four frustrating weeks, racing through all kinds of materials, which simply by chance included some sermons preached before the popes in the Sistine Chapel. I paid no attention to them—preaching was a dull subject, after all. I was, however, getting frantic and thought of withdrawing from the conference. Then one day I stopped dead in my tracks. Wait a minute! Those sermons! They were completely different from what I had been led to believe preaching was like in this period before the Reformation. They were neither the tightly organized and cerebral Scholastic sermons, filled with citations from Aristotle and other learned sources, nor the popular or penitential sermons, those grab bags of miracle stories and long-winded calls to conversion and penance. These sermons were short, inspirational pieces couched in elegant yet easily comprehensible Latin. During my time left in Rome, I located about fifty of them in print, and practically all of them conformed to that pattern.

Paul Oskar Kristeller participated in the conference at which I gave my paper, and he encouraged me to pursue the topic, but this time paying as much attention to the rhetorical form of the sermons as to their content. I had no interest in doing anything more with the sermons, let alone delving into the esoteric (for me) subject of rhetoric. Nonetheless, Helen North, professor of classics at Swarthmore, a great friend from academy days and a specialist in the history of classical rhetoric, gradually interested me in the subject.

I was prepared, therefore, when in the Vatican Library three years later I by accident ran across a passage—an aside, really—in a Renaissance treatise on epistolography describing the sermons in the Sistine Chapel and the style of rhetoric that shaped them. Eureka! All at once I saw how the sermons were put together and why in their aims, their tone, their vocabulary, and their uplifting spiritual message they were so different from medieval sermons. It was the rhetorical form that did it. The form framed and affected everything in them.

I immediately cast aside the project I was working on and set to work on a book that was published under the title *Praise and Blame in Renaissance Rome*. The book sent me into a period in which writing about rhetoric and preaching is what especially occupied me, but something more profound had happened to me that has only deepened with the passing of the years. Working on the book got me to realize in a new way that, in understanding texts, discourses, and people, as much attention must be paid to form and to style as to anything else. Style, I realized, more deeply and experimentally, is not a mere ornament of thought but an expression of meaning. It both manifests deep value systems and helps form them. That is indeed a basic premise of my recent *Four Cultures of the West*.

At the very time I was working on *Praise and Blame*, John Padberg, a Jesuit friend of mine, had become president of the Weston School of Theology in Cambridge, Massachusetts, whose purpose was to give basic and advanced training in theology to Jesuits and to any others who were interested in church service or theological careers. I at first resisted John's blandishments but gradually became more attracted to the idea, and finally I asked for permission to go to Weston. It was another happy decision, as the fact that I remained on the Weston faculty from 1979 until 2006 testifies.

Like my book on Giles, *Praise and Blame* caught the attention of some Renaissance art historians because it provided a theological context for their research. At a certain point Leo Steinberg initiated a correspondence with me about sermons preached in the Sistine Chapel on 1 January, the feast of the circumcision of Christ. A fair number of such sermons survived, and I tried to answer Leo's questions as best I could. Shortly thereafter I received an invitation from Columbia University to act as a respondent to a lecture by Steinberg titled "The Sexuality of Christ in Renaissance Art and Modern Oblivion." The sexuality of Christ! Did I want publicly to comment on "the sexuality of Christ"?

Curiosity overcame cowardice. As it turned out, I liked Steinberg's lecture and gave it two thumbs up. When Steinberg later published a book on the subject, my comments were included as a postscript. Reviews of the book were mixed, with Catholic publications generally favorable, but with others sometimes more reserved or even negative. For myself, I'm proud of my little postscript, which some people said served as Steinberg's *nihil obstat* or imprimatur.

Meanwhile, John Shearman, the great expert on Raphael, became chair of the fine arts department at Harvard, and we soon struck up a friendship. I thus found myself more and more drawn into the art historians' circle. I liked being there.

When I first began my doctorate, I had a vague idea of someday writing on the early history of the Jesuits, but I never quite got around to it. Just after I arrived at Weston I received an invitation to join an ongoing, in-house seminar that the Jesuits were running for themselves on their history and spirituality. I accepted the invitation. At that very moment, the Society of Jesus experienced a severe and unprecedented crisis. Pedro Arrupe, the order's beloved superior general, had a bad stroke, and it soon became clear that, though he would survive it, he would never be able to return to his position.

The Jesuits have from the beginning of the order had clear provisions for such an emergency: a vicar is always standing by to move in when necessary to set in motion the procedures for the election of a new superior general. In this instance the vicar was Father Vincent O'Keefe, an American Jesuit, a friend of mine, and a close collaborator of Father Arrupe's.

Out of the blue, however, Pope John Paul II intervened. Without warning he set aside Father O'Keefe and appointed his own vicar to manage the affairs of the Society into the indefinite future. The intervention was, obviously an act of profound distrust of the Society. It was a terrible shock for us and left us wondering, "What next?"

For several meetings of the seminar, the papal intervention dominated our conversations. Should we publish something on the matter? If so, what? One question kept coming back: What in this situation is the import of our so-called fourth vow? Besides the usual three vows of poverty, chastity, and obedience, Jesuits have another, which is to obey the pope "regarding missions."

Should the seminar take a look at that vow and say something about its relevance—or its irrelevance—in the present crisis? All eyes in the seminar were, unfortunately, turned to me.

With considerable reluctance I agreed to try my hand at something. Once I began the research, I was stunned at how little had been written about it and how sloppy most of the talk about the vow had been. I worked hard and was able to show that the vow was essentially a vow to be on call as missionaries and, as such, had nothing to do with the present crisis.

Thanks to the prudent management of Father Paolo Dezza, the Jesuit whom the pope appointed as his vicar in place of Vincent O'Keefe, the Society was able within two years to resume its normal procedures. John Paul II apparently expected a mass rebellion on the part of the Jesuits and, when that did not happen, realized he had badly misread the situation. In 1983 I was elected to the meeting that elected the new general, Peter-Hans Kolvenbach. More important for my life of learning, the work in the seminar got me into the Jesuit sources in an intense, urgent, yet professional way, and it turned out to be the doorway that led to my spending the next decade working largely on Jesuit subjects.

At about the same time, however, James McConica and Ronald Schoeffel, who had recently launched with the University of Toronto Press the project of translating into English the works of Erasmus, contacted me and asked me to help. Myron Gilmore was a great fan of Erasmus, and he had sparked the same interest in me. I had and still have a large print of Holbein's portrait of Erasmus hanging in my office. I readily accepted the invitation, pitched in with some odds and ends connected with the series, and eventually edited three volumes, which only increased my admiration of "the prince of the humanists." I found in Erasmus a kindred soul.

As I was working on Erasmus and dabbling in Jesuit history on the side, I became aware that 1990–1991 would mark two big anniversaries for the Society of Jesus—the five hundredth anniversary of the birth of Ignatius of Loyola in 1491 (we think!) and the four hundred fiftieth of the official founding of the Society in 1540. I wanted to contribute something to the celebration. After several false starts I conceived the idea of writing a sort of "basic book" about the early years of the Jesuits. For years I'd been annoyed at how off the mark most accounts were, whether from friend or foe, and how they located the story in misleading frameworks.

The anniversaries came and went without my book seeing the light of day. The project was, of course, bigger and more complicated than I anticipated, and I often felt overwhelmed by it. Ah, me! The Jesuits were into everything, it seemed, and I had to try to school myself in subjects about which I knew nothing—and in a few about which nobody seemed to know anything. Writing this book was a very different experience from writing *Praise and Blame*. I had a contract with Harvard, but deadline after deadline passed. One day panic; the next day despair; the next day exaltation; the next day writer's block. Then the cycle repeated itself. Sound familiar?

The moral of the story: Hang in there, and try to write something every day, no matter how banal or stupid you think it is going to sound. When you come back the next day, you might be able to salvage a paragraph or two, and, thus, agonizing paragraph by agonizing paragraph, the book gets written. *The First Jesuits* was finally published in 1993, and it went on to do well with critics and even at the box office.

I was happy, but I took a mighty oath, repeated again and again to anybody who would listen, that I would never, never, never, never ever again—no, never!—write another book. Why would I put myself through such agony and anguish again? The oath didn't work. I have, since *The First Jesuits*, edited volumes and produced more monographs. Father Young, my master of novices, used to tell us that once you got printers' ink on your fingers, you could never get it off. How right he was!

In 2000 I published *Trent and All That*, a book about what to call the Catholic side of the sixteenth and seventeenth centuries: Counter-Reformation, Catholic Reform, or what? It is an honest book in that it developed out of a number of real-life dilemmas in which I had found myself involved—for instance, in a committee to decide what entries to suggest from the Catholic side for the *Oxford Encyclopedia of the Reformation*.

I began to see how right Whitehead was when he said that names are the most important part of a subject because they are shorthand definitions of it. I suppose what I was really trying to do with *Trent and All That* was to shake things up a little bit, make us take a look at some received wisdom—or maybe received clichés—and then to question some conventional patterns of dealing with sixteenth-century Catholicism. To give a pedestrian but revealing instance, why do the Jesuits appear on the syllabus only after all the lectures on the Reformation? It's neat, but is it right? It says the Jesuits are meaningful only insofar as they related to the Reformation.

In 2005 I published *Four Cultures of the West*. I was talked into writing it by my editor at Harvard after a casual mention I made of the cultures at a lunch we had together. Nobody in this room is probably more wary of such grand narratives than I am, and that kind of book is certainly about as unfashionable in academe today as it is possible to be. Yet I'm glad I wrote it, because it tried to make historical scholarship relevant beyond professional historians and also because it drives home what has become one of the ongoing themes of my life of learning: style and content cannot be separated. We fail to understand content at its deepest level if we fail to take style into account.

* * *

As I look back, several things strike me about my life of learning. The first is the purifying or transforming aspect of the learning process. When I finished the dissertation, I said to myself, "You will never be the same again." I now knew what it was to know something that had taken me to the ledge where nobody had been before. Ah, yes, a razor-thin little ledge, but nonetheless I was alone there. What I said on that ledge was not an act of faith in what others had said, but rather an affirmation of what I myself had discovered and that I now put out to the world as my stance. I felt that in a new way I knew what it was to know. The process of getting there had tried my soul and, I think, purified it by making me constantly reexamine my assumptions, even my values, and putting me through the painful process of reassessing them. It had reshaped me by forcing me into a physical and psychological discipline I had never known before to such a degree.

I have to take issue with St. Paul. Knowledge, he said, puffs one up. That is not my experience. The dissertation revealed to me how little I knew and how very much I did not know—and would never know. In the process of writing it, I soon came to realize that I had to humble myself to ask great scholars what I knew were naïve questions. The questions were naïve because I did not know enough to ask any other kind. I soon came to realize that good scholarship perforce takes scholars into unknown territories, which they enter, if they have any sense, with fear and trembling and with the sure presentiment that they will soon have to cry out desperately for help. We get no place in scholarship without one another.

Why have I—or now let me say, why do *we* stick it out? The short answer is because, despite the costs, we enjoy it. Learning is fun. As is often said, it's great to get paid for pursuing your hobby. But there's something more involved than the thrill of "eureka!" There is for us historians the satisfaction of getting some glimmer of how the world we know got to be the way it is. And then there is the satisfaction of helping others get some glimmer of how we got to be the way we are.

That last is an aspect of our life of learning that up to this point I have not mentioned; yet for most of us it is the part that takes up most of our time and energy and perhaps gives us most satisfaction. I mean teaching. In the classroom and outside the classroom we see students light up, and we light up with them. The experience satisfies our souls. Teaching, we realize, is broader than the subject we teach and more meaningful than the purveying of intellectual comprehension. When we enter the classroom, we realize we are dealing with minds and hearts, sometimes with neuroses and psychoses, but always with human beings who are in front of us because they believe we have something to give them . . . and maybe something more than a passing grade.

Our first task, of course, is to teach the discipline, which day to day is pretty low down, such as, for instance, how the St. Bartholomew's Day Massacre happened or what's special about Shakespeare's sonnets. That's crucially important, but we know from study after study that this is not what most of the students will remember even six months later.

There is, therefore, something deeper and further that we try to communicate, which is surely specifically different for each discipline. In almost every case, though, it boils down to something like being able to recognize evidence, learning methods for organizing and testing it, and acquiring similar skills that are pertinent beyond the course and even beyond the classroom.

We are trying to impart useful skills and, beyond that, to spark little mental or even spiritual transformations that will stick for a lifetime and make their lives more satisfying.

There is more. We know that *we* are in the classroom, even more impressively than is our discipline. Students will probably remember the former longer and more vividly than they do the latter, and the former may have more profound impact on them. My litany of those I especially remember goes, in its most severely abbreviated form, something like this: Myron Gilmore, Heiko Oberman, Giles Constable, Paul Oskar Kristeller, Helen North, Father Young, Miss Funari, Mr. Kerr.

Students see in *us* what the discipline means on a human plane and, indeed, what effect a life of learning has had on us as human beings. In a few minutes, they figure out our style—fair, kind, honest, selflessly concerned for the good of the students—something like that, we hope.

My point: Our life of learning, when taken in its full amplitude, is a life that takes us beyond learning and, indeed, beyond ourselves. It takes us into hearts and minds and souls. It is a vocation worth dedicating one's life to.

ACKNOWLEDGMENTS

I have of course incurred debts of gratitude as I compiled this collection. I am especially grateful to my editor at Rowman & Littlefield, Sarah Stanton, who has deftly guided me through the publication process. I am also grateful to those generous souls who have come to my aid in moments of electronic-media desperation and have extricated me from what seemed to me unsolvable problems. Special among them are Joshua Cansona, Nelise Jeffrey, and Alan Mitchell.

I must also acknowledge the publishers who generously gave permission to republish articles or chapters that originally appeared in their journals or books. I list the pieces in the order that they appear in this book:

1. "The Millennium and the Papalization of Catholicism," *America* (8 April 2000): 8–16.
2. "Papal Job Descriptions: Yesterday and Today," *Theology Digest* 54 (2010): 103–16.
3. "Cardinals in Conclave: A Troubled History," *America* (18 April 2005): 23–27.
4. "Reform of the Roman Curia: Historical and Theological Perspectives," *Il Regno* 58 (15 September 2013): 482–84.
5. "The Beatification of Pope Pius IX," *America* (26 August and 2 September 2000): 6–11.
6. "Two Popes: Benedict and Francis," in *History of the Popes*, to be published in 2016 as *Une histoire des papes* (Brussels: Lessius).

7. "The Council of Trent: Myths, Misunderstandings, and Unintended Consequences," *Gregoriana* 4 (12 March 2013): 3–19.
8. "Bishops and Theologians at the Council of Trent: A Lesson for Today," *America* (31 October 2011): 11–13.
9. "The Council of Trent and Michelangelo's *Last Judgment* (1541)," *Proceedings of the American Philosophical Society* 156 (2012): 388–97.
10. "Ten Sure-Fire Ways to Mix Up the Teaching of Vatican II," *America* (4 February 2003): 25–27.
11. "What Happened and Did Not Happen at Vatican II," *Theology Digest* 53 (2006): 331–44.
12. "Dialog and the Identity of Vatican II," *Origins* 42 (22 November 2012): 398–403.
13. "Two Councils Compared: Trent and Vatican II," in *The Council of Trent: Reform and Controversy in Europe and Beyond* (tentative title), ed. Wim François and Violet Soen (forthcoming).
14. "Some Basics about Celibacy," *America* (28 October 2002): 7–11.
15. "Were Medieval Universities Catholic?" *America* (24 September 2012): 27–29.
16. "Excommunicating Politicians," *America* (27 September 2004): 7–11.
17. "One Priesthood, Two Traditions," in *A Concert of Charisms: Ordained Ministry in Religious Life* (New York: Paulist, 1997), 9–24.

"Epilogue: My Life of Learning," *Catholic Historical Review* 93 (2007): 576–88.

INDEX

accommodation, 204–205
Acta Ecclesiae Mediolanensis, 202
aggiornamento, 119, 121–122
Albrecht V (duke of Bavaria), 85, 86, 173
Alexander III (pope), 39
Ambrose, Saint, 35–36, 96, 184–185
Antonelli, Cardinal Giacomo, 57
Aretino, Pietro, 100
Aristotle, 17, 137
assertion, 133–135, 137
Athens culture, 136–137
Aubert, Canon Roger, 53
Augustine, Saint, 96
Augustine of Canterbury, Saint, 19

Baronio, Cardinal Cesare, 88
Basil, Saint, 18
Baumgartner, Sigismund, 85–86, 174
Benedict VIII (pope), 22–23
Benedict X (pope), 37
Benedict XV (pope), 31
Benedict XVI (pope): background, 60–64;
   bridge-building efforts, 32, 33; election
   of, 60; John Paul's relationship with,
   59, 62; and Muslims, 32, 64–65; papacy
   of, 64–65; resignation of, 65–66; on
   Vatican II, 113
Benedictines, 203–204
Bergoglio, Jorge Mario. *See* Francis
Bernard, Saint, 44
Bertano, Bishop Pietro, 83

Biaggio da Cesena, 100
Bible versions, 82–84
bishops: appointment of, 13, 15, 16, 27–29;
   center-periphery relations, 122–125;
   reforms affecting, 78, 199; from upper
   social strata, 96. *See also* cardinal
   bishops; Council of Trent; Vatican
   Council II
Bologna. *See* University of Bologna
Boniface VIII (pope), 186
Borromeo, Carlo, Saint, 193, 201–202, 206
Borromeo, Federico, 193
Bossy, John, 202
breviary, 93
Buber, Martin, 142

canonization of saints, 27, 49
canons, 127–128; on celibacy, 174; from
   Council of Elvira, 169–170; from
   Council of Trent, 154–155, 174; from
   Lateran I, 192; Vatican II not issuing,
   128, 155
capital punishment, 57
cardinal bishops: collegiality of, 48;
   Commission of Cardinals, 46; decree
   establishing, 43; role in conclaves,
   38–40. *See also* conclaves; Roman
   Curia; Vatican Council II
Cassian, John, 192
Catherine de' Medici, Queen, 103